Glass Tumblers

1860s to 1920s

IDENTIFICATION

AND

VALUE GUIDE

Tom Bredehoft

COLLECTOR BOOKS

A Division of Schroeder Publishing Co., Inc.

Front cover, reading left to right from the top of the book:
First row – Mother-of-Pearl Diamond Quilted; second row –
Florette; Mario; third row – Wedding Bells, Prince of Wales
Plumes; forth row – Beatty Rib; Dolly Madison

Back cover reading left to right from the top of the book:
First row – Cone, Toquay, Florette; Prince of Wales/Plumes;
second row – Inverted Fan & Feather, Sunken Buttons,
Mother-of-Pearl Diamond Quilted; third row – Dewdrop,
Fine Rib Swirl; fourth row – Beatty Rib, Tortise Shell,
Irish Cross; fifth row – Waffle, Guattate, Leaf Medallion;
sixth row – Royal Ivy, Bull's-eye & Fan, Wedding Bells,
Dolly Madison, Mario

Cover design by Beth Summers
Book design by Mary Ann Hudson

COLLECTOR BOOKS
P.O. Box 3009
Paducah, Kentucky 42002-3009

www.collectorbooks.com

Copyright © 2004 Tom Bredehoft

The current values in this book should be used only as a guide. They are not
intended to set prices, which vary from one section of the country to another.
Auction prices as well as dealer prices vary greatly and are affected by condition
as well as demand. Neither the author nor the publisher assumes responsibility
for any losses that might be incurred as a result of consulting this guide.

Searching For A Publisher?

We are always looking for people knowledgeable within their fields. If
you feel that there is a real need for a book on your collectible subject
and have a large comprehensive collection, contact Collector Books.

Contents

Acknowledgments

It's almost impossible to recognize all who gave assistance
and support to research. Below are those who stand out:

JoAnne and Earl Autenreith	Ralph Roland Collection
Bob Costa	Rusty Roland
Betty Daniels	Scott Roland
Doug and Coila Hales	Bob Sanford
Herb Johnson	Ray Secrist
Bob and Helen Jones	Dean Six
Dane Moore	Gay Taylor

Most of the help and encouragement for
this book came from my wife, Neila.

A special thank you goes to Becky Lyle for her work in organizing
a database from which much information has been extracted.

And thanks to all others who offered and gave help.

William McGuffin Photographer
Green Valley Auctions, Inc.

Introduction

In this study of glass tumblers, certain parameters have been established. Both pressed and blown tumblers will be examined. Only tumblers of about 3" diameter and 4" height will be considered. The volume of about ½ pint, or 1 cup (8 oz.), is one of the determining factors. Juice glasses and iced tea glasses have been ignored.

With minor exceptions, this study will limit itself to those tumblers made between the close of the Civil War and the beginning of World War I. Some tumblers made in the middle years of the twentieth century are included, having been made in imitation of earlier pieces. Whether they were made to deceive or simply because the shape or color was popular will be left for the reader to decide.

The name and the history of tumblers will be touched upon, but only lightly.

It is hoped that the reader will gain an understanding of the different techniques of manufacture and a feel for the difficulties of manufacture of tumblers of all kinds.

The Word Tumbler

In the twelfth century, the term "drinking glass" could be applied to what are now known as tumblers. By 1400, "tumbler" referred to a person who performed feats of gymnastic ability. In the mid-1600s, "tumbler" also referred to a spherical silver vessel which would right itself when allowed to roll freely. By 1700, mention is made of a "Venice glass tumbler," and by 1778, writing mentioned a "common water glass or tumbler." By 1827, when Deming Jarves developed a machine to make a pressed glass tumbler, the name was firmly established.

Blown Tumblers

The history of the blown tumbler is lost, but the blown tumbler probably had its beginning in pre-Christian Roman times. It must have been round or cylindrical — a blown bubble of glass will be fairly round. It must have had a fairly flat bottom, so that it could be put down without falling over. This form has come forward in time, unchanged, to the present. To be certain, modifications were made as glass workers developed their skills and as technology advanced. The first molds were cavities carved in hinged pieces of wood, which were eventually followed by iron molds. The iron molds, which left a mold mark, were improved by putting a layer of "paste" inside the mold. The paste held water, and the steam generated between the hot glass and the water-filled paste kept the hot glass from actually touching the surface of the mold, thus eliminating the unsightly mold seam.

Pressed Tumblers

"Mr. Deming Jarves, in his *Reminiscences of Glass Making*, gives an account of the invention of the American glass press in 1827, and describes the manufacture of the first tumbler..." *American Glass Worker*, July 31, 1885.

Ruth Webb Lee, in *Sandwich Glass*, tells the story. In 1827, a carpenter approached Deming Jarves, owner and operator of the Boston & Sandwich Glass Co., and asked to have a particular piece of glass made. Jarves replied that it couldn't be blown; what the man wanted was impossible. The carpenter suggested that perhaps a machine could be made to press the glass. A rough machine was eventually made and the first item, a tumbler, was pressed.

This first tumbler stayed in the possession of Mr. Jarves for almost 50 years.* It was taken to the

---

* Deming Jarves, *Reminiscences of Glass-Making*, 1865, page 85. "The writer has in his possession the first tumbler made by machine in this or any other country."

A drawing modified from *Sandwich Glass* by Ruth Webb Lee.

A tumbler thought to be from this first mold. *Top Diameter:* 3", *Bottom Diameter:* 2⅝", *Height:* 3¹/₁₆". There are twelve tapered ribs on the bottom, ending in a circle ⅝" in diameter.

Centennial Exhibition in Philadelphia in 1876. While being discussed by several glass manufacturers, John H. Hobbs of Hobbs Brockunier & Co. accidentally broke it. A drawing of this first pressed tumbler appears in Mrs. Lee's book. Presented here and on the preceding page are both a representation of this drawing and a photograph of a tumbler that may have been from this first pressing of glass.

Once the concept of pressing glass had been explored and accepted, pressing quickly became the standard method of glass manufacture in this country.

Crystal Glass Co. jelly tumbler with glass cover

The Crystal Glass Co., in Pittsburgh, existed for about 20 years. It was founded in 1869, and it burned in 1890. In 1875, it advertised what was probably the first tumbler to be advertised in the United States.

Three handled tumblers

A whimsy hat

When pressed tumblers come from the mold, they must have their top edges fire polished to be acceptable as a drinking vessel. At this time, it is very easy for the worker who is doing this fire polishing to do just a bit more. The top is soft; if he spins the punty rod, the top will spread out. With a bit of tooling, the glass makes an attractive hat. Or by tooling it inward, the piece can be used as an ink well. If he is a little more adventurous, the worker can add a handle and make a mug from the tumbler. Once there is a handle, a bit more tooling and the tumbler becomes a creamer. Both ink wells and mugs have been made in production, but the hats have always been whimsies, just for fun. Marmalades have been made from tumblers by adding a silver plate top, but a silver company, not the original manufacturer, would do this.

Intent

It is the intent of this book to present a variety of tumblers to the reader. The collection of tumblers is not confined to those shown it this volume. This is only a start. Regretfully, only a small percentage of available tumblers can be illustrated in one volume. One collector suggested that this volume could be the "First 1000," followed by several more volumes. He was told those were his responsibility.

Names

With very few exceptions, we have attempted to use existing common names or, where possible, original names. In a few cases, we developed names to help organize the sections. We have tried to avoid the use of names using colors of the glass; the same tumbler in another color would then need a different name, and this would be confusing.

With very minor exceptions, this book has been divided into pressed and blown sections, with divisions in both categories. Opalescent tumblers occur in both portions, as do various other tumblers created with the popular decorations of the times. Imitation cut tumblers have been organized by how far up the side the pattern goes, starting with the full pattern and ending with those with very little pattern. The Daisy & Button tumblers have been put in their own section for ease of comparison. As opposed to imitation cut, the figured tumblers have a design raised upon the surface. Both pressed and blown tumblers have sections devoted to smooth outer surfaces. Cut glass and carnival glass have largely been ignored. These fields of interest have their own devotees and literature.

Pressed

The tumbler was an easy piece to press. The mold consisted of a truncated cone with a cap ring forming the top edge, and a plunger, a smaller, truncated cone. The plunger was smooth, designed to be drawn easily from the finished tumbler and leave a smooth interior surface. After pressing, the mold was opened and the tumbler was inverted, picked up on a punty rod, and warmed-in in a glory hole. This polished the top rim and made it wonderfully smooth.

The bottom of the tumbler changed over time as technology developed. After the top rim was smoothed, the tumbler was broken from the punty rod, leaving a scar. The tumbler was then annealed. Using a spherical grinding wheel, the punty rod scar could be polished away, leaving a "ground pontil." It was soon found that if the valve (the bottom of the mold) was cut to form a ribbed star, the scar would only be on the ribs of the star and would be virtually unnoticeable.

Some manufacturers apparently decided that even this little roughness was unacceptable. They found that by sticking up the tumbler on the bottom rim, on a bare punty rod (one with no additional glass), they could finish the piece and then break it off, and the rim could be ground and polished with little effort. There were even machines developed and built to grind tumblers this way. Eventually, the bottom of the tumbler became pretty well standardized, with a multi-pointed star in the middle and a ground or fire-polished bottom rim.

Machines were developed to fire polish tumblers, obviating the need to stick them up, but some manufacturers continued to grind and polish the bottom rims of tumblers. It seems to have been an effort at enhanced quality.

Eventually, in efforts to reduce costs, both tops and bottoms were sometimes left unfinished. Most manufacturers, however, still felt the need to fire polish the top rim to make it comfortable to use.

Old Fashioned

"How changeable are our tastes as to tumblers! When this generation was young, tumblers were shorter and wider, not as they are now, narrow and tall, almost resembling a part of a straight gas chimney. Why is this? Have our hands ceased to grasp the wider variety from deterioration of our muscle, or have we given way to the idea that such a thing, to be elegant, must be tall and thin?

"A few days ago, we had occasion to sit at a well-filled board, and we were regaled with our liquid, be it water or "three X," in one of these old cut tumblers, and we confess we were more astonished why this tall tumbler ever came in, and we promised ourselves the pleasure of calling the attention of our manufacturers to this grand old tumbler, asking them to get up patterns in the old style instead of the modern flimsy substitute; it will bear the cutting better, and look more solid and brilliant. And so we leave it with our Stourbridge friends to try and resuscitate the old ship tumbler to our tables and our homes, giving us plenty of glass — fine crystal — and good deep cutting" (*Pottery Gazette*," as quoted in *China, Glass & Lamps*, December 23, 1896).

Tumblers made before about 1875 were broader and shorter than they are today.

Tumblers of this shape were called "old fashioned" sometime after 1880, referring to the way the tumblers looked. Later, the alcoholic drink was named after the glasses they were served in.

AKA: Six Flute

Color: Crystal
Value: $20.00 – 25.00
Description — Top: Poorly fire polished Bottom: Unfinished
Dimensions — Top: 4" Bottom: 2½" Height: 4½"
Additional Notes: Flint.

AKA: Alternating Flutes

Date: Ca. 1865
Color: Amethyst
Value: $60.00 – 100.00
Description — Top: Fire polished Bottom: Unfinished Bottom Figure: Sharp pontil
Dimensions — Top: 3⁵⁄₁₆" Bottom: 2⁵⁄₁₆" flat to point Height: 3½"
Additional Notes: Non-flint. Shown in Knittle, plate 38, no discussion.

AKA: Plain with Star Bottom

Color: Crystal
Value: $35.00 – 50.00
Description — Top: Fire polished Bottom: Rough Bottom Figure: 24-point star
Dimensions — Top: 3⅜" Bottom: 2¹⁵⁄₁₆" Height: 3¹³⁄₁₆"
Decoration: Engraved Masonic figures.
Additional Notes: Non-flint glass.

AKA: Diamond Thumbprint

Manufacturer: Imperial Glass Co. Date: 1900s
Color: Crystal
Value: $35.00 – 50.00
Description — Top: Fire polished Bottom: Unfinished
Dimensions — Top: 3½" Bottom: 2⁹⁄₁₆" Height: 3¾"
Additional Notes: 3³⁄₁₆" top of figure. Marked MMA in bottom. Made by Imperial
  as a reproduction for the Metropolitan Museum of Art.

AKA: Ovals

Color: Crystal
Value: $45.00 – 60.00
Description — Top: Fire polished **Bottom:** Ground rim
Dimensions — Top: 3¼" **Bottom:** 2⁷⁄₁₆" across flats **Height:** 3¹³⁄₁₆"
Additional Notes: 3⅛" top of figure.

AKA: Excelsior

Manufacturer: Ihmsen, McKee & Co. **Date:** 1851, 1859 – 1860
Color: Crystal
Value: $75.00 – 100.00
Description — Top Rim: Imperfectly fire polished **Bottom Rim:** Ground
Dimensions — Top: 3½" **Bottom:** 2⅞" **Height:** 3¹⁵⁄₁₆"
Additional Notes: Flint.

AKA: Bull's-eye Variant

Color: Crystal
Value: $45.00 – 60.00
Description — Top: Fire polished **Bottom Rim:** Ground **Bottom Figure:** 18-point star
Dimensions — Top: 3⁹⁄₁₆" **Bottom:** 3" **Height:** 3¹³⁄₁₆"
Additional Notes: Flint, unidentified from literature.

AKA: Bull's-eye

Color: Crystal
Value: $75.00 – 100.00
Description — Top: Fire polished **Bottom:** Ground pontil
Dimensions — Top: 3⁹⁄₁₆" **Bottom:** 2¹⁄₁₆" rim **Height:** 3⁷⁄₁₆"
Additional Notes: Nine panels, similar to New England's Laurence, non-flint.

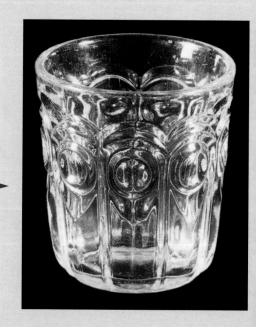

AKA: Bull's Eye Variant

Manufacturer: Rochester Tumbler Co.
Color: Crystal
Value: $75.00 – 100.00
Description — Top: Fire polished **Bottom:** Unfinished **Bottom Figure:** 14-point star
Dimensions — Top: 3⁵⁄₁₆" **Bottom:** 2½" **Height:** 3⅝"
Additional Notes: 3⅛" top of figure, nine panels cut about base

AKA: Chilson

Color: Crystal
Value: $45.00 – 60.00
Description — Top: Fire polished **Bottom:** Ground pontil
Dimensions — Top: 2⅜" **Bottom:** 2¼" **Height:** 3⅝"
Additional Notes: 3¹⁄₁₆" top of figure, flint.

AKA: Early Thistle, Scotch Thistle

Manufacturer: Bryce, McKee & Co. **Date:** Ca. 1872
Color: Crystal
Value: $80.00 – 120.00
Description — Top: Fire polished **Bottom:** Unfinished **Bottom Figure:** 12-point star
Dimensions – Top: 3⅜" **Bottom:** 2¹¹⁄₁₆" **Height:** 3⅞"

AKA: Grape Band, Ashburton & Grape Band

Manufacturer: Bryce, McKee & Co.
Color: Crystal
Value: $45.00 – 60.00
Description — Top: Fire polished **Bottom:** Ground **Bottom Figure:** 12-point star
Dimensions — Top: 3⁵⁄₁₆" **Bottom:** 2⅝" **Height:** 3⅝"

AKA: Halley's Comet

Color: Crystal
Value: $75.00 – 100.00
Descriptions — Top: Fire
polished **Bottom:** Unfinished
Dimensions — Top: 3⅛"
  Bottom: 2¾" **Height:** 3¹³⁄₁₆"
Additional Notes: 3³⁄₁₆" top of
  figure.

AKA: Gooseberry

Color: Crystal
Value: $35.00 – 50.00
Description — Top: Fire polished **Bottom:** Unfinished
  Bottom Figure: Stick-up scars
Dimensions — Top: 3¼" **Bottom:** 2⅝" **Height:** 3¹⁵⁄₁₆"
Additional Notes: 3" top of figure.

AKA: Gooseberry

Color: Crystal
Value: $35.00 – 50.00
Description — Top: Fire polished **Bottom:** Unfinished
Dimensions — Top: 3¼" **Bottom:** 2⅝" **Height:** 3¹¹⁄₁₆"
Additional Notes: Known with sharp pontil scar.

Original Name: Palace
AKA: Moon & Stars

Manufacturer: Weishar (Island Mould) **Date:** Ca. 1995
Color: Light Blue
Value: $5.00 – 20.00
Description — Top: Fire polished **Bottom:** Unfinished **Bottom Figure:** Script
  "Weishar"
Dimensions — Top: 3⅛" **Bottom:** 2¹⁵⁄₁₆" **Height:** 3⅝"
Additional Notes: 3⅛" top of figure, mold made by Weishar (Island Mould,
  Wheeling, W. Va.). Copy of Adams & Co.'s Palace.

AKA: Bellflower

Manufacturer: Several **Date:** Ca. 1874
Color: Crystal
Value: $80.00 – 120.00
Description — Top: Imperfectly fire polished **Bottom:** Pontil scars
Dimensions — Top: 3¼" **Bottom:** 2½" **Height:** 3⅝"
Additional Notes: Non-flint.

Original Name: No. 10
AKA: Block & Picket

Manufacturer: Challinor, Taylor & Co. **Date:** Ca. 1885
Color: Crystal
Value: $35.00 – 50.00
Description — Top: Fire polished **Bottom:** Ground and polished
   Bottom Figure: 24-point star
Dimensions — Top: 3¹⁄₁₆" **Bottom:** 2½" **Height:** 3½"
Additional Notes: Five horizontal by six vertical blocks alternate
   with two pickets. Three repeats, non-flint.

Front

Back

AKA: Bumper to the Union

Date: Civil War Era
Color: Crystal
Value: $75.00 – 100.00
Description — Top: Fire polished **Bottom:** Unfinished **Bottom Figure:** Polished pontil
Dimensions — Top: 2¾" **Bottom:** 2" **Height:** 3¼"
Additional Notes: Flint, clasped hands, "Union Forever" on one side; flag, shield, "Bumper to the Union" on the other side.

Front

Back

AKA: Shield, Campaign

Manufacturer: Bay State Glass Co. **Date:** Civil War Era, 1861
Color: Crystal
Value: Seller's choice
Description — Top: Fire polished **Bottom:** Unfinished **Bottom Figure:** Polished pontil
Dimensions — Top: 3¼" **Bottom:** 2½" across points **Height:** 4¹⁄₁₆"
Additional Notes: Flint, backside has shield.

Color: Crystal (lead)
Value: $45.00 – 55.00
Description — Top: Fire polished **Bottom Figure:** Polished pontil
Dimensions — Top: 3⅛" **Bottom:** 2¾" **Height:** 3⁹⁄₁₆"
Decoration: Cut diamonds and sunbursts
Additional Notes: 2¹⁵⁄₁₆" top of figure.

Colonials

Before the pressing of glass, it was common practice to embellish blown glass by cutting flutes on the sides of pieces. Except for the first two tumblers below, the following are pressed representations of this style. The first of the pressed colonial patterns was perhaps Huber, a pattern of flats around the piece. Sometime around the turn of the twentieth century, the name *Colonial* was applied to this style. By 1920, almost every company making tumblers had introduced its own Colonials.

AKA: Biedermier Style

Manufacturer: Bohemia **Date:** 1840 – 1845
Color: Canary
Value: $225.00 – 300.00
Description — Top: Ground and polished **Bottom:** Full ground **Bottom Figure:** 16-point cut star.
Dimensions — Top: 3⁷⁄₁₆" **Bottom:** 1⅞" **Height:** 4¹¹⁄₁₆"
Decoration: Six different engraved scenes, one on each panel.
Additional Notes: Blown, entire outer surface ground and polished.

Inner Color: Crystal **Outer Color:** Cobalt Blue, cut to clear
Value: $600.00 – 700.00
Description — Top: Ground and polished **Bottom:** Ground and polished
Bottom Figure: 8-point cut star
Dimensions — Top: 3¾" over points **Bottom:** 2½" rim **Height:** 4¼"
Decoration: Four cut circles, each with different design.
Additional Notes: Entirely cut on outer surface. One circle engraved "C. B. den 26, July 1837."

Original Name: No. 339
AKA: Continental

Manufacturer: A. H. Heisey & Co. **Date:** 1903 – 1910
Color: Crystal
Value: $40.00 – 70.00
Description — Top: Fire polished **Bottom:** Full ground **Bottom Figure:** 20-point star
Dimensions — Top: 3¼" **Bottom:** 2" across flutes **Height:** 3¾"
Additional Notes: 2¹¹⁄₁₆" top of figure, signed with Diamond H inside bottom.

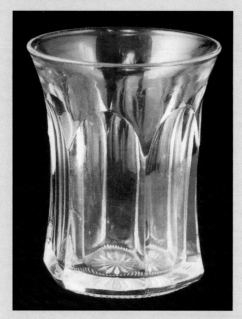

Original Name: No. 300
AKA: Peerless

Manufacturer: A. H. Heisey & Co. **Date:** 1897
Color: Crystal
Value: $40.00 – 70.00
Description — Top: Fire polished **Bottom:** Full ground **Bottom Figure:** 16-point star
Dimensions — Top: 3⅛" **Bottom:** 2⅜" **Height:** 3¹⁵⁄₁₆"
Additional Notes: 3⅛" top of figure, Diamond H inside, many pleats around bottom.

Original Name: No. 300
AKA: Peerless

Manufacturer: A. H. Heisey & Co. **Date:** 1897
Color: Crystal
Value: $35.00 – 50.00
Description — Top: Fire polished **Bottom:** Full ground
Dimensions — Top: 3⅛" **Bottom:** 2⁷⁄₁₆" across flutes **Height:** 3¾"
Additional Notes: Signed with Diamond H. Lacks star bottom and pleats of preceding tumbler.

Original Name: No. 300½
AKA: Peerless

Manufacturer: A. H. Heisey & Co. **Date:** 1897
Color: Crystal
Value: $35.00 – 50.00
Description — Top: Fire polished **Bottom:** Full ground
Dimensions — Top: 3" **Bottom:** 2⁵⁄₁₆" across flutes **Height:** 4⅛"
Additional Notes: 3³⁄₁₆" top of figure, Diamond H outside bottom.

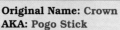

Original Name: Crown
AKA: Pogo Stick

Manufacturer: Lancaster Glass Co. **Date:** 1910
Color: Crystal
Value: $40.00 – 70.00
Description — Top: Fire polished **Bottom:** Ground and polished
   Bottom Figure: 24-point star
Dimensions — Top: 3¹⁄₁₆" **Bottom:** 3¹¹⁄₁₆" over figure **Height:** 4⅛"

Original Name: No. 15134
AKA: Elephant Toes

Manufacturer: United States Glass Co. **Date:** 1912
Color: Crystal
Value: $40.00 – 70.00
Dimension — Top: 3³⁄₁₆" **Bottom:** 3" over figure **Height:** 4¹⁄₈"
Description — Top: Fire polished **Bottom:** Unfinished **Bottom Figure:** 12-point irregular star
Decoration: Gold decoration.

Original Name: Huber
AKA: Nine Panel

Manufacturer: Gillinder & Sons **Date:** 1876
Color: Crystal
Value: $35.00 – 50.00
Description — Top: Imperfectly fire polished **Bottom:** Ground pontil
Dimensions — Top: 3³⁄₁₆" **Bottom:** 2⁵⁄₈" **Height:** 3¾"
Additional Notes: Flint, nine panels.

Original Name: Nestor

Manufacturer: National Glass Co. **Date:** 1902
Color: Amethyst
Value: $40.00 – 70.00
Description — Top: Fire Polished **Bottom:** Unfinished **Bottom Figure:** 22-point star
Dimensions — Top: 2⁷⁄₈" **Bottom:** 2⁵⁄₁₆" **Height:** 3¹³⁄₁₆"
Decoration: Gold on pattern, top rim; enamel design on alternating panels.
Additional Notes: 3³⁄₁₆" top of figure, eight panels.

Original Name: No. 15047 Colonial

Manufacturer: United States Glass Co. **Date:** 1896
Color: Dewey Blue
Value: $35.00 – 50.00
Description — Top: Fire polished **Bottom:** Full ground **Bottom Figure:** 22-point star
Dimensions — Top: 2⁷⁄₈" **Bottom:** 2⁷⁄₁₆" **Height:** 3¾"
Decoration: Gold rim.
Additional Notes: 2¹⁵⁄₁₆" top of figure, eight panels.

Colonials

Original Name: No. 97
AKA: Old Colony

Manufacturer: New Martinsville Glass Co. **Date:** 1906
Color: Crystal
Value: $45.00 – 55.00
Description — Top: Fire polished **Bottom:** Ground and polished
Dimensions — Top: 3" **Bottom:** 2⅜" **Height:** 3¾"
Decoration: Ruby stained.
Additional Notes: 3" top of figure.

Original Name: No. 140
AKA: Colonial

Manufacturer: A. H. Heisey & Co.
Color: Crystal
Value: $50.00 – 60.00
Description — Top: Fire polished **Bottom:** Ground and polished
   Bottom Figure: Diamond H outside
Dimensions — Top: 3" **Bottom:** 2⁷⁄₁₆" across ridges **Height:** 3⅞"
Additional Notes: 2⅞" top of figure, eight flutes, cross optic.

AKA: Seven Panels

Manufacturer: Hazel-Atlas Glass Co.
Color: Crystal
Value: $15.00 – 25.00
Description — Top: Fire polished
   Bottom: Unfinished
Dimensions — Top: 3⅛" **Bottom:** 2¼"
   Height: 4¹⁄₁₆"
Additional Notes: Signed with HA logo, narrow optic.

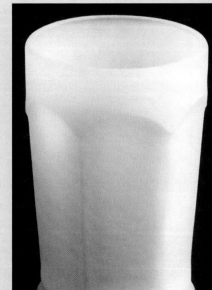

AKA: Six Panel

Manufacturer: Fenton Art Glass Co. **Date:** 1990s
Color: Jade Green
Value: $5.00 – 15.00
Description — Top: Unfinished **Bottom:** Unfinished **Bottom Figure:** Fenton logo
Dimensions — Top: 2⅞" **Bottom:** 2⁹⁄₁₆" **Height:** 4³⁄₁₆"
Decoration: Sandblasted.
Additional Notes: Made as sample for Martha Stewart Inc.

18

AKA: Ladders

Manufacturer: Tarentum Glass Co. **Date:** 1901
Color: Crystal
Value: $25.00 – 35.00
Description — Top: Fire Polished **Bottom:** Ground and polished **Bottom Figure:** 24-
  point star
Dimensions — Top: 3¼" **Bottom:** 2⁹⁄₁₆" across flutes **Height:** 3¾"

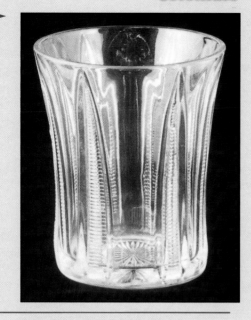

Original Name: No. 300
AKA: Madeira

Manufacturer: Tarentum Glass Co. **Date:** 1912
Color: Crystal
Value: $50.00 – 60.00
Description — Top: Fire Polished **Bottom:** Ground and polished **Bottom Figure:** Fancy
Dimensions — Top: 3¼" **Bottom:** 2⁷⁄₁₆" **Height:** 4"
Decoration: Ruby stained, gold above pattern.
Additional Notes: 3¼" top of figure.

Original Name: Mirror Plate, No. 15086
AKA: Galloway

Manufacturer: United States Glass Co. **Date:** 1904
Color: Crystal
Value: $35.00 – 45.00
Description — Top: Fire polished **Bottom Figure:** 20-point star
Dimensions — Top: 3³⁄₁₆" **Bottom:** 2" over rim **Height:** 3¹³⁄₁₆"
Decoration: Gold trim.
Additional Notes: Jefferson Glass in Toronto, Ont., illustrated in one catalog a sherbet
  glass which seems to be only similar to 15086; there is no indication of other pieces in the
  line. It appears that this line has NOT been reproduced.

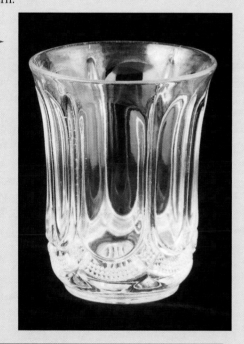

Original Name: Diamond
AKA: Chicken Wire, Sawtooth Honeycomb

Manufacturer: Steimer Glass Co.-Union Stopper Glass Co. **Date:** 1904
Color: Crystal
Value: $40.00 – 70.00
Dimensions — Top: 3³⁄₁₆" **Bottom:** 2⁹⁄₁₆" across flats **Height:** 3⅞"
Description — Top: Fire polished **Bottom:** Ground and polished **Bottom Figure:** Hobstar
Decoration: May be Ruby stained.
Additional Notes: 3⅛" top of figure.

Original Name: Spiral
AKA: Texas Star

Manufacturer: Steimer Glass Co. **Date:** 1905
Color: Crystal
Value: $75.00 – 100.00
Description — Top: Fire polished **Bottom:** Stone ground **Bottom Figure:** Swirled hobstar
Dimensions — Top: 3⅛" **Bottom:** 2⅞" across flats **Height:** 4⅛"
Additional Notes: 3¼" top of figure, eight panels.

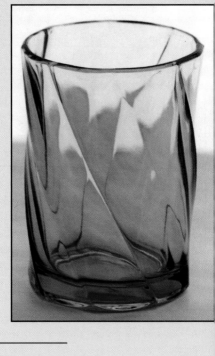

Original Name: No. 1252
AKA: Twist

Manufacturer: A. H. Heisey & Co. **Date:** 1929 – 1935
Color: Crystal, Green, Pink, Yellow
Value: $40.00 – 70.00
Description — Top: Fire polished **Bottom:** Ground and polished **Bottom Figure:** Diamond H outside center.
Dimensions — Top: 2⅞" **Bottom:** 2½" across flats **Height:** 3⅞"

Original Name: Columbia
AKA: Prism Buttress

Manufacturer: Columbia Glass Co. **Date:** 1890
Color: Crystal
Value: $40.00 – 70.00
Description — Top: Fire polished **Bottom:** Unfinished

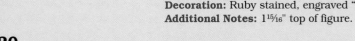

AKA: Bar & Flute

Manufacturer: Probably Riverside Glass Co. **Date:** 1892
Color: Crystal
Value: $40.00 – 70.00
Description — Top: Fire polished **Bottom:** Ground
Dimensions — Top: 3" **Bottom:** 1⅞" rim **Height:** 3¾"
Decoration: Ruby stained, engraved "World's Fair 1893."
Additional Notes: 1¹⁵⁄₁₆" top of figure.

Original Name: No. 56
AKA: Blocked Thumbprint Band

Manufacturer: Duncan & Miller Glass Co.
  Date: 1904
Color: Crystal
Value: $35.00 – 45.00
Description — Top: Fire polished **Bottom:** Ground
  and polished **Bottom Figure:** 8-point unequal
  star
Dimensions — Top: 2¹³⁄₁₆" **Bottom:** 2¹¹⁄₁₆" across
  flats **Height:** 3¹⁵⁄₁₆"
Decoration: Two fine gold bands.
Additional Notes: 1⅝" top of figure.

Original Name: No. 56
AKA: Blocked Thumbprint Band

Manufacturer: Duncan & Miller Glass Co.
  Date: 1904
Color: Crystal
Value: $40.00 – 70.00
Description — Top: Fire polished **Bottom:** Ground
  and polished **Bottom Figure:** 8-point unequal star
Dimensions — Top: 2¹⁵⁄₁₆" **Bottom:** 2⅝"
  Height: 3¹³⁄₁₆"
Decoration: Ruby stained, engraved "Fannie 1905."
Additional Notes: 1⅝" top of figure.

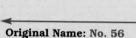

Original Name: No. 2003
AKA: Zipper Slash

Manufacturer: Geo. Duncan Sons & Co. **Date:** 1893
Color: Crystal
Value: $40.00 – 70.00
Description — Top: Fire polished **Bottom:** ground **Bottom Figure:** 24-point star
Dimensions — Top: 2⅞" **Bottom:** 2¼" **Height:** 3⁹⁄₁₆"
Decoration: Ruby stained, engraved.
Additional Notes: 1¼" top of figure.

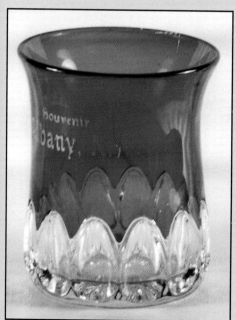

Original Name: No. 15091
AKA: Arched Ovals, Almond Thumbprint

Manufacturer: U. S. Glass Co. **Date:** 1905
Color: Crystal
Value: $35.00 – 50.00
Description — Top: Fire polished **Bottom:** Ground **Bottom Figure:** 26-point star
Dimensions — Top: 3⅛" **Bottom:** 2½" **Height:** 3⅝"
Decoration: Ruby stained, printed "Souvenir of Albany, NY."
Additional Notes: 1½" top of figure.

Original Name: No. 15091
AKA: Arched Ovals, Almond Thumbprint

Manufacturer: U. S. Glass **Date:** 1905
Color: Crystal
Value: $35.00 – 50.00
Description — Top: Fire polished **Bottom:** Full ground **Bottom Figure:** 26-point star
Dimensions — Top: 3¹⁄₁₆" **Bottom:** 2⁵⁄₁₆" **Height:** 3¹³⁄₁₆"
Decoration: May have stain on ovals. Ruby stained on body, gold bands. "Souvenir of Clarksburg, W.Va." written in gold. Also see preceding.

Original Name: No 11
AKA: Eyebrows

Manufacturer: Doyle & Co. **Date:** 1890
Color: Crystal
Value: $40.00 – 70.00
Description — Top: Fire polished **Bottom:** Unfinished **Bottom Figure:** 12-point star
Dimensions — Top: 2¹³⁄₁₆" **Bottom:** 2½" **Height:** 3¾"
Decoration: Ruby stained.
Additional Notes: 1¹¹⁄₁₆" top of figure.

AKA: 14 Panels

Date: Ca. 1906
Color: Crystal
Value: $35.00 – 45.00
Description — Top: Fire polished **Bottom:** Unfinished
Dimensions — Top: 2¹¹⁄₁₆" **Bottom:** 2⅛" **Height:** 3½"
Decoration: Ruby stained, engraved "Ella 1906."
Additional Notes: 1³⁄₁₆" top of figure, 14 panels.

AKA: 20 Flutes

Color: Crystal
Value: $35.00 – 50.00
Description — Top: Fire Polished **Bottom:** Unfinished
Dimensions — Top: 2⁵⁄₁₆" **Bottom:** 2¹⁄₁₆" **Height:** 3⅝"
Decoration: Ruby stained, printed "You Never Can Tell About A Woman, You Shouldn't Anyhow." Gold rim.

Color: Crystal
Value: $35.00 – 50.00
Description — Top: Fire polished **Bottom:** Unfinished
Dimensions — Top: 2⅞" **Bottom:** 2⅛" **Height:** 3¹¹⁄₁₆"
Decoration: Ruby stained, printed "Souvenir of Romeo."
Additional Notes: 1⅝" top of figure.

Original Name: No. 188

Manufacturer: A. H. Heisey & Co. **Date:** 1914 – 1920
Color: Crystal
Value: $35.00 – 50.00
Description — Top: Fire polished **Bottom:** Full ground **Bottom Figure:** 18-point star
Dimensions — Top: 2¾" **Bottom:** 2⁷⁄₁₆" across flats **Height:** 3¹³⁄₁₆"
Additional Notes: 2¼" top of figure, eight repeats, signed with Diamond H inside bottom.

AKA: Colonial with Ad

Color: Crystal
Value: $20.00 – 25.00
Description — Top: Fire polished **Bottom Figure:** "Arcade Mfg. Co. Freeport Ill."
Dimensions — Top: 2⅞" **Bottom:** 2⅜" **Height:** 3¾"
Additional Notes: 2³⁄₁₆" top of figure. poor quality glass, eight flutes.

Advertising in Base

Original Name: No. 439
AKA: Raised Loop

Manufacturer: A. H. Heisey & Co. **Date:** 1912
Color: Crystal
Value: $75.00 – 100.00
Description — Top: Fire polished **Bottom:** Full ground **Bottom Figure:** 18-point star
Dimensions — Top: 2⅞" **Bottom:** 2⅝" **Height:** 3¾"
Additional Notes: 2¹³⁄₁₆" top of figure, six repeats. Signed with Diamond H inside bottom.

Original Name: No. 150
AKA: Banded Flute

Manufacturer: A. H. Heisey & Co. **Date:** 1907
Color: Crystal
Value: $40.00 – 70.00
Description — Top: Fire polished **Bottom:** Ground and polished **Bottom Figure:** Diamond H inside center bottom
Dimensions — Top: 2¹³⁄₁₆" **Bottom:** 2½" **Height:** 3¾"
Additional Notes: 3" to top of grooves, six grooves, 20 flutes.

Original Name: No. 379½
AKA: Urn

Manufacturer: A. H. Heisey & Co.
Date: 1923 – 1927
Color: Crystal
Value: $40.00 – 70.00
Description — Top: Fire polished **Bottom:** Full ground **Bottom Figure:** 18-point star
Dimensions — Top: 2¹⁵⁄₁₆" **Bottom:** 2½" across flats **Height:** 3¹⁵⁄₁₆"
Additional Notes: 2¹³⁄₁₆" top of figure, eight flutes, signed with Diamond H inside bottom.

Original Name: No. 451
AKA: Cross-lined Flute

Manufacturer: A. H. Heisey & Co. **Date:** 1914
Color: Crystal
Value: $40.00 – 70.00
Description — Top: Fire polished **Bottom:** Full ground **Bottom Figure:** 16-point star
Dimensions — Top: 2⅞" **Bottom:** 2⁷⁄₁₆"
Height: 3¹³⁄₁₆"
Additional Notes: 3" top of figure. Signed with Diamond H inside bottom.

Name: No. 437
AKA: Ribbon Candy

Manufacturer: A. H. Heisey & Co. **Date:** 1912
Color: Crystal
Value: $125.00 – 175.00
Description – Top: Fire polished **Bottom:** Full ground **Bottom Figure:** 16-point star
Dimensions — Top: 2¹⁵⁄₁₆" **Bottom:** 2⁹⁄₁₆" **Height:** 3¾"
Additional Notes: 2⅞" top of figure, 12 flutes. Signed with Diamond H.

Original Name: No. 433
AKA: Greek Key

Manufacturer: A. H. Heisey & Co.
    Date: 1910 – 1917
Color: Crystal
Value: $75.00 – 100.00
Description — Top: Fire polished **Bottom:** Full
    ground **Bottom Figure:** 18-point star
Dimensions — Top: 3" **Bottom:** 2⅜" across flats
    Height: 3¹⁵⁄₁₆"
Additional Notes: 2¹⁵⁄₁₆" top of figure, eight flutes.
    Signed with Diamond H inside bottom.

Original Name: No. 208

Manufacturer: A. H. Heisey & Co. **Date:** 1924
Color: Crystal
Value: $25.00 – 35.00
Description — Top: Fire polished **Bottom:** Ground polished **Bottom Figure:** Diamond H
Dimensions — Top: 2⅞" **Bottom:** 2⁹⁄₁₆" **Height:** 3¹³⁄₁₆"
Additional Notes: 3" top of figure, 18 ribs.

Original Name: No. 15078 State of New York
AKA: U. S. Rib

Manufacturer: U. S. Glass Co. **Date:** 1902
Color: Crystal, Emerald Green
Value: $20.00 – 30.00
Description — Top: Fire polished **Bottom:** Unfinished **Bottom Figure:** 20-point star
Dimensions — Top: 3" **Bottom:** 2⁵⁄₁₆" **Height:** 4⅛"
Decoration: Gold rim.
Additional Notes: 3¼" top of figure.

Original Name: No. 417
AKA: Double Rib and Panel

Manufacturer: A. H. Heisey & Co. **Date:** 1924
Color: Crystal, Pink, Green
Value: $25.00 – 35.00
Description — Top: Fire polished **Bottom:** Ground and polished **Bottom Figure:** Diamond H center bottom (outside)
Dimensions — Top: 2⅞" **Bottom:** 2⁹⁄₁₆" over figure **Height:** 3¾"
Additional Notes: 2⅞" top of figure.

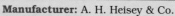

Manufacturer: A. H. Heisey & Co.
   Date: 1923
Color: Crystal
Value: $35.00 – 50.00
Description — Top: Fire polished
   Bottom: Ground and polished
   Bottom Figure: Diamond H
Dimensions — Top: 2⅞" **Bottom:** 2⁹⁄₁₆"
   Height: 3¾"
Additional Notes: 2⅞" top of figure, six repeats. See also Heisey's No. 417, above.

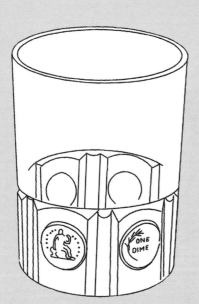

Original Name: No. 15005
AKA: U. S. Coin, Silver Age

Manufacturer: United States Glass Co., Central Glass Co. **Date:** 1892
Color: Crystal
Value: $300.00 – 350.00
Description — Top: Fire polished **Bottom Figure:** Multi-point star

Base of Tumbler with Coin

Original Name: Coin
AKA: U. S. Coin

Manufacturer: Imported by AA Importing **Date:** 1972
Color: Crystal
Value: $35.00 – 50.00
Description — Top: Fire polished **Bottom Figure:** Liberty Head dollar dated 1892
Dimensions — Top: 3" **Bottom:** 2⅜" **Height:** 3¹¹⁄₁₆"
Additional Notes: The U. S. Glass No. 15005 Silver Age Tumbler has dimes around the sides. A. J. Beatty and others made a plain tumbler with a dollar in the bottom, dated 1878, 1882. See also A. J. Beatty's No. 75.

Original Name: No. 1372, Coin

Manufacturer: Fostoria Glass Co. **Date:** 1958
Color: Crystal
Value: $35.00 – 45.00
Description — Top: Fire polished **Bottom Figure:** 14-point star
Dimensions — Top: 3⁵⁄₁₆" **Bottom:** 2½" across flats **Height:** 4¼"
Additional Notes: 9 oz.

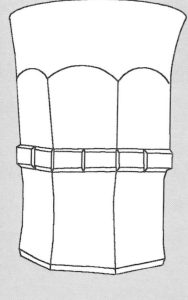

Original Name: Regal
AKA: Colonial Opalescent

Manufacturer: Northwood Glass Co. At Wheeling **Date:** 1906
Color: Crystal, Green and Blue Opalescent
Value: $35.00 – 45.00

AKA: Colonial Whimsy

Manufacturer: A. H. Heisey & Co.
Color: Crystal
Value: $75.00 – 95.00
Description — Top: Fire polished **Bottom:** Rough
   Bottom Figure: Diamond H outside
Dimensions – Bottom: 2⅛" across flat **Height:** 3"

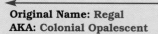

AKA: Colonial Eight Panel Whimsy Hat

Manufacturer: A. H. Heisey & Co.
Color: Crystal
Value: $75.00 – 95.00
Description – Top: Fire polished **Bottom:** Rough, stuck-up
   Bottom Figure: Diamond H outside
Dimensions — Top: 4¹¹⁄₁₆" across **Bottom:** 2⅛"
Additional Notes: Top rim flared out.

27

Original Name: No. 8
AKA: Whimsy Hat

Manufacturer: Hocking Glass Co.
Color: Crystal
Value: $35.00 – 50.00
Description — Top: Fire polished **Bottom:** Stuck-up **Bottom Figure:** 17-point star
Dimensions – Bottom: 2⁷⁄₁₆" **Height:** 2¹⁄₁₆"
Additional Notes: 16 grooves.

AKA: Whimsy Hat

Color: Crystal
Value: $50.00 – 65.00
Description — Top: Fire polished **Bottom:** Rough, stuck-up **Bottom Figure:** Star
Dimensions — Top: 5¹⁄₁₆" across **Bottom:** 2½"
Additional Notes: Top rim flared out, folded under.

Blocks & Diamonds

These tumblers, whether Block pattern or Diamond pattern, are grouped together for ease of identification.

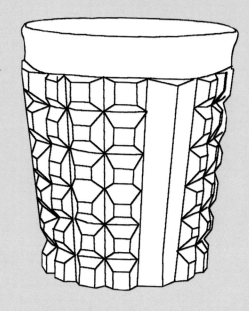

AKA: Waffle

Color: Crystal
Value: $159.00 – 200.00
Description — Top: Fire polished
Dimensions — Top: 3¼" **Bottom:** 2½" **Height:** 3¾"
Additional Notes: Described as Sandwich; brought $197.00 on eBay in 2002. Compare the top rim with other similar tumblers. Flint.

Original Name: No. 138
AKA: Waffle & Convex Bar

Manufacturer: King, Son & Co. **Date:** 1880s
Color: Crystal
Value: $75.00 – 100.00
Description — Top: Fire Polished **Bottom:** Rough, stuck-up **Bottom Figure:** 24-point star
Dimensions — Top: 3" **Bottom:** 2⁷⁄₁₆" **Height:** 3¹³⁄₁₆"
Additional Notes: Note that the bars and miters go to the top.

AKA: Block, Six Rows 16 Around.

Color: Crystal
Value: $25.00 – 35.00
Description — Top: Imperfectly fire polished **Bottom:** Unfinished
   Bottom Figure: 24-point star
Dimensions — Top: 2¹⁵⁄₁₆" **Bottom:** 2⁵⁄₁₆" rim **Height:** 3¹³⁄₁₆"
Additional Notes: 3¹¹⁄₁₆" top of figure.

Original Name: No. 331
AKA: Late Block

Manufacturer: Geo. Duncan & Sons **Date:** 1889
Color: Crystal
Value: $40.00 – 70.00
Description — Top: Fire polished **Bottom:** Ground **Bottom Figure:** 9-point star
Dimensions — Top: 2⅝" **Bottom:** 2⅜" **Height:** 3¾"
Decoration: Ruby stained.
Additional Notes: 2¹³⁄₁₆" top of figure.

AKA: Waffle

Manufacturer: Atterbury Glass Co. **Date:** 1880s
Color: Opaque Blue
Value: $75.00 – 100.00
Description — Top: Not fire polished **Bottom:** Unfinished **Bottom Figure:** 18-petaled flower
    with ½" circle around center
Dimensions — Top: 2⅞" **Bottom:** 2⁷⁄₁₆" rim **Height:** 3⅞"
Additional Notes: 3⅛" top of figure. Seven squares high, 18 around.

Original Name: No. 327
AKA: Quartered Block with Stars

Manufacturer: Hobbs Glass Co. **Date:** 1889
Color: Crystal
Value: $40.00 – 70.00
Description — Top: Fire polished **Bottom:** Ground and polished **Bottom Figure:** Two sets
    criss-cross.
Dimensions — Top: 2⅞" **Bottom:** 2⅜" **Height:** 3¹⁵⁄₁₆"
Decoration: Amber stained top rim, frosted below, Frances decoration.
Additional Notes: 3⅜" top of figure.

AKA: Block & Star

Color: Crystal
Value: $40.00 – 70.00
Description — Top: Fire polished **Bottom:** Ground and polished **Bottom Figure:** 24-point star
Dimensions — Top: 3" **Bottom:** 2¾" **Height:** 4³⁄₁₆"
Additional Notes: Twelve flutes around bottom.

Original Name: No. 28
AKA: Clark, Prism & Block Band

Manufacturer: King, Son & Co. **Date:** 1889
Color: Crystal
Value: $40.00 – 70.00
Description — Top: Fire polished **Bottom:** Unfinished **Bottom Figure:** IXIXI
Dimensions — Top: 3" **Bottom:** 2⅞" **Height:** 3¹¹⁄₁₆"
Decoration: Copper wheel engraved.

Original Name: No. 1425 Victorian

Manufacturer: A. H. Heisey & Co. **Date:** 1933
Color: Crystal, Yellow, Blue
Value: $40.00 – 70.00
Description — Top: Fire polished
Dimensions — Top: 2¹¹⁄₁₆" **Bottom:** 2³⁄₁₆" **Height:** 4⅛"
Additional Notes: 3⅜" top of figure. Signed with Diamond H outside bottom.

Original Name: No 77
AKA: Truncated Cube

Manufacturer: Thompson Glass Co., Ltd. **Date:** 1894
Color: Crystal
Value: $40.00 – 70.00
Description — Top: Fire polished **Bottom:** Ground **Bottom Figure:** 18-point star
Dimensions — Top: 3¹⁄₁₆" **Bottom:** 2⁵⁄₁₆" **Height:** 3⅞"
Decoration: Ruby stained.
Additional Notes: 2⅛" top of figure.

Original Name: Verona
AKA: Block & Star

Manufacturer: Tarentum Glass Co. **Date:** 1910
Color: Crystal
Value: $40.00 – 70.00
Description — Top: Fire polished **Bottom:** Ground **Bottom Figure:** 24 rays
Dimensions — Top: 2⅞" **Bottom:** 2¹¹⁄₁₆" **Height:** 4"
Decoration: Ruby stained.
Additional Notes: 3¹³⁄₁₆" top of figure.

Original Name: Hidalgo

Manufacturer: Adams & Co. **Date:** 1890
Color: Crystal
Value: $55.00 – 75.00
Description — Top: Fire polished **Bottom:** Unfinished **Bottom Figure:** Fancy
Dimensions — Top: 2⅝" **Bottom:** 1⅞" **Height:** 3¾"
Decoration: Ruby stained.
Additional Notes: 1⅝" top of figure.

Original Name: Oregon
AKA: Skilton

Manufacturer: Richards & Hartley Glass Co. **Date:** 1890
Color: Crystal
Value: $55.00 – 75.00
Description — Top: Fire polished **Bottom:** Unfinished **Bottom Figure:** Fancy fans
Dimensions — Top: 2⅞" **Bottom:** 2⁷⁄₁₆" **Height:** 3⁹⁄₁₆"
Decoration: Ruby stained.
Additional Notes: 2⅜" top of figure.

Original Name: No. 335
AKA: Hexagonal Block

Manufacturer: Hobbs Glass Co. **Date:** 1890
Color: Crystal
Value: $40.00 – 70.00
Description — Top: Fire polished **Bottom:** Ground and polished **Bottom Figure:** 8-point sta
Dimensions — Top: 2⅞" **Bottom:** 2³⁄₁₆" **Height:** 3⅞"
Decoration: Etched, Amber stained, also Ruby stained.
Additional Notes: 2⁷⁄₁₆" top of figure.

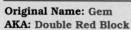

Original Name: Gem
AKA: Double Red Block

Manufacturer: Model Flint Glass Co. **Date:** 1889
Color: Crystal, Blue, Amber (green shards found at factory site)
Value: $40.00 – 70.00
Description — Top: Fire polished **Bottom:** Ground **Bottom Figure:** 6-point gem star
Dimensions — Top: 2⁹⁄₁₆" **Bottom:** 2⅜" **Height:** 3⅝"
Decoration: Ruby stained.
Additional Notes: 2⅜" top of figure.

AKA: Red Block
Date: 1886

Color: Crystal
Value: $40.00 – 55.00
Description — Top: Fire polished **Bottom:** Unfinished **Bottom Figure:** 6-point star
Dimensions — Top: 2¹³⁄₁₆" **Bottom:** 2½" **Height:** 3¹¹⁄₁₆"
Decoration: Ruby stained.
Additional Notes: 2⅝" top of figure. In 1888, this pattern — originally made by Doyle & Co. and called No. 250 — was copied almost exactly by Fostoria Glass Co. of Fostoria, Ohio, and called Virginia. In 1893, United States Glass Co. reissued Doyle's No. 250.

AKA: Double Block

Color: Crystal
Value: $40.00 – 55.00
Description — Top: Fire polished **Bottom:** Unfinished **Bottom Figure:** 6-point star
Dimensions — Top: 2¹¹⁄₁₆" **Bottom:** 2⅛" **Height:** 3⁹⁄₁₆"
Decoration: Ruby stained.
Additional Notes: 2⁷⁄₁₆" top of figure. This is not Red Block; compare with Red Block, above, and Gem on the preceding page.

AKA: Block Lattice

Inner **Color:** Crystal
Value: $40.00 – 70.00
Description — Top: Fire polished **Bottom:** Ground and polished
Dimensions — Top: 2¹⁵⁄₁₆" **Bottom:** 2¼" **Height:** 3¹¹⁄₁₆"
Decoration: Amber stained.
Additional Notes: 2⅛" top of figure.

Original Name: No. 9
AKA: Big Button

Manufacturer: Crystal Glass Co. **Date:** Early 1890s
Color: Crystal
Value: $60.00 – 90.00
Description — Top: Fire polished **Bottom:** Ground **Bottom Figure:** Figure
Dimensions — Top: 2¹³⁄₁₆" **Bottom:** 2¼" **Height:** 3⅞"
Decoration: Ruby stained, Amber stained.
Additional Notes: 2³⁄₁₆" top of figure.

AKA: Hexagon

Color: Crystal
Value: $40.00 – 70.00
Description — Top: Fire polished Bottom: Ground Bottom Figure: *
Dimensions — Top: 3³⁄₁₆" Bottom: 2¼" Height: 4⅛"
Additional Notes: 3¹¹⁄₁₆ top of figure, mold marked "Krystol" inside. Krystol trademark was used by Ohio Flint Glass Co., Jefferson Glass Co., and Central Glass Co., in that order.

Original Name: No. 15001
AKA: O'Hara's Diamond

Manufacturer: U. S. Glass Co., O'Hara Glass Co. Date: 1892
Color: Crystal
Value: $60.00 – 80.00
Description — Top: Fire polished Bottom: Unfinished Bottom Figure: 20-point star
Dimensions — Top: 2⅞" Bottom: 2⅞" Height: 3⅞"
Decoration: Ruby stained.
Additional Notes: 1¹⁵⁄₁₆" top of figure.

Original Name: No. 15001
AKA: O'Hara's Diamond

Manufacturer: U. S. Glass Co., O'Hara Class Co. Date: 1892
Color: Crystal
Value: $45.00 – 55.00
Description — Top: Fire polished Bottom: Unfinished Bottom Figure: 20-point star
Dimensions — Top: 3" Bottom: 2⅞" Height: 3¹⁵⁄₁₆"
Decoration: Engraved flower and leaf.
Additional Notes: 2" top of figure.

Original Name: No. 325
AKA: Pillows

Manufacturer: A. H. Heisey & Co. **Date:** 1901
Color: Crystal
Value: $75.00 – 100.00
Description — Top: Fire polished **Bottom:** Full ground **Bottom Figure:** Uneven 10-point star
Dimensions — Top: 3⅛" **Bottom:** 2½" **Height:** 3⅞"
Additional Notes: 2⅞" top of figure. Signed With Diamond H inside bottom.

Original Name: No. 9
AKA: Block & Double Bar

Manufacturer: Findlay Flint **Date:** 1890
Color: Crystal
Value: $75.00 – 90.00
Description — Top: Fire polished **Bottom:** Unfinished
Dimensions — Top: 2⅝" **Bottom:** 2⅜" **Height:** 3¾"
Decoration: Ruby stained.
Additional Notes: 2⁹⁄₁₆" top of figure.

AKA: Incised Cross

Color: Opaque Blue
Value: $75.00 – 100.00
Description — Top: Fire polished **Bottom:** Ground
Dimensions — Top: 3¼" **Bottom:** 2⁵⁄₁₆" **Height:** 3¹³⁄₁₆"
Additional Notes: 3⅜" top of figure, nine panels.

Original Name: Roanoke

Manufacturer: D. C. Ripley & Co., Gillinder & Sons **Date:** 1888
Color: Crystal
Value: $40.00 – 70.00
Description — Top: Fire polished **Bottom:** Unfinished **Bottom Figure:** Figure
Dimensions — Top: 2¾" **Bottom:** 2⅝" **Height:** 3¾"
Decoration: Ruby stained.
Additional Notes: 2¾" top of figure. Both factories made very similar tumblers.

Original Name: No. 311 Dunmoyle
AKA: Panel with Diamonds

Manufacturer: U. S. Glass Co. **Date:** Ca. 1926
Color: Crystal
Value: $40.00 – 70.00
Description — Top: Fire polished **Bottom:** Full ground **Bottom Figure:** 16-point star
Dimensions — Top: 3" **Bottom:** 2⅜" **Height:** 3¹⁵⁄₁₆"
Decoration: Gold band and heavy green, blue, and white enamel.
Additional Notes: 3" top of figure.

AKA: Shepherd's Plaid

Manufacturer: Model Flint **Date:** 1890s
Color: Crystal
Value: $40.00 – 70.00
Description — Top: Fire polished **Bottom:** Unfinished
Dimensions — Top: 2¹³⁄₁₆" **Bottom:** 2¾" **Height:** 3¹⁵⁄₁₆"
Additional Notes: 3¹¹⁄₁₆" top of figure.

Daisy & Button

This pattern was first designed as a cut pattern, patented by T. G. Hawkes & Co., June 20, 1882. On May 1, 1884, Geo. Duncan & Sons were reported as having "an exceedingly handsome berry dish....octagon rosette." Hobbs Brockunier & Co., on Oct. 9, 1884, called attention to "the 101 set in all colors..." Both of these patterns are now called Daisy & Button. Soon, most pressed glass houses had a pattern based upon this wondrous design. It has been said that this pattern was the death knell for rich cut glass. Some authors have claimed that this pattern was sold at the 1876 Centennial Celebration, but the dates of development show that this earlier dating is in error. This pattern is so popular that it has been made almost continuously since its introduction.

Original Name: No. 307
AKA: Daisy & Button

Manufacturer: Geo. Duncan & Sons **Date:** 1884
Color: Crystal, Blue, possibly Amber, Canary
Value: $40.00 – 70.00
Description — Top: Fire polished **Bottom:** Ground and polished
  Bottom Figure: Multi-point star
Dimensions — Top: 2¾" **Bottom:** 2½" **Height:** 4"

Original Name: No. 308
AKA: Daisy & Button

Manufacturer: Geo. Duncan & Sons **Date:** 1884
Color: Crystal, possibly Amber, Blue, Canary
Value: $30.00 – 40.00
Description — Top: Fire polished **Bottom:** Ground and polished **Bottom Figure:** 24-point star
Dimensions — Top: 2¹³⁄₁₆" **Bottom:** 2³⁄₁₆" **Rim Height:** 3¹³⁄₁₆"
Additional Notes: 3¹¹⁄₁₆" top of figure. Note that No. 307 (above) is taller than No. 308.

Original Name: No. 101
AKA: Daisy & Button

Manufacturer: Hobbs, Brockunier & Co. **Date:** 1884
Color: Crystal, Marine Green, Sapphire Blue, Amber, Canary, possibly others
Value: $40.00 – 70.00
Description — Top: Fire polished **Bottom:** Ground and polished
   Bottom Figure: Five hobs, four daisies
Dimensions — Top: 2¹⁵⁄₁₆" **Bottom:** 2¹¹⁄₁₆" **Height:** 4⅛"
Additional Notes: 2⁵⁄₁₆" top of figure.

AKA: Daisy & Button

Color: Blue, Amber
Value: $35.00 – 50.00
Description — Top: Fire polished **Bottom:** Ground **Bottom Figure:** 20-point star.
Dimensions — Top: 2⅞" to 3" **Bottom:** 2⅜" **Height:** 3¹¹⁄₁₆" to 3¾"
Additional Notes: 2" top of figure.

Original Name: Fashion
AKA: Daisy & Button

Manufacturer: Bryce Bros. **Date:** 1884
Color: Blue, possibly Amber, Canary, Sea Green, Amethyst
Value: $35.00 – 50.00
Description — Top: Fire polished **Bottom:** Stuck-up, rough
   Bottom Figure: Five daisies, four hobs
Dimensions — Top: 2⁹⁄₁₆" **Bottom:** 1¹³⁄₁₆" **Height:** 3⅝"
Decoration: Amber stained band and upper portion of figure.
Additional Notes: 2¾" top of figure.

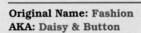

Original Name: Fashion
AKA: Daisy & Button

Manufacturer: Bryce Bros. **Date:** 1884
Color: Crystal
Value: $80.00 – 100.00
Description — Top: Fire polished **Bottom:** Ground Buttons
   Bottom Figure: Five daisies, four hobs
Dimensions — Top: 2⅝" **Bottom:** 1¹³⁄₁₆" rim **Height:** 3⁹⁄₁₆"
Decoration: Ruby stained.
Additional Notes: 2¹³⁄₁₆" top of figure.

Original Name: Fashion
AKA: Daisy & Button

Manufacturer: Bryce Bros. **Date:** 1884
Color: Crystal
Value: $80.00 – 100.00
Description — Top: Fire polished **Bottom:** Ground **Bottom Figure:** Five daisies, four hobs
Dimensions — Top: 2⁹⁄₁₆" **Bottom:** 1¾" **Height:** 3⁹⁄₁₆"
Decoration: Allover Ruby stained.
Additional Notes: 2¹³⁄₁₆" top of figure.

AKA: Daisy & Button

Color: Sapphire Blue
Value: $35.00 – 50.00

Original Name: Elrose
AKA: Daisy & Buttons with Amber Panels

Manufacturer: Geo. Duncan & Sons **Date:** 1886
Color: Crystal
Value: $70.00 – 90.00
Description — Top: Fire polished **Bottom:** Flat ground **Bottom Figure:** 24-point star
Dimensions — Top: 2⅞" **Bottom:** 2⁵⁄₁₆" **Height:** 3⅛"
Decoration: Amber stained.

Original Name: No. 58
AKA: Clover

Manufacturer: Duncan & Miller Co. **Date:** 1904
Color: Crystal
Value: $45.00 – 65.00
Dimensions — Top: 3¹⁄₁₆" **Bottom:** 2⅜" **Height:** 3¹⁵⁄₁₆"
Description — Top: Fire polished **Bottom:** Full ground **Bottom Figure:** 20-point star
Additional Notes: 3³⁄₁₆" top of figure.

Original Name: No. 86
AKA: Daisy & Button and Thumbprint Panel

Manufacturer: Adams & Co. **Date:** 1886
Color: Amber, probably others
Value: $40.00 – 70.00
Description — Top: Fire polished **Bottom Figure:** Pattern continues to center
Dimensions — Top: 3" **Bottom:** 2¹³⁄₁₆" **Height:** 4⅛"

Original Name: No. 555 Van Dyke
AKA: Daisy & Button with V Ornament

Manufacturer: A. J. Beatty & Sons **Date:** 1886
Color: Crystal, Amber, Blue, Canary
Value: $35.00 – 45.00
Description — Top: Fire polished **Bottom:** Ground buttons in figure **Bottom Figure:** Daisy & Button figure
Dimensions — Top: 2¹⁵⁄₁₆" **Bottom:** 2⁹⁄₁₆" **Height:** 3⅞"
Additional Notes: Nos. 555 and 558 are similar, but No. 555 has pattern in the bottom and 558 does not.

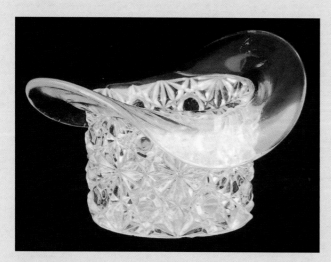

AKA: Daisy & Button Whimsy Hat

Color: Canary
Value: $75.00 – 95.00
Description — Top: Fire polished **Bottom:** Ground
   Bottom Figure: Five daisies, four buttons
Dimensions — Bottom Diameter: 2½"
Additional Notes: 1¹⁵⁄₁₆" top of figure.

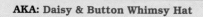

AKA: Daisy & Button Whimsy Hat

Color: Amber
Value: $40.00 – 70.00
Description — Top: Fire polished **Bottom:** Ground
   Bottom Figure: Five daisies, four buttons
Dimensions — Bottom Diameter: 2³⁄₁₆"
Additional Notes: 1¹¹⁄₁₆" top of figure.

Imitation Cut

It didn't start with Daisy & Button, but that was the first truly major imitation cut pattern. Companies began to vie with each other to make the pressed pattern that most realistically appeared to be cut. Trade quotes at the time were fond of the expression "only an expert can tell," implying that if you were to purchase such a piece, any guests you might later have would assume it was cut. These patterns began in the 1850s and continued into the 1920s. Obviously, they were very successful.

Original Name: No. 124
AKA: Wigwam

Manufacturer: A. H. Heisey & Co. **Date:** 1897
Color: Crystal
Value: $40.00 – 70.00
Description — Top: Fire polished **Bottom:** Ground rim **Bottom:** 20-point star
Dimensions — Top: 2¹³⁄₁₆" **Bottom:** 2½" **Height:** 3⅞"
Additional Notes: 3¹¹⁄₁₆" top of figure.

Original Name: No. 113
AKA: Diamond Point & Fan

Manufacturer: A. H. Heisey & Co. **Date:** 1897
Color: Crystal
Value: $40.00 – 70.00
Description — Top: Fire polished **Bottom:** Ground rim **Bottom:** 20-point star
Dimensions — Top: 2¾" **Bottom:** 2⁹⁄₁₆" **Height:** 3¾"
Additional Notes: 3¼" top of figure.

AKA: Divided Diamonds

Color: Crystal
Value: $35.00 – 50.00
Description — Top: Fire polished **Bottom:** Full ground
  Bottom Figure: 24-point star
Dimensions — Top: 3¹⁄₁₆" **Bottom:** 2⁷⁄₁₆" **Height:** 3⅞"

Original Name: No. 100
AKA: Boxed Star

Manufacturer: Kokomo Glass Co. **Date:** 1902
Color: Crystal
Value: $20.00 – 25.00
Description — Top: Fire polished **Bottom Figure:** 18-point star
Dimensions — Top: 2⅞" **Bottom:** 2⅝" **Height:** 3¹³/₁₆"

Original Name: Tacoma
AKA: Jeweled Diamond & Fan

Manufacturer: Greensburg Glass Co. **Date:** 1894
Color: Crystal
Value: $55.00 – 70.00
Descriptions — Bottom: Ground **Bottom Figure:** 30-point star
Dimensions — Top: 2⅞" **Bottom:** 2½" **Height:** 3⅝"
Decoration: Ruby stained.
Additional Notes: 3⁷/₁₆" top of figure, second manufacturer was National/Model Flint; they called it No. 907.

Original Name: No. 15046 Victor
AKA: Shoshone

Manufacturer: United States Glass Co. **Date:** 1896
Color: Crystal
Value: $55.00 – 70.00
Description — Top: Fire polished **Bottom:** Ground **Bottom Figure:** 24-point star
Dimensions — Top: 2¹¹/₁₆" **Bottom:** 2½" **Height:** 3⁹/₁₆"
Decoration: Ruby stained.
Additional Notes: 3⅜" top of figure.

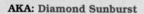

AKA: Diamond Sunburst

Color: Crystal
Value: $40.00 – 70.00
Description — Top: Fire polished **Bottom:** Ground **Bottom Figure:** 20-point star
Dimensions — Top: 2¾" **Bottom:** 2½" **Height:** 3¾"
Decoration: Ruby stained.
Additional Notes: 3¹¹/₁₆" top of figure. Compare with Champion on page 46.

Original Name: No. 300
AKA: Fancy Arch

Manufacturer: National Glass Co. at McKee Works **Date:** 1901
Color: Crystal
Value: $45.00 – 60.00
Descriptions — Bottom: Ground **Bottom Figure:** 24-point star.
Dimensions — Top: 2¾" **Bottom:** 2½" **Height:** 3¹³⁄₁₆"
Decoration: Ruby stained.
Additional Notes: 3³⁄₁₆" top of figure.

Original Name: Atlanta

Manufacturer: Tarentum Glass Co. **Date:** 1894
Color: Crystal
Value: $40.00 – 55.00
Description — Top: Fire polished **Bottom:** Ground **Bottom Figure:** Fancy
Dimensions — Top: 2¾" **Bottom:** 2⅝" **Height:** 3⅞
Decoration: Ruby stained.
Additional Notes: 3¹¹⁄₁₆" top of figure.

Original Name: Carmen

Manufacturer: Fostoria Glass Co. **Date:** 1896
Color: Crystal
Value: $40.00 – 70.00
Description — Top: Fire polished **Bottom:** Rough, stuck-up
Dimensions — Top: 3³⁄₁₆" **Bottom:** 2⁷⁄₁₆" **Height:** 3¹¹⁄₁₆"
Decoration: Exists with Amber stain and engraved flowers on plain panels.

Original Name: Carmen

Manufacturer: Fostoria Glass Co.
Color: Crystal
Value: $40.00 – 70.00
Dimensions — Top: 2⁷⁄₈" **Bottom:** 2½" across plain flats **Height:** 3¹³⁄₁₆"
Description — Top: Fire polished **Bottom:** Ground rim
Decoration: Amber stain, painted floral.
Additional Notes: 1⅞" top of figure.

AKA: Sunken Buttons

Date: Mid-1880s
Color: Crystal, Amber, Blue, Canary
Value: $35.00 – 50.00
Description — Top: Fire polished **Bottom:** Ground and polished
   Bottom Figure: 20-point star
Dimensions — Top: 3" **Bottom:** 2⁹⁄₁₆" **Height:** 3¾"
Additional Notes: This tumbler was made in a two-part mold.

Original Name: Harvard
AKA: Harvard Yard

Manufacturer: Tarentum Glass Co. **Date:** 1896
Color: Crystal
Value: $40.00 – 70.00
Description — Top: Fire polished **Bottom:** Ground and polished **Bottom Figure:** Hobstar
Dimensions — Top: 2⅞" **Bottom:** 2¾" **Height:** 3¹³⁄₁₆"
Decoration: Gold.
Additional Notes: Earlier researchers confused this with another Tarentum pattern,
   originally called Columbia, which they renamed Harvard.

Original Name: Harvard
AKA: Harvard Yard

Manufacturer: Tarentum **Date:** 1896
Color: Crystal, possibly other colors
Value: $75.00 – 95.00
Description — Top: Fire polished **Bottom:** Ground **Bottom Figure:** 24-point star
Dimensions — Top: 2¹⁵⁄₁₆" **Bottom:** 2¼" **Height:** 3¹⁵⁄₁₆"
Decoration: Ruby stained.
Additional Notes: 3" top of figure. Variant of preceding tumbler.

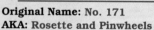

Original Name: No. 171
AKA: Rosette and Pinwheels

Manufacturer: Indiana Glass Co. **Date:** Ca. 1905
Color: Crystal
Value: $15.00 – 25.00
Description — Top: Imperfectly fire polished **Bottom:** Unfinished
   Bottom Figure: Ornate pinwheel
Dimensions — Top: 3⅛" **Bottom:** 2⁷⁄₁₆" **Height:** 4³⁄₁₆"

Original Name: No. 123
AKA: Caned Waffle

Manufacturer: A. H. Heisey & Co. **Date:** 1897
Color: Crystal
Value: $35.00 – 50.00
Description — Top: Fire polished **Bottom:** Ground rim **Bottom Figure:** 20-point star
Dimensions — Top: 2⅞" **Bottom:** 2½" **Height:** 3¹¹⁄₁₆"
Additional Notes: 3¹⁄₁₆" top of figure.

Original Name: Virginia No. 15071
AKA: Banded Portland

Manufacturer: United States Glass Co. **Date:** 1901
Color: Crystal
Value: $30.00 – 40.00
Description — Top: Fire polished **Bottom:** Full ground **Bottom Figure:** 24-point star
Dimensions — Top: 3¹⁄₁₆" **Bottom:** 2" across flats **Height:** 3⅞"
Decoration: Gold, Blush.

Original Name: No. 367
AKA: Prison Stripe

Manufacturer: A. H. Heisey & Co. **Date:** 1906
Color: Crystal
Value: $75.00 – 100.00
Description — Top: Fire polished **Bottom:** Full ground **Bottom Figure:** 20-point star
Dimensions — Top: 3³⁄₁₆" **Bottom:** 2⁹⁄₁₆" across flats **Height:** 3⅞"
Additional Notes: 3" top of figure, eight flutes. Signed with Diamond H inside bottom.

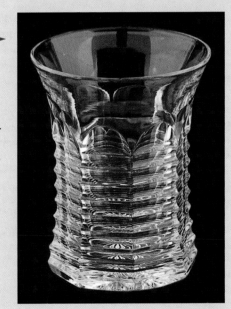

Original Name: No. 102
AKA: Maltese and Ribbon

Manufacturer: Hobbs, Brockunier & Co. **Date:** 1886
Color: Crystal, Canary, Sapphire, Amber, possibly Ruby
Value: $40.00 – 70.00
Description — Top: Unfinished **Bottom:** Unfinished **Bottom Figure:** Complex star, logo
Dimensions — Top: 3" **Bottom:** 2⁷⁄₁₆" **Height:** 4"
Decoration: May have yellow stain.
Additional Notes: Probably made by United States Glass Co. after the merger, has advertising, says, "USE WHITERIVER FLOUR." Production tumblers by Hobbs, Brockunier do not have advertising.

Original Name: No. 68
AKA: King Arthur

Manufacturer: Duncan & Miller Co. **Date:** 1908
Color: Crystal
Value: $40.00 – 50.00
Description — Top: Fire polished **Bottom:** Ground **Bottom Figure:** 16-point star
Dimensions — Top: 2⅞" **Bottom:** 2½" **Height:** 4"

Color: Crystal
Value: $20.00 – 30.00
Description — Top: Fire polished **Bottom:** Ground and polished **Bottom Figure:** 16-point star
Dimensions — Top: 2¹⁵⁄₁₆" **Bottom:** 2⁷⁄₁₆" **Height:** 4³⁄₁₆"
Additional Notes: 3⁷⁄₁₆" top of figure. Very similar to Duncan & Miller's King Arthur, see above.

Original Name: Champion

Manufacturer: McKee Bros. **Date:** 1894
Color: Crystal
Value: $65.00 – 85.00
Description — Top: Fire polished **Bottom:** Ground **Bottom Figure:** 24-point star
Dimensions — Top: 2¾" **Bottom:** 2⁹⁄₁₆" **Height:** 3⅞"
Decoration: Ruby stained.
Additional Notes: 3¾" top of figure.

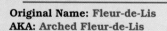

Original Name: Fleur-de-Lis
AKA: Arched Fleur-de-Lis

Manufacturer: Bryce, Higbee & Co. **Date:** 1989
Color: Crystal
Value: $35.00 – 60.00
Description — Top: Fire polished **Bottom Figure:** Complex ellipse with rays
Dimensions — Top: 2⅞" **Bottom:** 2⅝" **Height:** 3¾"
Additional Notes: 3⁵⁄₁₆" top of figure.

Original Name: Fleur-de-Lis
AKA: Arched Fleur-de-Lis

Manufacturer: Bryce Higbee & Co. **Date:** 1898
Color: Crystal
Value: $75.00 – 95.00
Description — Top: Fire polished **Bottom:** Unfinished **Bottom Figure:** Fancy
Dimensions — Top: 2⅞" **Bottom:** 2⅝" **Height:** 3¾"
Decoration: Ruby stained.
Additional Notes: 3¼" top of figure.

Original Name: No. 51
AKA: Two-ply Swirl

Manufacturer: Duncan & Miller Glass Co. **Date:** 1902
Color: Crystal
Value: $40.00 – 70.00
Description — Top: Fire polished **Bottom:** Ground **Bottom Figure:** 24-point star
Dimensions — Top: 2⅞" **Bottom:** 2¼" **Height:** 3⅛"
Decoration: May be Amber or Ruby stained.
Additional Notes: 3" top of figure.

Original Name: No. 213
AKA: Scroll with Cane Band

Manufacturer: West Virginia Glass Co. **Date:** 1894
Color: Crystal
Value: $40.00 – 50.00
Description — Top: Fire polished **Bottom:** Ground and polished
   Bottom Figure: 24-point star
Dimensions — Top: 3⅛" **Bottom:** 2¹¹⁄₁₆" **Height:** 3¾"
Decoration: May have Amber stain on central band.
Additional Notes: 3⁵⁄₁₆" top of figure.

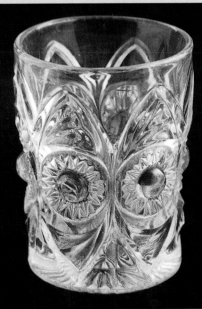

Original Name: No. 15090
AKA: Bull's-eye & Fan

Manufacturer: United States Glass Co. **Date:** 1904
Color: Crystal
Value: $40.00 – 50.00
Description — Top: Fire polished, irregularly round **Bottom:** Unfinished
   Bottom Figure: 30-point star
Dimensions — Top: 2¹⁵⁄₁₆" **Bottom:** 2½" **Height:** 3¹³⁄₁₆"
Decoration: Red luster on dots, gold on top band.
Additional Notes: 3½" top of figure.

Original Name: No. 15090
AKA: Bull's-eye & Fan

Manufacturer: United States Glass Co. **Date:** 1904
Color: Deep Copper Blue
Value: $40.00 – 70.00
Description — Top: Fire polished, irregularly round **Bottom:** Unfinished
    Bottom Figure: 30-point star
Dimensions — Top: 3" **Bottom:** 2⁹⁄₁₆" **Height:** 3¹³⁄₁₆"
Decoration: Gold on dots, top band.
Additional Notes: 3½" top of figure.

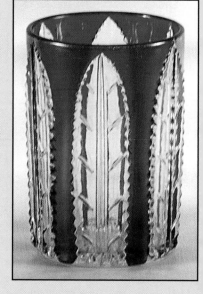

Original Name: No. 323
AKA: Lattice Leaf

Manufacturer: Co-Operative Flint Glass Co. **Date:** 1906
Color: Crystal
Value: $75.00 – 95.00
Description — Top: Fire polished **Bottom:** Unfinished **Bottom Figure:** 20-point star
Dimensions — Top: 2¾" **Bottom:** 2⁷⁄₁₆" **Height:** 3⅞"
Decoration: Ruby stained.
Additional Notes: 3⅛" top of figure.

Original Name: No. 90
AKA: Zippered Block

Manufacturer: Geo. Duncan & Sons **Date:** 1887
Color: Crystal
Value: $70.00 – 90.00
Description — Top: Fire polished **Bottom:** Ground **Bottom Figure:** 24-point star
Dimensions — Top: 2⅞" **Bottom:** 2⁷⁄₁₆" **Height:** 3⅞"
Decoration: Ruby stained.

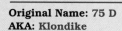

Original Name: 75 D
AKA: Klondike

Manufacturer: Dalzell, Gilmore & Leighton Glass Co. **Date:** 1898
Color: Crystal
Value: $150.00 – 200.00
Description — Top: Fire polished **Bottom Figure:** Figure
Dimensions — Top: 3" **Bottom:** 2½" **Height:** 4"
Decoration: Deep Amber stain, frosted panels.

Original Name: No. 15093 The States
AKA: Cane & Star Medallion

Manufacturer: United States Glass Co. **Date:** 1905
Color: Crystal
Value: $40.00 – 55.00
Description — Top: Fire polished **Bottom:** Ground and polished
  Bottom Figure: Irregular 30-point star
Dimensions — Top: 3¹⁄₁₆" **Bottom:** 2¹¹⁄₁₆" over lobes **Height:** 3⅞"
Decoration: Gold above figure.
Additional Notes: 3¼" top of figure.

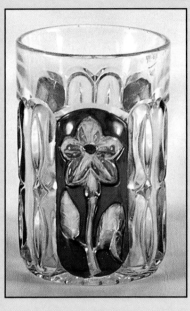

Original Name: Florida
AKA: Sunken Primrose

Manufacturer: Greensburg Glass Co. **Date:** 1894
Color: Crystal
Value: $50.00 – 70.00
Description — Top: Fire polished
  Bottom: Ground **Bottom Figure:** 20-point star
Dimensions — Top: 2½" **Bottom:** 2³⁄₁₆"
  Height: 3⅞"
Decoration: Ruby stained panels and Amber
  stain in flowers.
Additional Notes: 3¹⁄₁₆" top of figure, patented,
  called *Painted Amberina.*

AKA: Flower with Hexagons

Color: Crystal
Value: $20.00 – 30.00
Description — Top: Fire polished **Bottom:** Unfinished **Bottom Figure:** 16-point star
Dimensions — Top: 2¹⁵⁄₁₆" **Bottom:** 2¼" **Height:** 4¼"
Additional Notes: 3⅜" top of figure.

Original Name: No. 2760
AKA: Daisy

Manufacturer: Cambridge Glass Co. **Date:** 1910
Color: Crystal
Value: $40.00 – 70.00
Description — Top: Fire polished **Bottom:** Unfinished **Bottom Figure:** Figure
Dimensions — Top: 3³⁄₁₆" **Height:** 4⅛"
Decoration: Gold above figure, Ruby stained.
Additional Notes: 3⁵⁄₁₆" top of figure, "Nearcut" inside bottom.

Original Name: No. 50
AKA: Block & Rosette

Manufacturer: Duncan & Miller Glass Co. **Date:** 1902
Color: Crystal
Value: $40.00 – 70.00
Description — Top: Fire polished **Bottom:** Ground and polished
   Bottom Figure: 32-point star
Dimensions — Top: 2⅞" **Bottom:** 2½" **Height:** 4⅛"
Additional Notes: 3⅜" top of figure.

Original Name: No. 15125
AKA: Intaglio Sunflower

Manufacturer: United States Glass Co. **Date:** Ca. 1911
Color: Crystal
Value: $40.00 – 50.00
Dimensions — Top: 2¹⁵⁄₁₆" **Bottom:** 2⅝" across flats **Height:** 4"
Description — Top: Fire polished **Bottom:** Ground and polished
   Bottom Figure: 22-point star
Decoration: Gold, green ceramic glaze on flower.
Additional Notes: 3¼" top of figure, eight panels.

AKA: Diamond Panels

Color: Crystal
Value: $25.00 – 35.00
Description — Top: Fire polished **Bottom:** Rough, stuck-up
Bottom Figure: 24-point star
Dimensions — Top: 3" **Bottom:** 2⅝" **Height:** 3⅞"
Additional Notes: 2⅞" top of figure.

AKA: Flattened Diamonds

Color: Crystal
Value: $25.00 – 35.00
Description — Top: Fire polished **Bottom:** Unfinished **Bottom Figure:** 18-point star
Dimensions — Top: 3³⁄₁₆" **Bottom:** 2⅝" **Height:** 3¹¹⁄₁₆"
Additional Notes: 2¹³⁄₁₆" top of figure. See preceding tumbler.

Original Name: No. 550
AKA: High Hob

Manufacturer: Westmoreland Specialty Co. **Date:** 1915
Color: Crystal
Value: $60.00 – 70.00
Decoration: Ruby stained, gold above pattern.

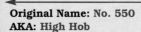

Original Name: No. 550
AKA: High Hob

Manufacturer: Westmoreland Specialty Co. **Date:** 1915
Color: Crystal
Value: $55.00 – 65.00 cut over, $25.00 - 35.00 uncut
Description — Top: Fire polished **Bottom:** Unfinished **Bottom Figure:** 6-point cut star
Dimensions — Top: 3¼" **Bottom:** 2⁷⁄₁₆" **Height:** 4⅝"
Decoration: This design has been cut over.

Original Name: No. 301, Lorraine
AKA: Flat Diamond Box

Manufacturer: Fostoria Glass Co. **Date:** 1893
Color: Crystal
Value: $40.00 – 70.00
Decoration: Ruby stained.

Original Name: No. 705
AKA: Klear-Kut

Manufacturer: New Martinsville Glass Co. **Date:** 1906
Color: Crystal
Value: $50.00 – 60.00
Description — Top: Fire polished **Bottom:** Ground **Bottom Figure:** Fancy rays
Dimensions — Top: 2⅞" **Bottom:** 2⁵⁄₁₆" **Height:** 3¾"
Decoration: Ruby stained.
Additional Notes: 2⅞" top of figure.

Original Name: No. 305
AKA: Punty & Diamond Point

Manufacturer: A. H. Heisey & Co. **Date:** 1899
Color: Crystal
Value: $65.00 – 85.00
Description — Top: Fire polished **Bottom:** Full ground **Bottom Figure:** Uneven 6-point star
Dimensions — Top: 3" **Bottom:** 2⁷⁄₁₆" **Height:** 3⅞"
Additional Notes: 3" top of figure.

Original Name: No. 1119 Sylvan

Manufacturer: Fostoria Glass Co. **Date:** 1902
Color: Crystal
Value: $25.00 – 35.00
Description — Top: Fire polished **Bottom:** Ground rim **Bottom Figure:** 24-point unequal star
Dimensions — Top: 2⅞" **Bottom:** 2⅜" **Height:** 3⅞"
Decoration: Gold on top rim.
Additional Notes: 2¹⁵⁄₁₆" top of figure.

Original Name: Doric
AKA: Feather

Manufacturer: McKee & Brothers **Date:** 1896
Color: Crystal
Value: $35.00 – 50.00
Description — Top: Fire polished **Bottom:** Unfinished **Bottom Figure:** 28-point star
Dimensions — Top: 2¹³⁄₁₆" **Bottom:** 2½" **Height:** 4¹⁄₁₆"
Additional Notes: Nearly identical pattern made by Beatty-Brady. Difficult to distinguish in the tumbler.

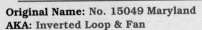

Original Name: No. 15049 Maryland
AKA: Inverted Loop & Fan

Manufacturer: United States Glass Co. **Date:** 1897
Color: Crystal
Value: $85.00 – 100.00
Description — Top: Fire polished **Bottom:** Unfinished **Bottom Figure:** 28 rays
Dimensions — Top: 2¾" **Bottom:** 2⁵⁄₁₆" **Height:** 3⅝"
Decoration: May have gold or Ruby stain.
Additional Notes: 3" top of figure.

Original Name: No. 185
AKA: Columned Thumbprints

Manufacturer: Westmoreland Specialty Co. **Date:** 1901
Color: Crystal
Value: $40.00 – 55.00
Description — Top: Fire polished **Bottom:** Unfinished
Dimensions — Top: 2¹¹⁄₁₆" **Bottom:** 2⅜" **Height:** 3⅞"
Decoration: Punties are cold stained.
Additional Notes: 3⅛" top of figure.

Original Name: No. 52
AKA: Ladder with Diamonds

Manufacturer: Duncan & Miller Glass Co. **Date:** 1902
Color: Crystal
Value: $25.00 - 35.00
Description — Top: Fire polished **Bottom:** Ground and polished **Bottom Figure:** 12-point star
Dimensions — Top: 3" **Bottom:** 2⁷⁄₁₆" **Height:** 3⅞"
Additional Notes: 3¼" top of figure. Duncan's tumbler has small diamonds in the large diamonds.

AKA: Ladder with Diamonds Variant

Manufacturer: Duncan & Miller Glass Co. **Date:** Ca. 1902
Color: Crystal
Value: $25.00 – 35.00
Description — Top: Fire polished **Bottom:** Rough **Bottom Figure:** 12-point star
Dimensions — Top: 3" **Bottom:** 2⁷⁄₁₆" **Height:** 3⅞"
Decoration: May have Gold or Ruby stain.
Additional Notes: 3³⁄₁₆" top of figure. This variant has small diamonds alternating with quartered blocks in the large diamonds.

AKA: Ladder with Diamonds

Manufacturer: Tarentum Glass Co. **Date:** 1903
Color: Crystal
Value: $40.00 – 70.00
Description — Top: Fire polished **Bottom:** Unfinished **Bottom Figure:** Fancy
Dimensions — Top: 3⅛" **Bottom:** 2⅝" **Height:** 3⅞"
Decoration: Gold above pattern, Ruby stained.
Additional Notes: 3⁷⁄₁₆" top of figure. Tarentum's tumbler has hexagonal cane motif in the large diamonds.

AKA: Fan & Hobstar

Color: Crystal
Value: $35.00
Description — Top: Fire polished **Bottom Figure:** Complex hobstar
Dimensions — Top: 3³⁄₁₆" **Bottom:** 2½" **Height:** 3¹⁵⁄₁₆"
Decoration: Gold above figure.
Additional Notes: 3" top of figure.

Original Name: Gladiator

Manufacturer: McKee & Brothers **Date:** 1897
Color: Emerald Green
Value: $45.00 – 55.00
Description — Top: Fire polished **Bottom:** Ground and polished
  Bottom Figure: 24-point star
Dimensions — Top: 2¹⁵⁄₁₆" **Bottom:** 2⁷⁄₁₆" **Height:** 3⁷⁄₈"
Decoration: Gold on top band.

Original Name: No. 125
AKA: Fancy Square

Manufacturer: A. H. Heisey & Co. **Date:** 1897
Color: Crystal
Value: $80.00 – 100.00
Description — Top: Fire polished **Bottom:** Ground and polished
  Bottom Figure: 20-point star
Dimensions — Top: 2⁷⁄₈" **Bottom:** 2½" **Height:** 3¾"
Additional Notes: 3¹⁄₁₆" top of figure.

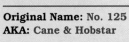

Original Name: No. 125
AKA: Cane & Hobstar

Manufacturer: A. H. Heisey & Co. **Date:** 1897
Color: Crystal
Value: $40.00 – 70.00
Description — Top: Fire polished **Bottom:** Ground and polished
  Bottom Figure: 20-point star
Dimensions — Top: 2⁷⁄₈" **Bottom:** 2½" **Height:** 3¾"
Additional Notes: 3⅛" top of figure.

AKA: Cane Octagon

Color: Crystal
Value: $30.00 – 40.00
Description — Top: Fire polished **Bottom:** Ground and polished rim
  Bottom Figure: 8-point star
Dimensions — Top: 3¼" **Bottom:** 2⁹⁄₁₆" **Height:** 3⅞"
Decoration: Gold on top band.
Additional Notes: 3³⁄₁₆" top of figure.

Original Name: No. 1205½
AKA: Fancy Loop

Manufacturer: A. H. Heisey & Co. **Date:** 1896
Color: Crystal
Value: $40.00 – 70.00
Description — Top: Fire polished **Bottom:** Full ground **Bottom Figure:** 20-point star
Dimensions — Top: 3" **Bottom:** 2½" **Height:** 3¹³⁄₁₆"
Additional Notes: 3⅛" top of figure. This is a variation of the standard 1205 pattern.

Original Name: Toltec

Manufacturer: National Glass Co., McKee & Brothers Glass Works **Date:** Ca. 1903
Color: Crystal
Value: $25.00 – 35.00
Description — Top: Fire polished **Bottom:** Unfinished **Bottom Figure:** 24-point uneven star
Dimensions — Top: 3" **Bottom:** 2⁷⁄₁₆" **Height:** 4"
Additional Notes: 3" top of figure. Marked "PRES CUT" inside bottom.

Original Name: No. 15048 Pennsylvania
AKA: Balder

Manufacturer: United States Glass Co. **Date:** 1897
Color: Crystal
Value: $75.00 – 90.00
Description — Top: Fire polished **Bottom:** Ground **Bottom Figure:** 24-point star
Dimensions — Top: 2⅞" **Bottom:** 2½" **Height:** 3¾"
Decoration: Ruby stained, engraved "To Julia from Tom."
Additional Notes: 3¹⁄₁₆" top of figure.

Original Name: No. 330

Manufacturer: Geo. Duncan & Sons **Date:** 1889
Color: Crystal
Value: $35.00 – 50.00
Description — Top: Fire polished **Bottom:** Unfinished **Bottom Figure:** Figure
Dimensions — Top: 2¹³⁄₁₆" **Bottom:** 2⅜" **Height:** 3¾"
Decoration: Ruby stained.
Additional Notes: 2¹³⁄₁₆" top of figure.

Original Name: Quintec

Manufacturer: McKee Glass Co. **Date:** 1910
Color: Crystal
Value: $50.00 – 60.00
Description — Top: Fire polished **Bottom:** Unfinished
Dimensions — Top: 3⅛" **Bottom:** 2⅝" **Height:** 4"
Decoration: Gold above pattern, ruby stained on panels
Additional Notes: 3⁵⁄₁₆" top of figure, "Prescut" inside base.

Original Name: No. 1
AKA: Three-in-One

Manufacturer: Imperial Glass Corp. **Date:** 1903
Color: Crystal
Value: $65.00 – 85.00
Dimensions — Top: 2⅞" **Bottom:** 2⅜" **Height:** 3¾"
Description — Top: Fire polished **Bottom:** Ground **Bottom Figure:** 22-point star
Decoration: Ruby stained.
Additional Notes: 3¼" Top of figure. Reintroduced by Imperial mid-century, in colors
    and iridized.

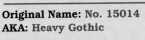

Original Name: No. 15014
AKA: Heavy Gothic

Manufacturer: United States Glass Co., Columbia Glass Co. **Date:** 1892
Color: Crystal
Value: $50.00 – 70.00
Dimensions — Top: 3⅛" **Bottom:** 3" across lobes **Height:** 3¾"
Description — Top: Fire polished **Bottom:** Unfinished **Bottom Figure:** 20-point star
Decoration: Ruby stained.
Additional Notes: 3¼" top of figure.

AKA: Crescent, Fringed Drape

Manufacturer: National Glass Co., McKee Brothers Glass Works **Date:** 1901
Color: Crystal
Value: $80.00 – 90.00
Description — Top: Fire polished **Bottom:** Ground **Bottom Figure:** Alternate long and short rays
Dimensions — Top: 2¹³⁄₁₆" **Bottom:** 2⅜" **Height:** 4"
Decoration: Ruby stained.
Additional Notes: 3¼" top of figure.

Original Name: No. 719
AKA: Old Glory

Manufacturer: New Martinsville Glass Co. **Date:** 1913
Color: Crystal
Value: $80.00 – 90.00
Description — Top: Fire polished **Bottom:** Ground
Dimensions — Top: 3" **Bottom:** 2⅛" **Height:** 4⅛"
Decoration: Gold above figure, Ruby stained.
Additional Notes: 3⁷⁄₁₆" top of figure.

Original Name: No. 23
AKA: Pioneer's 23, Loop & Block

Manufacturer: Thompson **Date:** 1893
Color: Crystal
Value: $50.00 – 70.00
Description — Top: Fire polished, irregularly round **Bottom:** Ground and polished
Bottom Figure: 18-point star
Dimensions — Top: 2¹⁵⁄₁₆" **Bottom:** 2½" **Height:** 4"
Decoration: Ruby stained.
Additional Notes: 3⁵⁄₁₆" top of figure.

AKA: Glenda

Date: Ca. 1908
Color: Crystal
Value: $70.00 – 90.00
Description — Top: Fire polished **Bottom:** Ground
Dimensions — Top: 3⅛" **Bottom:** 2⅜" **Height:** 4¹⁄₁₆"
Decoration: Ruby stain, gold band, inscribed "1908 Alex Conders."
Additional Notes: 3⅛" top of figure.

Imitation Cut

Original Name: No. 15004
AKA: Barred Oval

Manufacturer: United States Glass Co., Geo. Duncan & Sons **Date:** 1892
Color: Crystal
Value: $70.00 – 90.00
Description — Top: Fire polished **Bottom:** Unfinished **Bottom Figure:** 20-point star
Dimensions — Top: 2¹¹⁄₁₆" **Bottom:** 2⅛" **Height:** 3¹³⁄₁₆"
Decoration: Ovals may be frosted, Ruby stained.
Additional Notes: 3" top of figure. This pattern has been reproduced by Fenton in colors.

Original Name: No. 15021
AKA: Broken Column

Manufacturer: United States Glass Co., Columbia Glass Co. **Date:** 1893
Color: Crystal
Value: $145.00 – 175 .00
Description — Top: Fire polished **Bottom:** Unfinished **Bottom Figure:** Figure continues.
Dimensions — Top: 2¾" **Height:** 3⅞"
Decoration: Ruby stained.
Additional Notes: 3⁷⁄₁₆" top of figure.

AKA: Notched Circles

Color: Emerald Green
Value: $40.00 – 55.00
Description — Top: Fire polished **Bottom Figure:** Complex (4 Ellipses, Diamond Point, Ray
Dimensions — Top: 2¹⁵⁄₁₆" **Bottom:** 2⅜" **Height:** 3¹⁵⁄₁₆"
Decoration: Gold above figure.
Additional Notes: 3¼" top of figure.

Original Name: No. 15111
AKA: Peacock, Slewed Horseshoe

Manufacturer: United States Glass Co. **Date:** 1908
Color: Crystal
Value: $40.00 – 55.00
Description — Top: Fire polished **Bottom:** Ground **Bottom Figure:** 20-point star with fine
ribs between points of star.
Dimensions — Top: 3⅛" **Bottom:** 2¼" **Height:** 4"
Decoration: Gold band above figure.

Original Name: No. 132
AKA: Boonsboro

Manufacturer: A. H. Heisey & Co. **Date:** 1897
Color: Crystal
Value: $50.00 – 70.00
Description — Top: Fire polished **Bottom:** Ground and polished **Bottom Figure:** 20-point star
Dimensions — Top: 2¹⁵⁄₁₆" **Bottom:** 2⁵⁄₁₆" **Height:** 3¹⁵⁄₁₆"
Additional Notes: 3¼" top of figure. Signed inside with Diamond H.

AKA: Hobstar & Arches

Manufacturer: Cambridge Glass Co. **Date:** Ca. 1905
Color: Crystal
Value: $25.00 – 35.00
Description — Top: Fire polished **Bottom:** Ground **Bottom Figure:** 8-point uneven star
Dimensions — Top: 3¹⁄₁₆" **Bottom:** 2⁷⁄₁₆" **Height:** 4"
Additional Notes: 3" top of figure. Marked "NEAR CUT."

Original Name: No. 15104 Victoria
AKA: Buzzsaw & Parenthesis

Manufacturer: United States Glass Co. **Date:** 1907
Color: Crystal
Value: $35.00 – 45.00
Description — Top: Fire polished **Bottom Figure:** Complex hobstar
Dimensions — Top: 3¹⁄₁₆" **Bottom:** 2⁵⁄₈" **Height:** 3¹¹⁄₁₆"
Decoration: Gold.
Additional Notes: 3⅛" top of figure.

Original Name: No. 15104 Victoria

Manufacturer: United States Glass Co. **Date:** 1892
Color: Crystal
Value: $35.00 – 45.00
Description — Top: Fire polished **Bottom:** Unfinished **Bottom Figure:** Complex hobstar
Dimensions — Top: 2¹⁵⁄₁₆" **Bottom:** 2¹¹⁄₁₆" **Height:** 3¾"
Decoration: Green ceramic glaze.
Additional Notes: 3³⁄₁₆" top of figure.

Original Name: Admiral
AKA: Ribbed Ellipse

Manufacturer: Bryce Higbee & Co. **Date:** 1899
Color: Crystal
Value: $30.00 – 40.00
Dimensions — Top: 2¹⁵⁄₁₆" **Bottom:** 2⁷⁄₁₆" rim **Height:** 3¹³⁄₁₆"
Description — Top: Fire polished **Bottom:** Unfinished **Bottom Figure:** 4-lobed figure
Additional Notes: 3⁷⁄₁₆" top of figure.

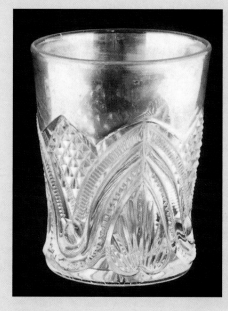

Original Name: No. 1901

Manufacturer: Co-Operative Flint Glass Co. **Date:** 1901
Color: Crystal
Value: $30.00 – 40.00
Description — Top: Fire polished **Bottom Figure:** 20-point star
Dimensions — Top: 3⅛" **Bottom:** 2⅝" **Height:** 3⅞"
Decoration: Gold.
Additional Notes: 2¹⁵⁄₁₆" top of figure.

Original Name: Swan

Manufacturer: Co-Operative Flint Glass Co. **Date:** 1900
Color: Crystal
Value: $120.00 – 150.00
Description — Top: Fire polished **Bottom:** Ground and polished **Bottom Figure:** Fancy
Dimensions — Top: 3¼" **Bottom:** 2⅜" **Height:** 3⅞"
Decoration: Gold above pattern, Ruby stained.
Additional Notes: 3¹⁄₁₆" top of figure.

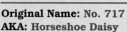

Original Name: No. 717
AKA: Horseshoe Daisy

Manufacturer: New Martinsville Glass Co. **Date:** 1917
Color: Crystal
Value: $30.00 – 40.00
Description — Top: Fire polished **Bottom:** Ground and polished
  Bottom Figure: 20-point star
Dimensions — Top: 3⅛" **Bottom:** 2¾" **Height:** 3⅞"

Original Name: No. 132

Manufacturer: National Glass Co., McKee & Brothers Glass Works **Date:** Ca. 1901
Color: Crystal
Value: $45.00 – 55.00
Dimensions — Top: 2¾" **Bottom:** 2⅜" **Height:** 3½"
Description — Top: Fire polished **Bottom:** Unfinished **Bottom Figure:** Circle inside points
Decoration: "Pan Am Expo 1901 Mother," Ruby stained.
Additional Notes: 2⅝" top of figure.

Original Name: No. 335 Prince of Wales, Plumes

Manufacturer: A. H. Heisey & Co. **Date:** 1902
Color: Crystal
Value: $75.00 – 100.00
Dimensions — Top: 3" **Bottom:** 2¹¹⁄₁₆" **Height:** 4"
Description — Top: Fire polished **Bottom:** Full ground **Bottom Figure:** Hobstar
Decoration: Gold.
Additional Notes: 3¼" top of figure, signed with Diamond H.

Original Name: No. 335 Prince of Wales, Plumes

Manufacturer: A. H. Heisey & Co. **Date:** 1902
Color: Crystal
Value: $140.00 – 170.00
Description — Top: Fire polished **Bottom:** Full ground **Bottom Figure:** Hobstar
Dimensions — Top: 2⅞" **Bottom:** 2¹¹⁄₁₆" **Height:** 4"
Decoration: Ruby stained, engraved "M. S. 1903."
Additional Notes: 3¼" top of figure.

Original Name: No. 484
AKA: Croesus

Manufacturer: Riverside Glass Co. **Date:** 1898
Color: Emerald Green
Value: $40.00 – 60.00
Description — Top: Fire polished **Bottom:** Ground
Dimensions — Top: 3⅛" **Bottom:** 2⁵⁄₁₆" **Height:** 4"
Decoration: Gold.
Additional Notes: Has been reproduced. Look for open ends in reproduced figures.

Original Name: No. 484
AKA: Croesus

Manufacturer: Riverside Glass Co. **Date:** 1898
Color: Royal Purple
Value: $50.00 – 70.00
Description — Top: Fire polished **Bottom:** Ground and polished
Dimensions — Top: 2⅞" **Bottom:** 2⅝" **Height:** 3⅞"
Decoration: Gold.
Additional Notes: 3⅝" top of figure. Has been reproduced.

AKA: Star in Teardrop

Color: Amber
Value: $35.00 – 45.00
Description — Top: Fire polished **Bottom Figure:** 36-point star
Dimensions — Top: 3" **Bottom:** 2⅝" **Height:** 3¹⁵⁄₁₆"
Additional Notes: 3" top of figure.

AKA: Wimpole

Date: Ca. 1900
Color: Crystal
Value: $55.00 – 70.00
Description — Top: Fire polished **Bottom:** Ground unfinished **Bottom Figure:** Figure
Dimensions — Top: 2⅞" **Bottom:** 2⁵⁄₁₆" **Height:** 3¹¹⁄₁₆"
Decoration: Ruby stained.
Additional Notes: 3³⁄₁₆" top of figure.

AKA: Ornate Star, Ladders & Diamonds with Star

Manufacturer: Tarentum Glass Co. **Date:** 1907
Color: Crystal
Value: $50.00 – 65.00
Description — Top: Fire polished **Bottom:** Ground **Bottom Figure:** Fancy
Dimensions — Top: 3" **Bottom:** 2⁷⁄₁₆" **Height:** 3¾"
Decoration: Ruby stained.
Additional Notes: 3³⁄₁₆" top of figure.

Original Name: Orion
AKA: Cathedral

Manufacturer: Bryce Bros. **Date:** 1884
Color: Crystal
Value: $30.00 – 40.00, $60.00 – 70.00 Ruby stained
Description — Top: Fire polished **Bottom:** Ground
 Bottom Figure: Body figure in square
Dimensions — Top: 3" **Bottom:** 2⅜" **Height:** 3⅞"
Decoration: May be Ruby stained.

Original Name: No. 321
AKA: Buttressed Sunburst

Manufacturer: Tarentum Glass Co. **Date:** 1909
Color: Crystal
Value: $50.00 – 70.00
Description — Top: Fire polished **Bottom:** Unfinished **Bottom Figure:** Star inside diamonds
Dimensions — Top: 3" **Height:** 3¾"
Decoration: Ruby stained.
Additional Notes: 3¹⁄₁₆" top of figure.

Original Name: No. 508
AKA: National Star

Manufacturer: National at Riverside Glass Works **Date:** 1901
Color: Crystal, Canary
Value: $50.00 – 70.00
Description — Top: Fire polished
Dimensions — Top: 2⅞" **Bottom:** 2½" **Height:** 3¹¹⁄₁₆"
Decoration: Ruby stained.
Additional Notes: 3⅛" top of figure.

Original Name: No. 1900 Peerless
AKA: Frost Crystal

Manufacturer: Tarentum Glass Co. **Date:** 1906
Color: Crystal
Value: $60.00 – 85.00
Description — Top: Fire polished **Bottom:** Ground **Bottom Figure:** 24-point star
Dimensions — Top: 3" **Bottom:** 2⅜" **Height:** 3⅞"
Decoration: Ruby stained.
Additional Notes: 3¹⁄₁₆" top of figure.

AKA: Nearcut Star

Manufacturer: Cambridge Glass Co. **Date:** Ca. 1905
Color: Crystal
Value: $50.00 – 65.00
Description — Top: Fire polished **Bottom:** Ground **Bottom Figure:** 8-point star
Dimensions — Top: 3" **Bottom:** 2⅜" **Height:** 4"
Decoration: Gold above pattern, Ruby stained.
Additional Notes: 3³⁄₁₆" top of figure.

Original Name: No. 62
AKA: Homestead

Manufacturer: Duncan & Miller Glass Co. **Date:** 1907
Color: Crystal
Value: $65.00 – 80.00
Decoration: Ruby stained.

AKA: Triple Thumbprint

Color: Crystal
Value: $30.00 – 40.00
Description — Top: Fire polished **Bottom:** Ground and polished **Bottom Figure:** 24-point star
Dimensions — Top: 2¹³⁄₁₆" **Bottom:** 2¾" **Height:** 3¹³⁄₁₆"
Decoration: Gold luster in thumbprints.
Additional Notes: 3⅜" top of figure.

Original Name: No. 15110 Sunshine
AKA: Rising Sun

Manufacturer: United States Glass Co. **Date:** 1908
Color: Crystal
Value: $50.00 – 70.00
Description — Top: Fire polished **Bottom:** Ground **Bottom Figure:** Figure
Dimensions — Top: 3" **Bottom:** 2³⁄₁₆" **Height:** 3¹⁵⁄₁₆"
Decoration: Various luster treatments, Ruby stained.
Additional Notes: 3⁷⁄₁₆" top of figure.

Original Name: No. 350
AKA: Pinwheel & Fan

Manufacturer: A. H. Heisey & Co. **Date:** 1910
Color: Crystal
Value: $30.00 – 40.00
Description — Top: Fire polished **Bottom:** Flat ground **Bottom Figure:** 14-point hobstar
Dimensions — Top: 3¹⁄₁₆" **Bottom:** 2⅝" **Height:** 3¹¹⁄₁₆"
Additional Notes: Marked with Diamond H inside bottom.

Original Name: No. 343
AKA: Sunburst

Manufacturer: A. H. Heisey & Co. **Date:** 1903
Color: Crystal
Value: $50.00 – 60.00
Description — Top: Fire polished **Bottom:** Full polished **Bottom Figure:** 14-point hobstar
Dimensions — Top: 2¹⁵⁄₁₆" **Bottom:** 2³⁄₁₆" **Height:** 3¹⁵⁄₁₆"
Additional Notes: 2¹¹⁄₁₆" top of figure. Signed inside with Diamond H.

Original Name: No. 79
AKA: Bordered Ellipse

Manufacturer: National Glass Co. at McKee Brothers Glass Works **Date:** 1901
Color: Crystal
Value: $60.00 – 70.00
Dimension — Top: 2¾" **Bottom:** 2¼" **Height:** 3¹³⁄₁₆"
Descriptions — Top: Fire polished **Bottom:** Unfinished **Bottom Figure:** 16-point star
Decoration: Ruby stained.
Additional Notes: 3⁵⁄₁₆" top of figure.

AKA: Pressed Ovals

Color: Crystal
Value: $20.00 – 30.00
Description — Top: Fire polished **Bottom:** Fire polished **Bottom Figure:** 22 rays
Dimensions — Top: 2¾" **Bottom:** 2⅜" **Height:** 3⅞"
Additional Notes: 2⅞" top of figure, eight repeats.

Original Name: Nogi

Manufacturer: Indiana Glass Co. **Date:** 1906
Color: Crystal
Value: $50.00 – 70.00
Description — Top: Fire polished **Bottom:** Unfinished **Bottom Figure:** Figure
Dimensions — Top: 2¹⁵⁄₁₆" **Bottom:** 2⅛" **Height:** 4"
Decoration: Ruby stained.
Additional Notes: 3⅛" top of figure.

Original Name: No. 423
AKA: Diamond Band

Manufacturer: A. H. Heisey & Co. **Date:** Ca. 1910
Color: Crystal
Value: $150.00 – 170.00
Description — Top: Fire polished **Bottom:** Full ground **Bottom Figure:** 16-point star
Dimensions — Top: 2¹⁵⁄₁₆" **Bottom:** 2½" **Height:** 3¾"
Decoration: Gold on upper portion and band
Additional Notes: 2¹³⁄₁₆" top of figure, 15 panels. A very similar pattern was cut by Val St. Lambert of Belgium.

Original Name: No. 100
AKA: Funnel Rosette

Manufacturer: Columbia Glass Co. **Date:** Ca. 1890
Color: Crystal
Value: $35.00 – 45.00
Description — Top: Fire polished **Bottom:** Rough, stuck-up **Bottom Figure:** 24-radial ribs
Dimensions — Top: 2¹³⁄₁₆" **Bottom:** 2½ rim **Height:** 3¹³⁄₁₆"
Additional Notes: 2¹¹⁄₁₆" top of figure.

AKA: Giant Fine Cut

Color: Crystal
Value: $25.00 – 35.00
Description — Top: Fire polished **Bottom:** Ground and polished
   Bottom Figure: Figure
Dimensions — Top: 2⅞" **Bottom:** 2⁹⁄₁₆" over figure **Height:** 3⁹⁄₁₆"
Additional Notes: 2½" top of figure.

AKA: Beaded Diamond

Color: Crystal
Value: $20.00 – 30.00
Description — Top: Fire polished **Bottom:** Ground **Bottom Figure:** 30-point star
Dimensions — Top: 2¹³⁄₁₆" **Bottom:** 2⁷⁄₁₆" **Height:** 3¹¹⁄₁₆"
Decoration: Gold band.

Original Name: Gaelic

Manufacturer: Indiana Glass Co.
Color: Crystal
Value: $35.00 – 50.00
Description — Top: Fire polished **Bottom Figure:** Complex hobstar
Dimensions — Top: 3¼" **Bottom:** 2⅜" **Height:** 4³⁄₁₆"
Decoration: Gold, stain on flower.
Additional Notes: 3¹¹⁄₁₆" top of figure.

Original Name: No. 711
AKA: Leaf & Star

Manufacturer: New Martinsville Glass Co. **Date:** 1909
Color: Crystal
Value: $75.00 – 95.00
Description — Top: Fire polished **Bottom:** Ground **Bottom Figure:** 16-point star
Dimensions — Top: 3" **Bottom:** 2⅛" **Height:** 4⅛"
Decoration: Gold above figure, Ruby stained.
Additional Notes: 3¹⁄₁₆" top of figure.

AKA: Diamonds with Double Fans

Color: Crystal
Value: $70.00 – 90.00
Description — Top: Fire polished **Bottom:** Unfinished **Bottom Figure:** 20 small rays
Dimensions — Top: 2⅔" **Bottom:** 2⁷⁄₁₆" **Height:** 3¾"
Decoration: Ruby stained.
Additional Notes: 2¹¹⁄₁₆" top of figure.

Original Name: No. 2653 Ribbon
AKA: Bridal Rosettes

Manufacturer: Cambridge Glass Co. **Date:** 1908
Color: Crystal
Value: $70.00 – 90.00
Description — Top: Fire polished **Bottom:** Ground and polished **Bottom Figure:** 6-point unequal star
Dimensions — Top: 3¼" **Bottom:** 1¹⁵⁄₁₆" rim **Height:** 4"
Decoration: Gold above, Ruby stained.
Additional Notes: 2⅞" top of figure.

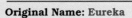

Original Name: Eureka

Manufacturer: National at McKee Works **Date:** 1901
Color: Crystal
Value: $70.00 – 90.00
Description — Top: Fire polished **Bottom Figure:** Multi-point star
Dimensions — Top: 2¾" **Bottom:** 2½" **Height:** 4"
Decoration: Ruby stained.
Additional Notes: 2¹⁵⁄₁₆" top of figure.

Original Name: No. 341 Victoria
AKA: Draped Top

Manufacturer: Riverside Glass Co. **Date:** 1895
Color: Crystal
Value: $75.00 – 95.00
Descriptions — Top: Fire polished **Bottom:** Unfinished
Dimensions — Top: 2¹¹⁄₁₆" **Bottom:** 1¹⁵⁄₁₆" rim **Height:** 3⁹⁄₁₆"
Decoration: Ruby or Amber stained.
Additional Notes: 2⅝" top of figure.

Original Name: No. 76
AKA: Triple Triangle

Manufacturer: Doyle & Co. **Date:** 1890
Color: Crystal
Value: $40.00 – 70.00
Description — Top: Fire polished **Bottom:** Unfinished **Bottom Figure:** Figure
Dimensions — Top: 2¾" **Bottom:** 2⁷⁄₁₆" **Height:** 3¾"
Additional Notes: 2⁹⁄₁₆" top of figure.

Original Name: Hobnail
AKA: Cane

Manufacturer: Gillinder & Sons and McKee Bros. **Date:** Ca. 1890
Color: Crystal
Value: $30.00 – 40.00
Description — Top: Fire polished **Bottom:** Unfinished
Dimensions — Top: 3¹⁄₁₆" **Bottom:** 2⁷⁄₁₆" **Height:** 3¹⁵⁄₁₆
Additional Notes: This tumbler pattern is reported to have been made
  by both Gillinder & Sons and McKee Bros.

Original Name: No. 15070 New Jersey
AKA: Loops & Drops

Manufacturer: U. S. Co. Glass **Date:** 1900
Color: Crystal
Value: $75.00 – 95.00
Description — Top: Fire polished **Bottom:** Unfinished **Bottom Figure:** 24 rays
Dimensions — Top: 2⅞" **Bottom:** 2⁷⁄₁₆" **Height:** 4"
Decoration: Ruby stained.
Additional Notes: 3¹⁄₁₆" top of figure.

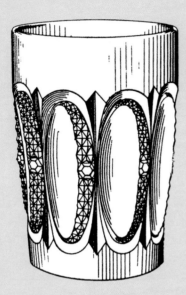

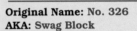

Original Name: Pearl

Manufacturer: Huntington Tumbler Co. **Date:** Ca. 1895
Color: Crystal
Value: $75.00 – 100.00
Decoration: May be found Ruby stained.

Original Name: No. 326
AKA: Swag Block

Manufacturer: Geo. Duncan & Sons **Date:** 1888
Color: Crystal
Value: $35.00 – 50.00
Description — Top: Fire polished **Bottom:** Ground
Dimensions — Top: 2⅞" **Bottom:** 2¹³⁄₁₆" **Height:** 3¹³⁄₁₆"
Decoration: Ruby stained, engraved.
Additional Notes: 2⅞" top of figure.

Original Name: No. 365
AKA: Queen Anne

Manufacturer: A. H. Heisey & Co. **Date:** 1907
Color: Crystal
Value: $90.00 – 150.00
Description — Top: Fire polished **Bottom:** Full ground **Bottom Figure:** 18-point star
Dimensions — Top: 3⅛" **Bottom:** 2⅝" **Height:** 4"
Decoration: Gold, Ruby stained.
Additional Notes: 2⁹⁄₁₆" top of figure.

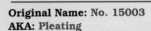

Original Name: No. 15003
AKA: Pleating

Manufacturer: U. S. Glass Co. **Date:** 1892
Color: Crystal
Value: $60.00 – 70.00
Description — Top: Fire polished **Bottom:** Ground
Dimensions — Top: 3⅛" **Bottom:** 2⁹⁄₁₆" **Height:** 3⁷⁄₁₆"
Decoration: Ruby stained.
Additional Notes: 2⁹⁄₁₆" top of figure.

AKA: Prism with Ball & Button

Color: Crystal
Value: $60.00 – 80.00
Description — Top: Fire polished **Bottom:** Unfinished
Dimensions — Top: 2¾" **Bottom:** 2¼" **Height:** 3⁹⁄₁₆"
Decoration: Ruby stained, engraved.
Additional Notes: 2¹¹⁄₁₆" top of figure.

AKA: Dalton

Manufacturer: Tarentum Glass Co. **Date:** 1904 – 1905
Color: Crystal
Value: $25.00 – 35.00
Description — Top: Fire polished **Bottom Figure:** 26-point star
Dimensions — Top: 3" **Bottom:** 2 ¹³⁄₁₆" **Height:** 3⅞"
Decoration: Trace of gold band.
Additional Notes: 3½" top of figure.

Original Name: Sextec

Manufacturer: McKee Bros. **Date:** 1894
Color: Crystal
Value: $40.00 – 70.00
Description — Top: Fire polished **Bottom:** Ground and polished
   Bottom Figure: Hobstar, inside marked "PRES CUT."
Dimensions — Top: 3¹⁄₁₆" **Bottom:** 2⁷⁄₁₆" **Height:** 4¹⁄₁₆"

Color: Crystal
Value: $25.00 – 35.00
Description — Top: Fire polished **Bottom:** Unfinished
   Bottom Figure: 10-point complex star
Dimensions — Top: 3⅛" **Bottom:** 2¹¹⁄₁₆" **Height:** 4⅛"
Additional Notes: 3³⁄₁₆" top of figure.

Original Name: Corona
AKA: Sunk Honeycomb

Manufacturer: Greensburg Glass Co. **Date:** 1894
Color: Crystal
Value: $50.00 – 60.00
Description – Bottom: Ground **Bottom Figure:** 20-point star
Dimensions — Top: 2¹¹⁄₁₆" **Bottom:** 2⅜" **Height:** 3⅞"
Decoration: Ruby stained, "Atlantic City 1897."
Additional Notes: 1⅞" top of figure.

Original Name: No. 15084 New Hampshire
AKA: Bent Buckle

Manufacturer: United States Glass Co. **Date:** 1903
Color: Crystal
Value: $35.00 – 50.00
Description — Top: Fire polished **Bottom:** Figured
Dimensions — Top: 2¹³⁄₁₆" **Bottom:** 2¹³⁄₁₆" **Height:** 3¹⁵⁄₁₆"
Decoration: Gold, Blush.

AKA: Daisy & Hexagon

Color: Amber
Value: $25.00 – 35.00
Description — Top: Fire polished **Bottom:** Unfinished
Dimensions — Top: 3⅛" **Bottom:** 2⁹⁄₁₆" **Height:** 4¼"
Additional Notes: 2⁵⁄₁₆" top of figure.

Original Name: No. 341
AKA: Mario

Manufacturer: Hobbs Glass Co. **Date:** 1890
Color: Crystal
Value: $40.00 – 70.00
Description — Top: Fire polished **Bottom:** Ground and polished
  Bottom Figure: Figure, 16 repeats
Dimensions — Top: 2 ¹³⁄₁₆" **Bottom:** 2⅜" rim **Height:** 3¹⁵⁄₁₆"
Decoration: Amber stain, vapor-etched leaves and flowers, also Ruby stained.
Additional Notes: 2³⁄₁₆" top of figure.

Original Name: No. 870
AKA: Star & Oval, Lens & Star

Manufacturer: O'Hara Glass Co. **Date:** 1887
Color: Crystal
Value: $25.00 – 35.00
Description — Top: Fire polished **Bottom:** Ground and polished **Bottom Figure:** Figure
Dimensions — Top: 2¹³⁄₁₆" **Bottom:** 2³⁄₁₆" rim **Height:** 3⅞"
Additional Notes: 1¹⁵⁄₁₆" top of figure.

Original Name: Crystal Wedding

Manufacturer: Adams & Co. **Date:** 1891
Color: Crystal
Value: $110.00 – 130.00
Description — Top: Fire polished **Bottom:** Unfinished
   Bottom Figure: Star surrounded by nine loops
Dimensions — Top: 3" **Bottom:** 2⅛" rim **Height:** 3¾"
Decoration: Ruby stained.
Additional Notes: 2¹⁄₁₆" top of figure.

AKA: Bull's-eye Variant

Color: Blue
Value: $45.00 – 55.00
Description — Top: Fire polished
   Bottom Figure: 8-point irregular star
Dimensions — Top: 3¼" **Bottom:** 2⁹⁄₁₆"
   Height: 3¾"
Additional Notes: 2¼" top of figure.

Original Name: No 1255
AKA: Pineapple & Fan

Manufacturer: A. H. Heisey & Co. **Date:** 1898
Color: Crystal, Emerald Green
Value: $35.00 – 45.00 Crystal with gold, $70.00 – 90.00 Crystal with Ruby stain
Description — Top: Fire polished **Bottom:** Ground and polished
   Bottom Figure: 16-point notched star
Dimensions — Top: 2¹⁵⁄₁₆" **Bottom:** 2¼" **Height:** 3¾"
Decoration: Gold, Ruby stained.
Additional Notes: 2⅜" top of figure.

Original Name: The Summit

Manufacturer: Thompson Glass Co. **Date:**1894
Color: Crystal
Value: $60.00 – 75.00
Description — Top: Fire polished **Bottom:** Unfinished
   Bottom Figure: 5-point snowflake
Dimensions — Top: 3¹⁄₁₆" **Bottom:** 2⅛" **Height:** 3¹³⁄₁₆"
Decoration: Ruby stained, engraved "Atlantic City 1895."
Additional Notes: 1¹³⁄₁₆" top of figure.

Original Name: Hanover
AKA: Star Block

Manufacturer: Richards & Hartley Glass Co. **Date:** 1888
Color: Amber
Value: $35.00 – 35.00
Description — Top: Fire polished **Bottom:** Unfinished **Bottom Figure:** Figure
Dimensions — Top: 2¹³⁄₁₆" **Bottom:** 2⁹⁄₁₆" **Height:** 3¾"
Additional Notes: 1¾" top of figure.

Color: Crystal
Value: $45.00 – 55.00
Description — Top: Fire polished **Bottom:** Unfinished **Bottom Figure:** Fancy
Dimensions — Top: 2⅞" **Bottom:** 2⁷⁄₁₆" **Height:** 3¹³⁄₁₆"
Decoration: Ruby stained.
Additional Notes: 1¹⁵⁄₁₆" top of figure. Figure is triangles and squares with
   narrow vertical bars.

Original Name: No. 800 Bag

Manufacturer: Geo. Duncan & Sons **Date:** 1883
Color: Crystal, Amber, Canary, blue
Value: $25.00 – 30.00
Description — Top: Fire polished **Bottom:** Ground **Bottom Figure:** 24-point star
Dimensions — Top: 2¹¹⁄₁₆" **Bottom:** 2½" **Height:** 3 ¹³⁄₁₆"
Additional Notes: 1¹³⁄₁₆" top of figure.

Original Name: No. 90 Puritan
AKA: Radiant Daisy

Manufacturer: Robinson Glass Co. **Date:** 1894
Color: Crystal
Value: $40.00 – 70.00
Description — Top: Fire polished **Bottom:** Ground and polished
  Bottom Figure: 10-point star
Dimensions — Top: 2^{15}/$_{16}$" **Bottom:** 2⅝" **Height:** 3¾"
Decoration: Ruby stained.
Additional Notes: 2¼" top of figure.

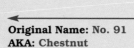

Original Name: No. 91
AKA: Chestnut

Manufacturer: Westmoreland Specialty Co. **Date:** 1898
Color: Crystal
Value: $60.00 – 75.00
Description — Top: Fire polished **Bottom:** Unfinished
  Bottom Figure: Hobstar with 20 rays
Dimensions — Top: 2¾" **Bottom:** 2½" **Height:** 3^{15}/$_{16}$"
Decoration: Ruby stained.
Additional Notes: 2^{7}/$_{16}$" top of figure.

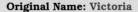

Original Name: Victoria

Manufacturer: Greensburg Glass Co. **Date:** Ca. 1892
Color: Crystal
Value: $70.00 – 80.00
Description — Top: Fire polished **Bottom:** Ground **Bottom Figure:** 18-point star
Dimensions — Top: 2^{11}/$_{16}$" **Bottom:** 2⅜" **Height:** 3¾"
Additional Notes: 1^{15}/$_{16}$" top of figure. Decorated by Pioneer with ruby stain.

Original Name: Victoria

Manufacturer: Greensburg Glass Co. **Date:** 1892
Color: Crystal
Value: $70.00 – 80.00
Description — Top: Fire polished **Bottom:** Ground **Bottom Figure:** 18-point star
Dimensions — Top: 2⅞" **Bottom:** 2½" **Height:** 4^{1}/$_{16}$"
Decoration: Ruby stained above figure.
Additional Notes: 2^{1}/$_{16}$" top of figure. Larger version, see above; there must have
  been two molds.

Original Name: No. 15026
AKA: Scalloped Swirl

Manufacturer: United States Glass Co. **Date:** 1893
Color: Crystal
Value: $70.00 – 80.00
Description — Top: Fire polished **Bottom:** Unfinished
Dimensions — Top: 2¹⁵⁄₁₆" **Bottom:** 2" rim **Height:** 3¹³⁄₁₆"
Decoration: Engraved, Ruby stained.
Additional Notes: 1¹⁵⁄₁₆" top of figure.

Original Name: Melrose
AKA: Diamond Beaded Band

Manufacturer: Brilliant Glass Co. **Date:** 1887
Color: Crystal
Value: $80.00 – 90.00
Description — Top: Fire polished **Bottom:** Unfinished
Dimensions — Top: 2¾" **Bottom:** 2" **Height:** 3⅞"
Decoration: Ruby stained, engraved flower and leaf.
Additional Notes: 2¹⁄₁₆" top of figure.

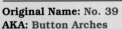

Original Name: No. 39
AKA: Button Arches

Manufacturer: Geo. Duncan's Sons & Co. **Date:** 1897
Color: Crystal
Value: $30.00 – 40.00
Description — Top: Fire polished **Bottom:** Ground **Bottom Figure:** 6-point star filled with buttons
Dimensions — Top: 2⅞" **Bottom:** 2⅞" **Height:** 3⅞"
Decoration: Ruby stained, engraved "Father."

Original Name: No. 39
AKA: Button Arches

Manufacturer: Duncan & Miller Glass Co. **Date:** 1897
Color: Crystal
Value: $35.00 – 45.00
Description — Top: Fire polished **Bottom:** Ground and polished **Bottom Figure:** 6-sided star
Dimensions — Top: 2⅞" **Bottom:** 2⁵⁄₁₆" **Height:** 3¹⁵⁄₁₆"
Decoration: Engraved "Summit, N. Y.," Ruby stained.
Additional Notes: 1¹¹⁄₁₆" top of figure. This tumbler was made by Jefferson Glass, ca. 1915, in a milky white "Clambroth" color.

Original Name: No. 139
AKA: Heart Band

Manufacturer: McKee Bros. **Date:** 1897
Color: Crystal
Value: $40.00 – 55.00
Description — Top: Fire polished **Bottom Figure:** 24-point star
Dimensions — Top: 3⅛" **Bottom:** 2⅜" rim **Height:** 3¹³⁄₁₆"
Decoration: Ruby stained.

Color: Crystal
Value: $35.00 – 45.00
Description — Top: Fire polished **Bottom:** Unfinished **Bottom Figure:** Fancy
Dimensions — Top: 3⅛" **Bottom:** 2½" **Height:** 3¹¹⁄₁₆"
Decoration: Ruby stained.
Additional Notes: 1¾" top of figure.

Original Name: No. 2005
AKA: Zipper Slash

Manufacturer: Geo. Duncan's Sons & Co. **Date:** 1894
Color: Crystal
Value: $40.00 – 50.00
Description — Top: Fire polished **Bottom:** Ground rim **Bottom Figure:** 24-point star
Dimensions — Top: 2⅞" **Bottom:** 2¼" **Height:** 3⅝"
Additional Notes: 1³⁄₁₆" top of figure.

Original Name: No. 67
AKA: Sunburst in Ovals

Manufacturer: Duncan & Miller Glass Co. **Date:** 1908
Color: Crystal
Value: $35.00 – 45.00
Description — Top: Fire polished **Bottom:** Ground and polished
  Bottom Figure: 12-point hobstar
Dimensions — Top: 2¹⁵⁄₁₆" **Bottom:** 2⅞" over figure **Height:** 3⅞"
Decoration: May be Ruby stained.
Additional Notes: 1¾" top of figure.

Original Name: No. 420
AKA: Box-in-Box

Manufacturer: Riverside Glass Co. **Date:** 1894
Color: Crystal
Value: $50.00 – 60.00
Description — Top: Fire polished **Bottom:** Unfinished
Dimensions — Top: 3" **Bottom:** 2¼" **Height:** 3¾"
Decoration: Ruby stained, engraved.
Additional Notes: 1¹¹⁄₁₆" top of figure.

Original Name: No. 15040
AKA: Diamond Bridges

Manufacturer: U. S. Glass Co. **Date:** 1895
Color: Crystal
Value: $25.00 – 35.00
Description — Top: Fire polished **Bottom:** Unfinished **Bottom Figure:** 8-point star figure
Dimensions — Top: 3" **Bottom:** 2⅜" over flats **Height:** 3⅞"
Additional Notes: 3⁷⁄₁₆" top of figure.

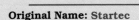

Color: Crystal
Value: $45.00 – 55.00
Description — Top: Fire polished **Bottom:** Unfinished **Bottom Figure:** Star and rays
Dimensions — Top: 2⅞" **Bottom:** 2 _" **Height:** 3⅞"
Decoration: Ruby stained, engraved.
Additional Notes: 1¾" top of figure.

Original Name: Startec

Manufacturer: McKee Glass Co. **Date:** 1910
Color: Crystal
Value: $40.00 – 50.00
Description — Top: Fire polished **Bottom:** Unfinished **Bottom Figure:** 24-point star
Dimensions — Top: 3⅛" **Bottom:** 2⅜" **Height:** 4"
Decoration: Gold on ellipses, Ruby stained band with enameled dots.
Additional Notes: 1¾" top of figure.

Original Name: Esther

Manufacturer: Riverside Glass Co. **Date:** 1896
Color: Green
Value: $55.00 – 70.00
Description — Top: Fire polished **Bottom:** Ground rim
Dimensions — Top: 2¹⁵⁄₁₆" **Bottom:** 2⅝" **Height:** 3¾"
Decoration: Gold in figure.
Additional Notes: 1¾" top of figure.

Original Name: NO. 82
AKA: Chandelier, Crown Jewels

Manufacturer: O'Hara Glass Co. **Date:** 1888
Color: Crystal
Value: $45.00 – 55.00
Description — Top: Fire polished **Bottom:** Unfinished
  Bottom Figure: 16-points, figure continues.
Dimensions — Top: 3¹⁄₁₆" **Bottom:** 2 ¹³⁄₁₆" over figure **Height:** 3⅞"
Additional Notes: 1⁹⁄₁₆" top of figure.

Original Name: No. 1908 Radiant
AKA: Diamond Band with Panels

Manufacturer: Co-Operative Flint Glass Co. **Date:** 1908
Color: Crystal
Value: $60.00 – 75.00
Description — Top: Fire polished **Bottom:** Ground **Bottom Figure:** 16-point star
Dimensions — Top: 2⅞" **Bottom:** 2½" **Height:** 3⅞"
Decoration: Ruby stained on panels.
Additional Notes: 1¾" top of figure.

Original Name: No. 857
AKA: Midway, Pillow Encircled

Manufacturer: Model Flint Glass Co. **Date:** 1891
Color: Crystal
Value: $35.00 – 45.00
Description — Top: Fire polished **Bottom:** Ground **Bottom Figure:** 20 swirled spokes
Dimensions — Top: 3" **Bottom:** 2¼" **Height:** 3⁹⁄₁₆"
Decoration: Ruby stained, engraved leaf.
Additional Notes: 1⅛" top of figure.

AKA: Hero, Pillow Encircled

Manufacturer: Elson Glass Co. **Date:** 1891
Color: Crystal
Value: $35.00 – 45.00
Description — Top: Fire polished **Bottom:** Ground **Bottom Figure:** Many rays
Dimensions — Top: 2¾" **Bottom:** 2¼" **Height:** 3⅝"
Decoration: Ruby stained, stenciled flower and leaf, Amber stained.
Additional Notes: 1⅛" top of figure. This pattern lacks the incised horizontal band of Model Flint's No. 857, see preceding.

Original Name: No. 1200
AKA: Cut Block

Manufacturer: A. H. Heisey & Co. **Date:** 1896
Color: Crystal
Value: $75.00 – 95.00
Description — Top: Fire polished **Bottom:** Ground **Bottom Figure:** 24-point star
Dimensions — Top: 2⅞" **Bottom:** 2⅝" **Height:** 3¹¹⁄₁₆"
Decoration: Ruby stained, engraved "Niagara Falls."
Additional Notes: 1⁵⁄₁₆" top of figure.

Original Name: Pavonia

Manufacturer: Ripley & Co. **Date:** 1885
Color: Crystal
Value: $40.00 – 70.00
Description — Top: Fire polished **Bottom:** Unfinished **Bottom Figure:** Figure
Dimensions — Top: 2 ¹³⁄₁₆" **Bottom:** 2¹⁵⁄₁₆" **Height:** 3⅞"
Decoration: Sandblast acorn, oak leaf, engraved leaves and vine.
Additional Notes: ¹³⁄₁₆" top of figure.

Original Name: *Pavonia*

Manufacturer: Ripley & Co. **Date:** 1886
Color: Crystal
Value: $50.00 – 60.00
Description — Top: Fire polished **Bottom:** Unfinished **Bottom Figure:** Figure
Dimensions — Top: 2¹¹⁄₁₆" **Bottom:** 2⅝" **Height:** 3⅞"
Decoration: Ruby stained, engraved "Sister Mamie 1894."
Additional Notes: ⅞" top of figure. Dated 1894, this piece was almost certainly sold, if not made, after Ripley joined U. S. Glass.

Original Name: No. 190
AKA: Bar & Diamond

Manufacturer: Richards & Hartley Glass Co. **Date:** 1885
Color: Crystal
Value: $60.00 – 70.00
Description — Top: Fire polished **Bottom:** Ground **Bottom Figure:** 27-point star
Dimensions — Top: 2⅞" **Bottom:** 2⅜" **Height:** 3⅝"
Decoration: Ruby stained, engraved "Clarence 1892."
Additional Notes: 3¹¹⁄₁₆" top of figure.

AKA: Niagara Falls

Color: Crystal
Value: $35.00 – 50.00
Dimensions — Top: 2⁷⁄₁₆" **Bottom:** 2¹¹⁄₁₆" **Height:** 3⅝"
Decoration: Ruby stained, gold on top rim. "Niagara Falls."

AKA: Calendar

Color: Crystal
Value: $40.00 – 55.00
Description — Top: Fire polished
Dimensions — Top: 2⁵⁄₁₆" **Bottom:** 2¹⁄₁₆" **Height:** 3⅝"
Decoration: Ruby stained, printed 1909 calendar, gold rim.

Pressed Figural

These patterns seem to have evolved sometime in the 1870s, as naturalistic designs that were often raised above the surface. In this section, the designs represent these more naturalistic themes, often flowers or leaves. This type of tumbler continued well beyond the 1920s.

AKA: Maple Leaf

Manufacturer: Northwood Glass Co., National Glass Co. **Date:** Ca. 1900
Color: Custard
Value: $75.00 – 100.00
Description — Top: Fire polished **Bottom:** Unfinished
Dimensions — Top: 3⅛" **Bottom:** 2⁷⁄₁₆" **Height:** 3⅞"
Additional Notes: Reproduced by L. G. Wright, may be marked with a *W* inside. Shards have been found at the Indiana, PA, site of Northwood/National/Dugan. At this time, there is no way to determine which company originated the pattern.

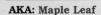

AKA: Maple Leaf

Manufacturer: Gillinder & Sons **Date:** Ca. 1885
Color: Crystal, Amber, blue, Canary
Value: $35.00 – 45.00 Crystal
Additional Notes: The design is grape leaf; finial is bunch of grapes. The pattern is misnamed.

AKA: Grape & Cable

Manufacturer: Northwood Glass Co.; Indiana, PA. **Date:** 1899
Color: Canary
Value: $15.00 – 25.00
Description — Top: Not fire polished **Bottom:** Unfinished **Bottom Figure:** 6-point unequal sta
Dimensions — Top: 2⅞" **Bottom:** 2⅜" **Height:** 4"
Additional Notes: Poor quality, glass is cloudy, unfinished piece. Marked with Circle N (no underline). This piece is probably a reproduction.

Original Name: No. 339
AKA: Leaf & Flower

Manufacturer: Hobbs Glass Co. **Date:** 1890
Color: Crystal
Value: $40.00 – 50.00
Description — Top: Fire polished **Bottom:** Ground and polished
  Bottom Figure: 6-petal flower
Dimensions — Top: 2¹³⁄₁₆" **Bottom:** 2¹¹⁄₁₆" **Height:** 4"
Decoration: Amber stain, frosted.
Additional Notes: 2¼" top of figure.

Original Name: No. 339
AKA: Leaf & Flower

Manufacturer: Hobbs Glass Co. **Date:** 1890
Color: Crystal
Value: $40.00 – 50.00
Description — Top: Fire polished **Bottom Figure:** 6-petal flower
Dimensions — Top: 2¹⁵⁄₁₆" **Bottom:** 2¾" **Height:** 4"
Decoration: Amber stain.

Original Name: No. 162
AKA: Boquet

Manufacturer: Indiana Glass Co. **Date:** 1917
Color: Crystal
Value: $35.00 – 50.00
Description — Top: Fire polished **Bottom:** Unfinished **Bottom Figure:** Ornate snowflake
Dimensions — Top: 3" **Bottom:** 2½" **Height:** 4⁵⁄₁₆"

Original Name: No. 140
AKA: Wildflower

Manufacturer: Adams & Co. **Date:** Ca. 1884
Color: Crystal, Amber, Blue, Canary, Light Green, Amethyst
Value: $20.00 – 35.00
Description — Top: Fire polished **Bottom:** Unfinished
  Bottom Figure: Figure like upper band
Dimensions — Top: 2¹³⁄₁₆" **Bottom:** 1¹³⁄₁₆" rim **Height:** 3¹³⁄₁₆"

Original Name: Wildflower

Manufacturer: L. G. Wright Glass Co. **Date:** late 1930s
Color: Amber, Blue, Purple, Vaseline
Value: $15.00 – 20.00
Description — Top: Fire polished **Bottom:** Unfinished
   Bottom Figure: Figure like upper band
Dimensions — Top: 3⅛" **Bottom:** 2½" rim **Height:** 3¹⁵⁄₁₆"

Original Name: No. 590

Manufacturer: A. J. Beatty & Sons **Date:** Ca. 1885
Color: Canary
Value: $50.00 – 60.00
Description — Top: Fire polished **Bottom:** Unfinished
Dimensions — Top: 3⅛" **Bottom:** 2⅝" **Height:** 3¹¹⁄₁₆"
Additional Notes: 1⁹⁄₁₆" top of figure. Design is comprised of tiny cones.

Original Name: No. 590
AKA: Hat Whimsy

Manufacturer: A. J. Beatty & Sons **Date:** Ca. 1885
Color: Canary
Value: $120.00 – 130.00
Description — Top: Fire polished **Bottom:** Unfinished
Dimensions — Top: 3⅛" **Bottom:** 2⅝" **Height:** 2⅞" to highest point
Additional Notes: 1⁹⁄₁₆" top of figure. Design is comprised of tiny cones.

AKA: Oriental Poppy

Manufacturer: Northwood Glass Co.; Wheeling, WV **Date:** Ca. 1911
Color: Transparent Blue or Green
Value: $40.00 – 50.00
Description — Top: Imperfectly fire polished **Bottom Figure:** 24-point star,
   N in circle inside bottom
Dimensions — Top: 3³⁄₁₆" **Bottom:** 2¹¹⁄₁₆" **Height:** 4¼"
Decoration: With gold, carnival colors.

Original Name: Art Navo
AKA: Paneled Dogwood

Manufacturer: Co-Operative Flint Glass Co. **Date:** 1905
Color: Crystal
Value: $30.00 – 40.00
Description — Top: Fire polished **Bottom:** Ground and polished
   Bottom Figure: 8-petal flower
Dimensions — Top: 2⅞" **Bottom:** 2⅝" **Height:** 4¹/₁₆"
Decoration: Aqua and white enamel.

AKA: Art Navo

Manufacturer: Co-Operative Flint Glass Co. **Date:** 1905
Value: $50.00 – 60.00
Description — Top: Fire polished **Bottom:** Ground **Bottom Figure:** 8-petal flower
Dimensions — Top: 2¾" **Bottom:** 2½" **Height:** 4"
Decoration: Gold in flowers; date in Spanish, 9/27/06. Ruby stained.
Additional Notes: 3¹¹/₁₆" top of figure.

AKA: Beaded Flower

Color: Crystal
Value: $35.00 – 50.00
Description — Top: Fire polished **Bottom:** Unfinished **Bottom Figure:** 20-point star
Dimensions — Top: 2⅞" **Bottom:** 2⁷/₁₆" **Height:** 4"
Decoration: Gold on figure.
Additional Notes: 3⅛" top of figure.

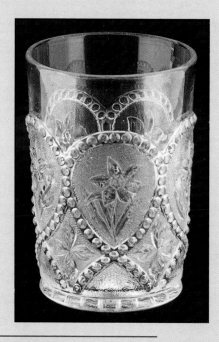

Original Name: La France

Manufacturer: Co-Operative Flint Glass Co. **Date:** 1902
Color: Emerald Green, possibly other colors
Value: $40.00 – 50.00
Description — Top: Fire polished **Bottom Figure:** 8-point hobstar and fans
Dimensions — Top: 3³/₁₆" **Bottom:** 2½" **Height:** 3⅞"
Decoration: Gold on figure, top band.
Additional Notes: 3⅛" top of figure.

Original Name: Puritan

Manufacturer: McKee Glass Co. **Date:** 1910
Color: Crystal
Value: $35.00 – 50.00
Description — Top: Fire polished **Bottom:** Ground **Bottom Figure:** Fancy, octagonal
Dimensions — Top: 3⁵⁄₁₆" **Bottom:** 2½" across flats **Height:** 4⅛"
Decoration: Ruby stained, gold above and on pattern.
Additional Notes: 3 ⁷⁄₁₆" top of figure.

AKA: Carnation

Manufacturer: New Martinsville Glass Co.
Color: Crystal
Value: $70.00 – 85.00
Description — Top: Fire polished **Bottom:** Ground **Bottom Figure:** 10-spoke pinwheel
Dimensions — Top: 3¹⁄₁₆" **Bottom:** 2⁵⁄₁₆" **Height:** 3¹⁵⁄₁₆"
Decoration: Some found with gold in pattern.
Additional Notes: 3⁹⁄₁₆" top of figure.

Original Name: No. 408
AKA: Chrysanthemum, Double Daisy

Manufacturer: Riverside Glass Co. **Date:** 1893
Color: Crystal
Value: $60.00 – 70.00
Description — Top: Fire polished **Bottom:** Unfinished **Bottom Figure:** Figure
Dimensions — Top: 3³⁄₁₆" **Bottom:** 2⅜" **Height:** 3¾"
Decoration: Ruby stained.
Additional Notes: 1⁹⁄₁₆" top of figure.

Original Name: W. B. Line
AKA: Teardrop Flower

Manufacturer: Northwood Glass Co.; Wheeling, WV **Date:** 1904
Color: Blue
Value: $50.00 – 60.00
Description — Top: Fire polished **Bottom:** Ground and polished rim
Dimensions — Top: 3⅛" **Bottom:** 2⁷⁄₁₆" **Height:** 4"
Decoration: Gold on top band and pattern.
Additional Notes: 3⁷⁄₁₆" top of figure.

Original Name: No. 80
AKA: Sunflower Patch

Manufacturer: Duncan & Miller Glass Co. **Date:** 1913
Color: Crystal
Value: $40.00 – 70.00
Description — Top: Fire polished **Bottom:** Ground **Bottom Figure:** Many rays
Dimensions — Top: 3¹⁄₁₆" **Bottom:** 2½" **Height:** 4¹⁄₁₆"
Decoration: Ruby stained, gold in figure.
Additional Notes: 3¾" top of figure.

AKA: Stippled Rose, Hundred-Leaved Rose

Manufacturer: Windsor Glass Co. **Date:** 1892
Color: Crystal
Value: $35.00 – 50.00
Description — Top: Fire polished **Bottom:** Unfinished
  Bottom Figure: 6-petaled stippled flower
Dimensions — Top: 2¹¹⁄₁₆" **Bottom:** 2½" **Height:** 3⁹⁄₁₆"
Additional Notes: 2" top of figure.

AKA: Stippled Daisy

Color: Crystal
Value: $35.00 – 50.00
Description — Top: Fire polished **Bottom:** Unfinished
Bottom Figure: 16 swirled ribs
Dimensions — Top: 2¾" **Bottom:** 2⁹⁄₁₆" **Height:** 3¹³⁄₁₆"
Additional Notes: 2⅞" top of figure.

Original Name: No. 436 Brilliant

Manufacturer: Riverside Glass Co. **Date:** 1895
Color: Crystal
Value: $40.00 – 50.00
Description — Top: Fire polished **Bottom:** Ground and polished
Dimensions — Top: 3" **Bottom:** 2¹¹⁄₁₆" **Height:** 3¾"
Decoration: Ruby stained, Amber stained.
Additional Notes: 3⅛" top of figure.

AKA: Brilliant

Manufacturer: Riverside Glass Co. **Date:** 1895
Color: Crystal
Value: $60.00 – 70.00
Description — Top: Fire polished **Bottom:** Unfinished
Dimensions — Top: 2¹⁵⁄₁₆" **Bottom:** 2⅝" **Height:** 3¾"
Decoration: Ruby stained
Additional Notes: 3⅛" top of figure.

Original Name: No. 127
AKA: Strawberry with Roman Key Band

Manufacturer: Indiana Glass Co. **Date:** 1911
Color: Crystal
Value: $30.00 – 40.00
Description — Top: Fire polished **Bottom:** Ground and polished
   Bottom Figure: Leaves and berries
Dimensions — Top: 3¼" **Bottom:** 2" across flats **Height:** 4⁵⁄₁₆"
Decoration: Gold with berries stained red/purple.
Additional Notes: 3⅝" top of figure.

Original Name: No. 166
AKA: Gothic Windows

Manufacturer: Indiana Glass Co. **Date:** 1920s
Color: Crystal
Value: $30.00 – 40.00
Description — Top: Fire polished **Bottom:** Unfinished **Bottom Figure:** 30-point star
Dimensions — Top: 3⅛" **Bottom:** 2⁷⁄₁₆" across flats **Height:** 4⁵⁄₁₆"
Decoration: Gold on rim, platinum on figure.

Original Name: Duquesne
AKA: Wheat & Barley

Manufacturer: Bryce Bros. **Date:** Ca. 1880s
Color: Amber
Value: $35.00 – 50.00
Description — Top: Fire polished **Bottom:** Unfinished **Bottom Figure:** 10-pointed center
   star surrounded by 16-pointed geometric design
Dimensions — Top: 2⅞" **Bottom:** 2½" **Height:** 2¹³⁄₁₆"

Original Name: No. 507
AKA: Heavy Paneled Grape

Manufacturer: Kokomo Glass Mfg. Co. **Date:** 1904
Color: Crystal
Value: $35.00 – 50.00
Description — Top: Fire polished **Bottom:** Unfinished **Bottom Figure:** 18-point star
Dimensions — Top: 2¹⁵⁄₁₆" **Bottom:** 2⁷⁄₁₆" **Height:** 3¹³⁄₁₆"
Additional Notes: Nine panels.

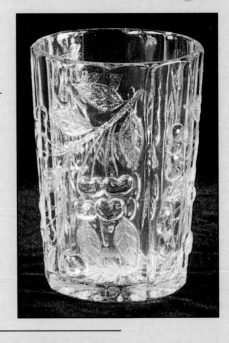

AKA: Cherry

Color: Crystal
Value: $35.00 – 50.00
Description — Top: Fire polished **Bottom:** Ground **Bottom Figure:** 16-point star
Dimensions — Top: 2⅞" **Bottom:** 2⁵⁄₁₆" **Height:** 3⅞"
Additional Notes: Twelve panels.

AKA: Cherry Lattice

Manufacturer: Northwood Glass Co., Wheeling, WV **Date:** Ca. 1910
Color: Crystal
Value: $40.00 – 70.00
Description — Top: Fire polished **Bottom Figure:** 28-point star
Dimensions — Top: 2¹⁵⁄₁₆" **Bottom:** 2½" **Height:** 4¹⁄₃₂"
Decoration: Gold and Blush.
Additional Notes: 3⅛" top of figure.

AKA: English Late Cherry

Color: Crystal
Value: $45.00 – 55.00
Dimensions — Top: 2⅞" **Bottom:** 2⁵⁄₁₆" **Height:** 4"
Decoration: Ruby stained.
Additional Notes: 3⅛" top of figure. "Compliments of Bailey Bros.," "9 AV OZ" embossed on outside.

AKA: Cherry & Cable

Manufacturer: Northwood Glass Co., Wheeling, WV **Date:** 1907
Color: Crystal
Value: $35.00 – 50.00
Description — Top: Fire polished
Dimensions — Top: 3¼" **Bottom:** 2⁷⁄₁₆" **Height:** 4¹⁄₁₆"
Decoration: Gold, Blush.
Additional Notes: 3³⁄₁₆" top of figure, signed with Circle N.

Original Name: No. 375
AKA: Dewberry

Manufacturer: Co-Operative Flint Glass Co. **Date:** 1905
Color: Crystal
Value: $30.00 – 40.00
Description — Top: Fire polished **Bottom Figure:** 18-point star
Dimensions — Top: 2^{15}/$_{16}$" **Bottom:** 2^{5}/$_{16}$" **Height:** 3^{5}/$_{8}$"
Decoration: Gold on figure.
Additional Notes: 2^{3}/$_{4}$" top of figure.

AKA: Plum & Leaf, Bartlett Pear

Color: Crystal
Value: $30.00 – 40.00
Description — Top: Fire polished **Bottom:** Ground and polished rim
Dimensions — Top: 2^{13}/$_{16}$" **Bottom:** 2" rim **Height:** 3^{7}/$_{8}$"
Decoration: Gold on top band and fruit.

Original Name: No. 2766
AKA: Nearcut Thistle, Late Thistle

Manufacturer: Cambridge Glass Co. **Date:** 1906
Color: Crystal
Value: $65.00 – 80.00
Description — Top: Fire polished **Bottom:** Ground **Bottom Figure:** Fancy
Dimensions — Top: 3^{1}/$_{8}$" **Bottom:** 2^{9}/$_{16}$" **Height:** 4"
Decoration: Ruby stained.
Additional Notes: 3^{7}/$_{16}$" top of figure, mold signed "Near Cut" inside.

Original Name: No. 2766
AKA: Inverted Thistle, Late Thistle

Manufacturer: Cambridge Glass Co. **Date:** 1906
Color: Emerald Green
Value: $65.00 – 80.00
Description — Top: Fire polished **Bottom Figure:** 24-point star
Dimensions — Top: 3^{1}/$_{4}$" **Bottom:** 2^{9}/$_{16}$" **Height:** 4^{1}/$_{8}$"
Decoration: Gold on figure.
Additional Notes: See also above.

Original Name: No. 2780
AKA: Inverted Strawberry

Manufacturer: Cambridge Glass Co. **Date:** 1905
Color: Crystal, also seen in Emerald Green with Gold
Value: $60.00 – 70.00
Description — Top: Fire polished **Bottom:** Unfinished
   Bottom Figure: Three flowers and leaves
Dimensions — Top: 2⅞" **Bottom:** 2⅜" **Height:** 3⅞"
Decoration: Ruby-stained bottom.
Additional Notes: 3¹⁄₁₆" top of figure.

Original Name: No. 2780
AKA: Inverted Strawberry

Manufacturer: Cambridge Glass Co. **Date:** 1905
Color: Crystal, Emerald Green
Value: $40.00 – 70.00
Description — Top: Fire polished **Bottom:** Unfinished
   Bottom Figure: Three flowers and leaves
Dimensions — Top: 2⅞" **Bottom:** 2⅜" **Height:** 3⅞"
Decoration: Gold rim, Ruby-stained top.
Additional Notes: 3³⁄₁₆ top of figure.

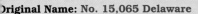

Original Name: No. 15,065 Delaware

Manufacturer: United States Glass Co. **Date:** 1899
Color: Emerald Green, also Crystal
Value: $40.00 – 70.00
Description — Top: Fire polished **Bottom:** Unfinished **Bottom Figure:** 20-point star
Dimensions — Top: 3⅛" **Bottom:** 2⁵⁄₁₆" **Height:** 3¾"
Decoration: Gold, various colored stains on crystal glass.

Original Name: No. 151
AKA: Giant Bull's-eye

Manufacturer: Bellaire Goblet Co. **Date:** 1989
Color: Crystal
Value: $35.00 – 50.00
Description — Top: Fire polished **Bottom Figure:** 16-point star
Dimensions — Top: 2¹³⁄₁₆" **Bottom:** 2⁷⁄₁₆" rim **Height:** 4⅛"
Additional Notes: 2⅝" top of figure.

Original Name: Royal

Manufacturer: Co-Operative Flint Glass Co. **Date:** 1894
Color: Crystal
Value: $40.00 – 50.00
Description — Top: Fire polished **Bottom:** Ground
Dimensions — Top: 2¾" **Bottom:** 2⅛" **Height:** 3⁷⁄₁₆"
Decoration: Ruby stained, engraved.
Additional Notes: 1³⁄₁₆" top of figure.

Original Name: No 355
AKA: Pinwheel

Manufacturer: King, Son & Co. **Date:** 1887
Color: Crystal
Value: $30.00 – 40.00
Description — Top: Fire polished **Bottom:** Rough, stuck-up
Dimensions — Top: 2¹⁵⁄₁₆" **Bottom:** 2⁷⁄₁₆" **Height:** 3⅞"
Additional Notes: 3⁷⁄₁₆" top of figure.

Original Name: No. 15002
AKA: Nail

Manufacturer: U. S. Glass Co. **Date:** 1892
Color: Crystal
Value: $70.00 – 80.00
Description — Top: Fire polished **Bottom:** Unfinished
Dimensions — Top: 2¾" **Bottom:** 2¼" rim **Height:** 3⅝"
Decoration: Ruby stained.
Additional Notes: 2³⁄₁₆" top of figure.

AKA: Roses & Leaves

Date: 1900
Color: Opal
Value: $45.00 – 60.00
Description — Top: Not fire polished **Bottom:** Unfinished
Dimensions — Top: 3¹⁄₁₆" **Bottom:** 2⅜" **Height:** 4⅛"
Decoration: Pink and green enamel.
Additional Notes: This tumbler bears a strong resemblance to Dithridge's Versailles.

Original Name: New York
AKA: Beaded Shell

Manufacturer: Dugan Glass Co., Mosser Glass Co. **Date:** Early/late 1900s.
Color: Canary
Value: $20.00 – 30.00
Description — Top: Fire polished
Dimensions — Top: 3⅛" **Bottom:** 2⁷⁄₁₆" **Height:** 3¹³⁄₁₆"
Additional Notes: This example marked on bottom edge with an *M* (Mosser).

Original Name: No. 1280
AKA: Winged Scroll

Manufacturer: A. H. Heisey & Co. **Date:** 1898
Color: Custard, Emerald Green
Value: $75.00 – 100.00
Description — Top: Fire polished
Dimensions — Top: 2⅞" **Bottom:** 2⁹⁄₁₆" **Height:** 3¹¹⁄₁₆"
Decoration: Gold.

Original Name: No. 607
AKA: Inverted Fan & Feather

Manufacturer: Dugan Glass Co. **Date:** 1901
Color: Pink Slag
Value: $250.00 – 375.00
Description — Top: Fire polished **Bottom:** Unfinished
Dimensions — Top: 3" **Bottom:** 2½" **Height:** 4"
Additional Notes: Circles on scroll detail are flat on originals, dome shaped on reproductions. Arrows on drawing below point to these.

Detail of Scroll

93

Original Name: No. 607
AKA: Inverted Fan and Feather

Manufacturer: Dugan **Date:** Ca. 1908 (color also introduced then)
Color: Blue Opalescent
Value: $80.00 – 120.00
Description — Top: Fire polished **Bottom:** Unfinished
Dimensions — Top: 3" **Bottom:** 2⁵⁄₁₆" **Height:** 3¹⁵⁄₁₆"
Decoration: Gold on figure.

Original Name: No. 99
AKA: Flora

Manufacturer: Beaumont Glass Co. **Date:** Ca. 1898
Color: Emerald Green, Canary, Custard
Value: $85.00 – 130.00
Description — Top: Imperfectly fire polished **Bottom:** Unfinished
Dimensions — Top: 2¹⁵⁄₁₆" **Bottom:** 2¾" **Height:** 3⅝"
Decoration: Gold on design.

Original Name: No. 99
AKA: Flora

Manufacturer: Beaumont Glass Co. **Date:** 1898
Color: Crystal
Value: $40.00 – 50.00
Description — Top: Fire polished
Dimensions — Top: 2¹³⁄₁₆" **Bottom:** 2¹³⁄₁₆" **Height:** 3⅝"
Decoration: Gold.
Additional Notes: 3⅜" top of figure.

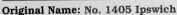

Original Name: No. 1405 Ipswich

Manufacturer: A. H. Heisey & Co. **Date:** 1931
Color: Crystal, Green, Yellow, Pink
Value: $50.00 – 70.00
Description — Top: Fire polished **Bottom:** Ground and polished rim
   Bottom Figure: Diamond H outside center
Dimensions — Top: 3" **Bottom:** 2" **Height:** 4¹⁄₁₆"
Additional Notes: 3³⁄₁₆" top of figure. This is often mistaken for
   Halley's Comet.

AKA: Fleur-de-Lis

Manufacturer: National Glass Co., Royal Glass Works **Date:** 1898
Color: Chocolate (Caramel Slag)
Value: $75.00 – 100.00
Description — Top: Fire polished **Bottom:** Unfinished **Bottom Figure:** 16-point star
Dimensions — Top: 2¾" **Bottom:** 2¼" **Height:** 3¹⁵⁄₁₆"
Additional Notes: This example made by National Glass, after the consolidation. Note worn mold work.

AKA: Fleur-de-Lis

Manufacturer: Royal Glass Co. **Date:** 1898
Color: Blue
Value: $40.00 – 70.00
Description — Top: Fire polished **Bottom Figure:** 16-point star
Dimensions — Top: 2¾" **Bottom:** 2¼" **Height:** 3¹⁵⁄₁₆"
Additional Notes: Note sharp mold work.

Original Name: No. 15009
AKA: Fleur-de-Lis and Drape

Manufacturer: United States Glass Co. **Date:** 1892
Color: Crystal, Emerald Green
Value: $40.00 – 50.00
Description — Top: Fire polished **Bottom:** Unfinished **Bottom Figure:** 20 ribs, or star
Dimensions — Top: 2¹³⁄₁₆" **Bottom:** 2⅛" **Height:** 3⅞"
Additional Notes: Green made after 1898.

Original Name: No. 789
AKA: Wedding Bells

Manufacturer: Fostoria Glass Co. **Date:** 1900
Color: Crystal
Value: $55.00 – 70.00
Description — Top: Fire polished **Bottom:** Stuck-up
Dimensions — Top: 3¹⁄₁₆" **Bottom:** 2½" **Height:** 3⅝"
Decoration: Pink luster.

AKA: Chrysanthemum Leaf

Manufacturer: National Glass Co. **Date:** 1901
Color: Chocolate
Value: $600.00 – 650.00
Description — Top: Fire polished **Bottom:** Unfinished
Dimensions — Top: 3" **Height:** 3⅞"

AKA: Spanish Fans

Manufacturer: Imported by AA Importing **Date:** 1974
Color: Crystal, Blue, Opalescent Blue, Opalescent White
Value: $25.00 – 30.00
Description — Top: Fire polished **Bottom Figure:** Circles and whorls
Dimensions — Top: 3¼" **Bottom:** 3¹⁄₁₆" **Height:** 3¾"
Additional Notes: This may be a copy of a much earlier tumbler; original would be flint.

AKA: French Lacy

Date: Ca. 1850
Color: Crystal, Blue Opaque
Value: $75.00 – 100.00
Description — Top: Fire polished **Bottom:** Ground, not polished
   Bottom Figure: Figure as upper half
Dimensions — Top: 2⅞" **Bottom:** 2⁹⁄₁₆" **Height:** 3⁷⁄₁₆"
Additional Notes: Appears in Ruth Webb Lee's *Sandwich Glass*, as fig. 171.

Original Name: Victoria

Manufacturer: Tarentum Glass Co. **Date:** 1900
Color: Crystal, Emerald Green, Custard, Opaque Green
Value: $40.00 – 50.00
Description — Top: Fire polished **Bottom:** Rough, stick-up scars
   Bottom Figure: 28-point star
Dimensions — Top: 3" **Bottom:** 2⁷⁄₁₆" **Height:** 3¹³⁄₁₆"
Additional Notes: 2⁵⁄₁₆" top of figure.

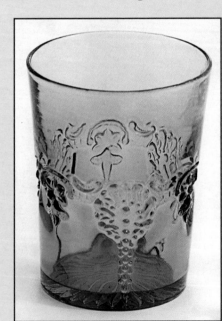

Original Name: No. 1
AKA: Fagot, Vera

Manufacturer: Robinson Glass Co. **Date:** 1893
Color: Crystal
Value: $80.00 – 100.00
Decoration: Ruby stained.
Dimensions — Top: 2¾" **Bottom:** 2½" **Height:** 3⅝"
Additional Notes: 2½" top of figure.

Original Name: No. 15016
AKA: Millard

Manufacturer: United States Glass Co. **Date:** 1893
Color: Crystal
Value: $45.00 – 55.00
Description — Top: Fire polished **Bottom:** Ground **Bottom Figure:** Fancy
Dimensions — Top: 2⅝" **Bottom:** 2½" **Height:** 3⁹⁄₁₆"
Decoration: Ruby stained, engraved floral.
Additional Notes: 2⅞" top of figure.

AKA: Tavern Scene

Manufacturer: National Glass Co., Indiana Tumbler & Goblet Works **Date:** 1901
Color: Crystal, Chocolate
Value: $500.00 – 550.00
Description — Top: Fire polished
Dimensions — Top: 3" **Height:** 3⅞"

Original Name: No. 500
AKA: King's 500

Manufacturer: King, Son & Co., United States Glass Co. **Date:** 1890
Color: Crystal, Dewey Blue
Value: $50.00 – 60.00
Description — Top: Fire polished **Bottom:** Ground and polished
Dimensions — Top: 3" **Bottom:** 2¹⁄₁₆" rim **Height:** 3⅝"
Decoration: Figure frosted.
Additional Notes: 1⅞" top of figure. Dewey Blue produced by Untied States Glass Co. after 1898.

Original Name: No. 15077 Michigan

Manufacturer: United States Glass Co. **Date:** 1902
Color: Crystal
Value: $65.00 – 75.00
Description — Top: Fire polished **Bottom:** Unfinished
Dimensions — Top: 3" **Bottom:** 2⅛" **Height:** 3¹³⁄₁₆"
Decoration: Ruby stained, also various color stains.
Additional Notes: 3⁵⁄₁₆" top of figure.

Original Name: No. 200
AKA: Beaded Lobe

Manufacturer: Greensburg Glass Co. **Date:** 1890
Color: Crystal
Value: $50.00 – 65.00
Description — Top: Fire polished **Bottom:** Unfinished **Bottom Figure:** Lobes
Dimensions — Top: 2⅝" **Bottom:** 2⅜" **Height:** 3¾"
Decoration: Ruby stained.
Additional Notes: 1⁷⁄₁₆" top of figure.

Original Name: Plume

Manufacturer: Adams & Co. **Date:** 1890
Color: Crystal
Value: $50.00 – 75.00
Description — Top: Fire polished **Bottom:** Unfinished
Dimensions — Top: 2¾" **Bottom:** 2⅛" **Height:** 3⅞"
Decoration: Ruby stained, engraved "World's Fair, 1893."
Additional Notes: This tumbler is pressed; there is a blown tumbler in this pattern, also (see page 190). 2¹⁄₁₆" top of figure.

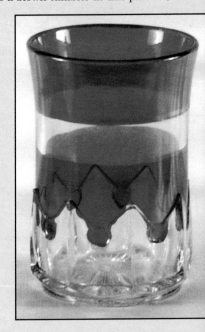

Original Name: Gothic
AKA: Spearpoint Band

Manufacturer: National Glass Co., McKee Bros. **Date:** 1902
Color: Crystal
Value: $50.00 – 75.00
Description — Top: Fire polished **Bottom:** Unfinished
Dimensions — Top: 2¹³⁄₁₆" **Bottom:** 2⁵⁄₁₆" **Height:** 4⅛"
Decoration: Ruby stained, gold.
Additional Notes: 1¾" top of figure.

AKA: Torpedo

Manufacturer: Thompson Glass Co. **Date:** 1889
Color: Crystal
Value: $70.00 – 80.00
Description — Top: Fire polished **Bottom:** Ground **Bottom Figure:** 20-point star
Dimensions — Top: 2¾" **Bottom:** 2⁵⁄₁₆" **Height:** 3¹⁵⁄₁₆"
Decoration: Ruby stained.
Additional Notes: 1¾" top of figure.

Original Name: No. 15074 Washington

Manufacturer: United States Glass Co. **Date:** 1901
Color: Crystal
Value: $50.00 – 60.00
Description — Top: Fire polished **Bottom:** Unfinished **Bottom Figure:** 24-point star
Dimensions — Top: 2¹⁵⁄₁₆" **Bottom:** 2¼" **Height:** 3¹¹⁄₁₆"
Decoration: Ruby stained.
Additional Notes: ⅞" top of figure.

Original Name: Ramona
AKA: Tip Toe

Manufacturer: McKee Glass Co. **Date:** 1910
Color: Crystal
Value: $25.00 – 35.00
Description — Top: Fire polished **Bottom:** Unfinished **Bottom Figure:** 24-point star
Dimensions — Top: 2¹⁵⁄₁₆" **Bottom:** 2⅞" over lobes **Height:** 3¹⁵⁄₁₆"
Decoration: Gold on lobes.
Additional Notes: 3⅜" top of figure.

Original Name: No. 722
AKA: Lorraine

Manufacturer: New Martinsville Glass Co. **Date:** 1913
Color: Crystal
Value: $75.00 – 85.00
Description — Top: Fire polished **Bottom:** Unfinished **Bottom Figure:** 20-point star
Dimensions — Top: 2⅞" **Bottom:** 2¼" **Height:** 3¹⁵⁄₁₆"
Decoration: Ruby stained.
Additional Notes: 3⁷⁄₁₆" top of figure.

Original Name: No. 724
AKA: Heart in Sand

Manufacturer: New Martinsville Glass Co. **Date:** 1915
Color: Crystal
Value: $275.00 – 325.00
Description — Top: Fire polished **Bottom:** Ground **Bottom Figure:** 16-point star
Dimensions — Top: 2⅞" **Bottom:** 2" **Height:** 3⅞"
Decoration: Ruby stained on hearts.
Additional Notes: 3¾" top of figure.

AKA: Teardrop and Tassel (Type 1)

Manufacturer: Greentown Glass Co. **Date:** Ca. 1898
Color: Crystal, other Greentown colors, known in Opaque Green
Value: $75.00 – 100.00
Description — Top: Unfinished **Bottom:** Unfinished
Dimensions — Top: 3¹⁄₁₆" **Bottom:** 2¼" **Height:** 3¹³⁄₁₆"
Additional Notes: Type 1 has full upper pattern; with Type II, the design has been polished from the mold.

AKA: Icicle

Color: Crystal
Value: $30.00 – 40.00
Description — Top: Fire polished **Bottom:** Unfinished
Dimensions — Top: 2¹⁵⁄₁₆" **Bottom:** 2" **Height:** 3¾"
Decoration: Gold, Ruby stained, printed "Fremont, Mich."
Additional Notes: 2³⁄₁₆" top of figure.

AKA: Icicle

Manufacturer: National Glass Co., Indiana Tumbler & Goblet Works **Date:** 1901
Color: Crystal, Chocolate
Value: $375.00 – 400.00 Chocolate
Description — Top: Fire polished
Dimensions — Top: 3" **Height:** 3⅞"

AKA: Picket and Band

Manufacturer: National Glass Co., Indiana Tumbler & Goblet Works **Date:** 1901
Color: Crystal, Chocolate
Value: $600.00 – 650.00 Chocolate
Description — Top: Fire polished
Dimensions — Top: 3" **Height:** 3⅞"
Additional Notes: Crystal known with "The E. C. Flaccus Co., Wheeling, WV"
   impressed in bottom.

Legend in Base.

Original Name: No. 15056 Florida
AKA: Emerald Green Herringbone

Manufacturer: United States Glass Co. **Date:** 1898
Color: Crystal, Emerald Green
Value: $25.00 – 35.00
Description — Top: Fire polished **Bottom Figure:** 24-point star
Dimensions — Top: 2¹³⁄₁₆" **Bottom:** 2⁷⁄₁₆" **Height:** 3¹³⁄₁₆ "
Additional Notes: At one time, authors insisted that the name of this pattern should be
   Emerald Green Herringbone, regardless of color.

Original Name: No. 450, Golden Agate
AKA: Holly Amber

Manufacturer: National Glass Co., Indiana Tumbler & Goblet Works **Date:** 1903
Color: Opalescent Amber
Value: $500.00 – 600.00
Additional Notes: Under blacklight it may fluoresce orange.

AKA: Cottage

Manufacturer: Windsor Glass Co. **Date:** 1892
Color: Crystal
Value: $25.00 – 35.00
Description — Top: Fire polished **Bottom:** Ground rim **Bottom Figure:** Figure
Dimensions — Top: 2¹³⁄₁₆" **Bottom:** 2⅜" **Height:** 3¹³⁄₁₆"
Additional Notes: 3⅜" top of figure.

Original Name: No. 157
AKA: Strawberry & Bird

Manufacturer: Indiana Glass (Dunkirk) **Date:** 1914
Color: Crystal
Value: $35.00 – 50.00
Description — Top: Fire polished **Bottom:** Hobstar
Dimensions — Top: 3¹⁄₁₆" **Bottom:** 3⁵⁄₁₆" **Height:** 4⅜"
Decoration: Blue, green, and red glaze.

Original Name: Hartford
AKA: Heart with Thumbprint

Manufacturer: Tarentum Glass Co. **Date:** 1899
Color: Crystal, Custard, Opaque Green
Value: $50.00 – 65.00
Description — Top: Fire polished **Bottom:** Rough **Bottom Figure:** Hobstar
Dimensions — Top: 3¹⁄₁₆" **Bottom:** 2⅝" **Height:** 3¹⁵⁄₁₆"
Decoration: Gold on pattern.
Additional Notes: 2¾" top of figure.

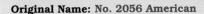

Original Name: No. 2056 American

Manufacturer: Fostoria Glass Co. **Date:** 1915
Color: Crystal
Value: $12.00 – 15.00
Description — Top: Fire polished **Bottom:** Unfinished **Bottom Figure:** 16-point star
Dimensions — Top: 3⅜" **Bottom:** 2⅝" **Height:** 4⁵⁄₁₆"
Additional Notes: 3⁵⁄₁₆" top of figure. This is probably a late-twentieth-century example,
  although the pattern has been made for most of the twentieth century.

Stippled & Beaded

Grouped together here for ease of comparison are tumblers that have prominent beads or areas of stippling.

Original Name: Fish
AKA: Seaweed & Fish

Manufacturer: Model Flint Glass Co. **Date:** Ca. 1890
Color: Crystal
Value: $60.00 – 70.00
Description — Top: Ground and polished, Chamfered inside
Dimensions — Top: 2¾" **Bottom:** 2⁵⁄₁₆" **Height:** 3¹¹⁄₁₆"
Decoration: Gold, blue stain on fish.
Additional Notes: 3¼" top of figure, made in emulation of Pomona, ten optics.

Original Name: Victor
AKA: Shell & Jewel

Manufacturer: Westmoreland Specialty Co. **Date:** 1893
Color: Crystal
Value: $25.00 – 35.00
Description — Top: Fire polished **Bottom:** Unfinished **Bottom Figure:** 16-petal flower
Dimensions — Top: 2¹³⁄₁₆" **Bottom:** 2½" **Height:** 3¹³⁄₁₆"
Additional Notes: 3-pint jug made by Fostoria in 1898 and called No. 618.

Original Name: Nugget

Manufacturer: Dominion Glass Co., Ltd. **Date:** Ca. 1900
Color: Crystal, Blue
Value: $25.00 – 35.00
Additional Notes: Note points in fan motif. Product of Canada. See Victor, above.

AKA: Festoon

Date: Ca. 1894
Color: Crystal
Value: $35.00 – 45.00
Description — Top: Fire polished **Bottom:** Unfinished
    Bottom Figure: Four rays in each quarter
Dimensions — Top: 2¾" **Bottom:** 2⅝" **Height:** 4"
Additional Notes: In Ward's catalog, 1894.

Original Name: Spanish American
AKA: Dewey, Admiral Dewey

Manufacturer: Beatty Brady Glass Co. **Date:** 1898
Color: Crystal
Value: $40.00 – 70.00
Description — Top: Imperfectly fire polished **Bottom:** May or may not be ground
    Bottom Figure: 28-point star
Dimensions — Top: 2¾" **Bottom:** 2½" **Height:** 3¹⁵⁄₁₆"
Additional Notes: Ornate mold work, cannon, ship, flags, Dewey, all against a stippled
    background. Has been reproduced; watch for rounded bottom corners on reproduction.

Original Name: No. 1218
AKA: Oriental

Manufacturer: A. J. Beatty & Sons
Color: Crystal
Value: $40.00 – 70.00
Description — Top: Fire polished **Bottom:** Unfinished **Bottom Figure:** 18-point star
Dimensions — Top: 2¾" **Bottom:** 2⁵⁄₁₆" over figure **Height:** 4³⁄₁₆"
Additional Notes: 3⅛" top of figure.

AKA: Posies & Pods

Manufacturer: Northwood Glass Co.; Wheeling, WV **Date:** 1905
Color: Crystal
Value: $140.00 – 160.00
Description — Top: Fire polished **Bottom:** Ground **Bottom Figure:** 24-point star
Dimensions — Top: 3⅛" **Bottom:** 2⅝" **Height:** 3⅞"
Decoration: Gold and blush.
Additional Notes: 2⁵⁄₁₆" top of figure.

Original Name: Dot
AKA: Stippled Forget-Me-Not

Manufacturer: Findlay Flint Glass Co. **Date:** 1890
Color: Amber, Crystal, Opal
Value: $75.00 – 100.00
Description — Top: Fire polished **Bottom:** Stuck-up **Bottom Figure:** 20-point star
Dimensions — Top: 2¾" **Bottom:** 2½" **Height:** 3⅝"

Original Name: Fleur-de-Lis

Manufacturer: King, Son & Co. **Date:** 1885
Color: Deep Emerald Green
Value: $35.00 – 45.00
Description — Top: Fire polished **Bottom:** Unfinished **Bottom Figure:** Raised 28-point star
Dimensions — Top: 2¾" **Bottom:** 2⁷⁄₁₆" **Height:** 3¾"
Decoration: Gold rim.
Additional Notes: Possibly by United States Glass Co., ca. 1898

Original Name: No. 15079 Wisconsin
AKA: Beaded Dewdrop

Manufacturer: U. S. Glass Co. **Date:** 1903
Color: Crystal
Value: $50.00 – 70.00
Description — Top: Fire polished **Bottom Figure:** 24-point star
Dimensions — Top: 2¾" **Bottom:** 2⁵⁄₁₆" **Height:** 3⅞"
Decoration: Gold on panels.
Additional Notes: 3⅜" top of figure.

AKA: Shimmering Star, Beaded Star

Manufacturer: Kokomo Glass Mfg. Co. **Date:** 1904
Color: Crystal
Value: $30.00 – 40.00
Description — Top: Imperfectly fire polished **Bottom Figure:** 8-point geometric design
Dimensions — Top: 2¹⁵⁄₁₆" **Bottom:** 2⁹⁄₁₆" **Height:** 3¾"

AKA: Sandwich

Manufacturer: Hocking Glass Co. **Date:** Mid-20th century
Color: Forest Green
Value: $15.00 – 25.00
Description — Top: Fire polished **Bottom:** Unfinished **Bottom Figure:** Star from figure
Dimensions — Top: 2¹⁵⁄₁₆" **Bottom:** 2¼" **Height:** 3⅞"
Additional Notes: 3³⁄₁₆" top of figure. Made in emulation of Bakewell, Page's Rochelle.

Original Name: No. 335
AKA: Beaded Swirl

Manufacturer: Geo. Duncan & Sons **Date:** Ca. 1890
Color: Crystal, Emerald Green
Value: $45.00 – 50.00
Description — Top: Fire polished **Bottom:** Ground
Dimensions — Top: 2⅞" **Bottom:** 2½" **Height:** 3½"
Decoration: Gold on beads.
Additional Notes: Green made by U. S. Glass, ca., 1898.

AKA: Bead Swirl Variant

Color: Crystal
Value: $30.00 – 40.00
Description — Top: Fire polished **Bottom:** Ground
Dimensions — Top: 2¹³⁄₁₆" **Bottom:** 2⅝" **Height:** 3¾"
Additional Notes: Resembles Duncan's Beaded Swirl. Note alternating widths of swirls.

Original Name: No. 1295
AKA: Bead Swag

Manufacturer: A. H. Heisey & Co. **Date:** 1898
Color: Opal; also Crystal, Emerald Green
Value: $50.00 – 60.00 Opal, $50.00 – 60.00 Ruby stained
Description — Top: Fire polished **Bottom:** Unfinished **Bottom Figure:** 18-point star
Dimensions — Top: 2¾" **Bottom:** 2⁹⁄₁₆" **Height:** 3¾"
Decoration: Purple cosmos, gold rim, beads in Opal, Ruby stained.

Original Name: No. 1295
AKA: Bead Swag

Manufacturer: A. H. Heisey & Co. **Date:** 1898
Color: Crystal, Emerald, Opal
Value: $50.00 – 75.00
Description — Top: Fire polished **Bottom:** Groundand polished
    Bottom Figure: 16-point star
Dimensions — Top: 2⅝" **Bottom:** 2½" **Height:** 3¾"
Decoration: Ruby stained, engraved band in center, gold.
Additional Notes: 1⅜" top of figure.

AKA: Beads & Drapes

Manufacturer: Monongah Glass Co./Indiana Glass Co.
Color: Crystal
Value: $30.00 – 40.00
Additional Notes: The same tumbler appears in both companys' catalogs.

Original Name: No. 350
AKA: Cord Drapery

Manufacturer: Greentown Glass Co. Date: 1898
Color: Crystal, other Greentown colors
Value: $75.00 – 100.00, $150.00 – 200.00 Blue
Description — Top: Fire polished Bottom: Unfinished
Dimensions — Top: 3⅛" Bottom: 2⁵⁄₁₆" Height: 3¹⁵⁄₁₆"
Additional Notes: This tumbler has an applied handle.

AKA: East Liverpool

Manufacturer: Attributed to East Liverpool Glass Co. Date: 1882
Color: Crystal
Value: $40.00 – 50.00
Description — Top: Fire polished Bottom: Unfinished Bottom Figure: 24-petal
    swirled flower
Dimensions — Top: 3³⁄₁₆" Bottom: 2⅝" Height: 3⁷⁄₁₆"
Decoration: Engraved.

Original Name: Russe

Manufacturer: Baccarat Date: Ca. 1930s
Color: Rose Tiente (Amberina)
Value: $65.00 – 80.00
Description — Top: Fire polished Bottom: Ground and polished
    Bottom Figure: 12-petal flower
Dimensions — Top: 2¹⁵⁄₁₆" Bottom: 2¹⁄₁₆" rim Height: 4"
Additional Notes: This is included because of its confusing color.

Original Name: No. 97
AKA: Teardrops

Manufacturer: Gillinder & Sons **Date:** 1885
Color: Crystal
Value: $35.00 – 45.00
Description — Top: Fire polished **Bottom:** Ground **Bottom Figure:** 19-point star
Dimensions — Top: 3" **Bottom:** 2¹³⁄₁₆" **Height:** 3¹¹⁄₁₆"
Additional Notes: 2⅜" top of figure.

Original Name: Scroll
AKA: Atterbury Scroll (Misnomer)

Manufacturer: Imperial Glass Corp. **Date:** Ca. 1960
Color: Blue
Value: $35.00 – 50.00
Description — Top: Fire polished
    Bottom: Unfinished
Dimensions — Top: 2½" **Bottom:** 2¹⁄₁₆" on rim
    Height: 3¹¹⁄₁₆"
Additional Notes: Note snap rim. Imperial made
    several pieces of this pattern for one of the major
    museums and continued to produce the pattern
    as a production item.

Original Name: No. 314
AKA: Scroll

Manufacturer: Challinor, Taylor & Co. **Date:** 1885
Color: Opal, Olive, Turquoise
Value: $50.00 – 60.00
Description — Top: Imperfectly fire polished **Bottom:** Rough
    Bottom Figure: 20-point star
Dimensions — Top: 2⅞" **Bottom:** 2⅝" rim **Height:** 3¹³⁄₁₆"
Additional Notes: Original on left.

Name: No. 15032
AKA: Thumbprints & Teardrops

Manufacturer: United States Glass Co. **Date:** 1895
Color: Dewey Blue with Gold
Value: $30.00 – 45.00
Description — Top: Fire polished **Bottom Figure:** Star
Dimensions — Top: 3" **Bottom:** 2¼" **Height:** 3⅝"
Additional Notes: 1¹⁄₁₆" top of figure.

Hobnail

What is today called hobnail was originally called Dew Drop. The pattern seems to have been introduced in the spring of 1886. There are several variations; the sizes and locations of the "drops" differ, and some pieces have a bump on top, some have several tiny bumps on top, and one tumbler has notches, or ribs, around the base. There is some thought that the pattern might be a pressed descendant of blown polka dot ware.

Ruby Sapphire

Value: $400.00 – 500.00

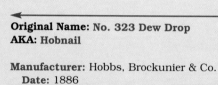

Original Name: No. 323 Dew Drop
AKA: Hobnail

Manufacturer: Hobbs, Brockunier & Co.
   Date: 1886
Inner Color: Ruby **Outer Color:** Pressed Sapphire
   Blue or Canary
Description — Top: Fire polished
   Bottom: Polished Pontil
Dimensions — Top: 2⅝" **Bottom:** 2¾" over figure
   Height: 3¹³⁄₁₆"
Additional Notes: The inner layer is blown
   into the pressed outer layer.

Rubina Verde

Value: $350.00 – 400.00

Ruby Opalescent

Value: $175.00 – 200.00

Original Name: No. 323 Dew Drop
AKA: Hobnail

Manufacturer: Hobbs, Brockunier & Co.
   Date: 1886
Description — Top: Fire polished
   Bottom: Unfinished
Dimensions — Top: 2⅝" **Bottom:** 2⅝" over pattern
   Height: 3¹⁵⁄₁₆"
Additional Notes: This tumbler was made in a wide
   range of colors, combinations of colors, and
   surface treatments.

Blue Opalescent

Value: $75.00 – 100.00

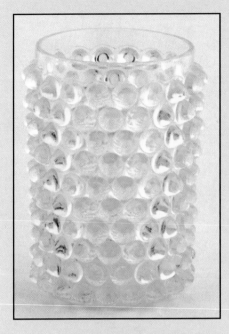

Original Name: No. 323 Dew Drop
AKA: Hobnail

Manufacturer: Hobbs, Brockunier & Co.
   Date: 1886
Description — Top: Fire polished
   Bottom: Unfinished
Dimensions — Top: 2⅝" **Bottom:** 2⅝" over pattern
   Height: 3¹⁵⁄₁₆"
Additional Notes: This tumbler was made in a wide
   range of colors, combinations of colors, and
   surface treatments.

Crystal, Decoration No. 7

Value: $55.00 – 65.00

Canary

Value: $65.00 – 75.00

Original Name: No. 100
AKA: Dewdrop/Hobnail

Manufacturer: A. J. Beatty & Sons **Date:** 1888
Color: White, Blue, Canary Opalescent
Value: $50.00 – 70.00 Opal, $75.00 – 85.00 Blue
Description — Top: Fire polished
   Bottom: Unfinished
Dimensions — Top: 2⁹⁄₁₆" **Bottom:** 2⁵⁄₁₆"
   Height: 4¹⁄₁₆"
Additional Notes: Nine vertical rows, 18 hobnails
   around.

Original Name: No. 150

Manufacturer: Doyle & Co. **Date:** 1885
Color: Amber
Value: $30.00 – 40.00
Description — Top: Fire polished **Bottom Figure:** One central hobnail, circle
    of eight, circle of fourteen
Dimensions — Top: 2⅝" **Bottom:** 2⅝" **Height:** 3⅞"
Additional Notes: Seven vertical rows of hobnails. Engraved "Lizzie, 1887."

Original Name: No. 150

Manufacturer: Doyle & Co., **Date:** 1885
Color: Crystal
Value: $45.00 – 55.00
Description — Top: Fire polished **Bottom:** Unfinished **Bottom:** One central hobnail,
    circle of eight, circle of fourteen
Dimensions — Top: 2¹¹⁄₁₆" **Bottom:** 2¼" **Height:** 3¾"
Additional Notes: Seven vertical rows of hobnails.

Sea Green

Crystal Opalescent

AKA: Hobnail

Manufacturer: Doyle & Co., **Date:** 1885
Color: Crystal
Value: $60.00 – 70.00
Description — Top: Fire polished **Bottom:** Unfinished **Bottom Figure:** Hobnails
Dimensions — Top: 2⁹⁄₁₆" **Bottom:** 2⅛" rim **Height:** 3⅞"
Decoration: Middle three bands of hobnails and top band are Ruby stained.
Additional Notes: 2¹¹⁄₁₆" top of figure. This tumbler probably made by United
    States Glass Co. in the 1890s.

Color: Crystal
Value: $20.00 – 30.00
Description — Top: Fire polished **Bottom:** Ground and polished
Dimensions — Top: 3¹⁄₁₆" **Bottom:** 2⅞" over figure **Height:** 3⅝"
Additional Notes: 1¹³⁄₁₆" top of figure. Five vertical rows of hobnail.

AKA: Printed Hobnail

Color: Crystal
Value: $30.00 – 40.00
Description — Top: Fire polished **Bottom Figure:** Figure
Dimensions — Top: 3" **Bottom:** 2⅝" rim **Height:** 3½"
Additional Notes: 2¾" top of figure. Note dots on top of hobnails.

AKA: Hobnail

Color: Amber
Value: $30.00 – 40.00
Description — Top: Ground and polished, chamfered inside and out **Bottom:** Flat ground
   Bottom Figure: Petaled flower extending onto sides
Dimensions — Top: 2¹¹⁄₁₆" over figure **Bottom:** 2¼" over figure **Height:** 3⅝"
Additional Notes: Seems to have been tooled into tumbler form from another
   shape. This tumbler seems to be of mid-twentieth century production.

Original Name: No. 335½
AKA: Hobnail in Square

Manufacturer: Aetna Glass Mfg. Co. **Date:** Ca. 1889
Color: Crystal Opalescent
Value: $60.00 – 70.00
Description — Top: Fire polished **Bottom:** Unfinished **Bottom Figure:** Hobnail star
Dimensions — Top: 2¾" **Bottom:** 2¾" over figure **Height:** 4¹⁄₁₆"

AKA: Hobnail

Manufacturer: Fenton Art Glass Co. **Date:** 1980s
Color: Mulberry Opalescent
Value: $35.00 – 50.00
Description — Top: Fire polished **Bottom:** Unfinished
 Bottom Figure: Fenton Logo plus *8*
Dimensions — Top: 3" **Bottom:** 2⅜" **Height:** 4³⁄₁₆"
Additional Notes: The *8* with the Fenton Logo
 indicates production in the 1980s. Note the
 snap ring, there to eliminate stick-up scars.

Original Name: Wyandotte
AKA: Umbilicated Hobnail

Manufacturer: Ripley & Co. **Date:** 1880s
Color: Crystal
Value: $50.00 – 60.00
Description — Top: Fire polished **Bottom:** Ground
 rim **Bottom Figure:** One pattern circle
Dimensions — Top: 2¹⁵⁄₁₆" **Bottom:** 2⅞"
 Height: 4⅛"
Decoration: Engraved leaf and berries, may be
 sandblasted (late).
Additional Notes: 1⅞" top of figure. Hobnails are
 depressed in center.

Original Name: No.25
AKA: Three Panel

Manufacturer: Richards and Hartley Glass Co.
 Date: Ca. 1883
Color: Crystal, Amber, Blue, Canary, Sea Green
Value: $45.00 – 55.00
Description — Top: Fire polished
 Bottom: Unfinished **Bottom Figure:** Figure
Dimensions — Top: 2¹³⁄₁₆" **Bottom:** 2¹¹⁄₁₆"
 Height: 3⅝"
Additional Notes: 2⁵⁄₁₆" top of figure, hobnails
 are alternately plain and 8-petal daisy.

AKA: Hobnail Band

Date: Ca. 1890
Color: Crystal
Value: $35.00 – 50.00
Description — Top: Fire polished
 Bottom: Ground **Bottom Figure:** One central
 hobnail, circle of five, circle of 12, circle of
 24 small
Dimensions — Top: 3⁵⁄₁₆" **Bottom:** 2⁵⁄₁₆"
 Height: 3⅝"
Additional Notes: Four vertical rows, 24 each
 row.

Original Name: Stardrop
AKA: Burred Hobnail

Manufacturer: Possibly Canton Glass C•
 Date: 1898
Color: Opal
Value: $40.00 – 50.00
Description — Top: Fire polished
 Bottom: Rough ground **Bottom**
 Figure: 17-point star
Dimensions — Top: 2½" **Bottom:** 2⅛"
 Height: 3¹¹⁄₁₆"
Decoration: Enamel flowers, cold gold
 on band and top rim.
Additional Notes: 1¾" top of figure.
 Each hobnail has many tiny ribs
 around its base.

Opalescent

The process of manufacturing opalescent glass involves putting a chemical (bone ash) in the batch. The mold must contain cavities that will allow the glass to form prominences. Once the glass is out of the mold, cool air is blown over the piece. The pressed tumbler needs only to be reheated and put in the lehr to anneal. The inside will be smooth and the raised design will be on the outside. Generally, the top rim and the raised design of these tumblers will be white, showing up nicely against the clear or colored background.

AKA: Swirl

Manufacturer: A. J. Beatty & Sons **Date:** 1889
Color: Crystal, Opalescent Blue, pieces in pattern known in Canary
Value: $55.00 – 65.00
Description — Top: Fire polished **Bottom:** Unfinished
 Bottom Figure: Three rings and center dot
Dimensions — Top: 2¾" **Bottom:** 2⅜" **Height:** 3¾"
Additional Notes: 3¼" top of figure. No documentation on manufacturer has been found.

Original Name: No. 87
AKA: Beatty Rib

Manufacturer: A. J. Beatty & Sons **Date:** 1889
Color: Crystal, Opalescent Blue
Value: $70.00 – 80.00
Description — Top: Fire polished **Bottom Figure:** Design continues to center.
Dimensions — Top: 2⅝" **Bottom:** 2⅝" over ribs **Height:** 3¾"
Additional Notes: 2¹⁵⁄₁₆" top of figure.

Original Name: No. 905 Manila
AKA: Shell & Wreath

Manufacturer: Model Flint Glass Co. **Date:** 1900
Color: Crystal, Canary, Blue, all may be Opalescent
Value: $60.00 – 70.00
Description — Top: Fire polished **Bottom:** Unfinished
Dimensions — Top: 2¹⁵⁄₁₆" **Bottom:** 2¹³⁄₁₆" **Height:** 3¹³⁄₁₆"
Additional Notes: 2¼" top of figure. This tumbler may have three feet instead of bottom rim, doubling the value.

Original Name: Iris
AKA: Wild Bouquet

Manufacturer: Northwood Glass Co.; Indiana, PA **Date:** 1898
Color: Opal, Blue, and Green Opalescent
Value: $75.00 – 100.00
Description — Top: Fire polished **Bottom:** Polished rim
Dimensions — Top: 2¹³⁄₁₆" **Bottom:** 2⁵⁄₁₆" **Height:** 3⅝"
Additional Notes: 3" top of figure. Pattern first made by Northwood in 1898, in Custard; later, by Dugan in opalescent colors.

Original Name: Victor
AKA: Jeweled Heart

Manufacturer: Dugan Glass Co. **Date:** 1904
Color: White, Blue, and Green Opalescent; Crystal, Blue, Apple Green. Carnival colors in 1909.
Value: $75.00 – 100.00
Description — Top: Fire polished **Bottom:** Unfinished **Bottom Figure:** 24-point star
Dimensions — Top: 3" **Bottom:** 2⅜" over figure **Height:** 3¾"
Additional Notes: 3¼" top of figure. Reproduced by L. G. Wright, difficult to distinguish.

Original Name: Intaglio

Manufacturer: Northwood Glass Co., Indiana PA **Date:** 1899
Color: White, Blue, and Canary Opalescent; Blue, Green, Custard
Value: $60.00 – 70.00
Description — Top: Fire polished **Bottom:** Unfinished
Dimensions — Top: 3" **Bottom:** 2¼" **Height:** 4"
Decoration: Gold on figure.

Original Name: No. 351
AKA: Buttons & Braids

Manufacturer: Fenton Art Glass Co. **Date:** 1910
Color: Blue, Green, and White Opalescent
Value: $50.00 – 60.00
Description — Top: Fire polished **Bottom:** Rough, stuck-up
Dimensions — Top: 3³⁄₁₆" **Bottom:** 2⅜" **Height:** 4"
Additional Notes: This item may have had a handle; it has a scar as if a handle had broken
off. Jefferson's version is blown. See also page 220.

Original Name: No. 271
AKA: Dolly Madison

Manufacturer: Jefferson Glass Co. **Date:** 1908
Color: Green, Blue, and White Opalescent; Crystal
Value: $60.00 – 90.00
Description — Top: Fire polished **Bottom:** Unfinished **Bottom Figure:** 48-point
unequal star
Dimensions — Top: 3¹⁄₁₆" **Bottom:** 2⅜" **Height:** 3¾"
Additional Notes: 3¹⁄₁₆" top of figure.

Original Name: No. 19 Encore
AKA: Jewel & Flower

Manufacturer: Northwood Glass Co., Wheeling, WV **Date:** 1904
Color: Blue Opalescent
Value: $65.00 – 75.00
Description — Top: Fire polished
Dimensions — Top: 3" **Bottom:** 2¾" **Height:** 4"
Decoration: Gold on figure.

Original Name: Nautilus
AKA: Argonaut Shell

Manufacturer: Northwood Glass Co., Indiana, PA **Date:** 1898
Color: Blue Opalescent, White Opalescent, Custard
Value: $75.00 – 100.00
Description — Top: Fire polished **Bottom:** Ground and polished
Dimensions — Top: 2⅞" **Bottom:** 2¼" **Height:** 3¹¹⁄₁₆"
Additional Notes: Reproduced by L. G. Wright, difficult to distinguish.

AKA: Circled Scroll

Manufacturer: Dugan Glass Co. **Date:** Ca. 1903
Color: Blue, Green, and White Opalescent
Value: $75.00 – 100.00
Description — Top: Fire polished **Bottom:** Unfinished **Bottom Figure:** Irregular 6-point star
Dimensions — Top: 2⅞" **Bottom:** 2½" **Height:** 3⅞"
Additional Notes: 3⅝" top of figure.

Original Name: National
AKA: S Repeat

Manufacturer: National Glass Co., Northwood Glass Works, Dugan Glass Co.
  Date: 1904,1909
Color: Blue Opalescent (1909)
Value: $50.00 – 65.00
Description — Top: Fire polished **Bottom:** Unfinished **Bottom Figure:** 30-point
  unequal star
Dimensions — Top: 3³⁄₁₆" **Bottom:** 2⁷⁄₁₆" **Height:** 3¹³⁄₁₆"
Additional Notes: 3¹⁄₁₆" top of figure. Made in transparent colors in 1904.

Opaque

These tumblers may also exist in crystal glass, but are shown here for ease of comparison.

Original Name: No. 15060 Vermont
AKA: Thumbprint with Flower Band

Manufacturer: United States Glass Co. **Date:** 1899
Color: Custard, Emerald Green, Crystal
Value: $70.00 – 80.00
Description — Top: Fire polished **Bottom Figure:** The pattern extends onto the bottom.
Dimensions — Top: 2¹³⁄₁₆" **Bottom:** 2½" exclusive of feet **Height:** 3¾"
Decoration: Green enamel, three different floral designs.
Additional Notes: 3³⁄₁₆" top of figure.

Original Name: Intaglio

Manufacturer: Northwood Glass Co., Indiana, PA **Date:** 1899
Color: Custard
Value: $45.00 – 55.00
Description — Top: Fire polished **Bottom:** Ground **Bottom Figure:** 20-point star
Dimensions — Top: 2⅞" **Bottom:** 2⅜" **Height:** 3¹⁵⁄₁₆"
Decoration: Gold on figure.

AKA: Stork & Rushes

Manufacturer: Dugan Glass Co., L. G. Wright Glass Co. **Date:** 1975
Color: Light Blue Opaque, Marigold Carnival
Value: $20.00 – 30.00
Description — Top: Imperfectly fire polished **Bottom:** Unfinished **Bottom Figure:** Wright logo (Circle W)
Dimensions — Top: 2¾" **Bottom:** 2⁷⁄₁₆" **Height:** 4¹⁄₁₆"
Additional Notes: Originally made by Dugan Glass, Ca. 1912. Reproduced by L. G. Wright.

Original Name: Pagoda
AKA: Chrysanthemum Sprig

Manufacturer: Northwood/Dugan **Date:** 1900
Color: Custard, also Blue Opaque
Value: Custard $45.00 – 55.00, Blue $150.00 – 200.00
Description — Top: Fire polished **Bottom:** Rough, stuck-up **Bottom Figure:** 20 ribs
Dimensions — Top: 2¹³⁄₁₆" **Bottom:** 2⅜" across points **Height:** 3¹³⁄₁₆"
Decoration: Gold, enamel possible.
Additional Notes: 3½" top of figure, 12 flutes.

AKA: Jackson

Manufacturer: Northwood Glass Co., Indiana, PA **Date:** 1898
Color: Ivory
Value: $50.00 – 60.00
Description — Top: Fire polished **Bottom:** Unfinished
Dimensions — Top: 2¹⁵⁄₁₆" **Bottom:** 2¼" **Height:** 4"
Decoration: Gold and red lacquer on flowers.

Original Name: No. 310
AKA: Ring Band

Manufacturer: A. H. Heisey & Co. **Date:** 1900
Color: Ivory (Pale Custard), Opal, Crystal (rare)
Value: $65.00 – 75.00
Description — Top: Fire polished **Bottom:** Rim ground and polished
Dimensions — Top: 2¹⁵⁄₁₆" **Bottom:** 2¹¹⁄₁₆" **Height:** 3¹¹⁄₁₆ "
Additional Notes: Signed with Diamond H. Original production had a ring about one-quarter of the way down the tumbler. Later souvenir pieces lack this ring.

AKA: St. Louis World's Fair

Date: 1904
Color: Opal
Value: $40.00 – 50.00
Description — Top: Fire polished **Bottom:** Unfinished **Bottom Figure:** 18-point star (with the number *2* inside bottom)
Dimensions — Top: 3⁵⁄₁₆" **Bottom:** 2⁵⁄₁₆" **Height:** 4¹⁵⁄₁₆"
Decoration: May have gold on figure.
Additional Notes: Shows several scenes of the fair. 4⅛" top of figure.

Original Name: No. 140
AKA: Diamond Peg

Manufacturer: McKee Bros. **Date:** 1894
Color: Custard
Value: $60.00 – 80.00
Description — Top: Fire polished **Bottom Rim:** Fire polished **Bottom Figure:** Hobstar
Dimensions — Top: 3³⁄₁₆" flared **Bottom:** 2³⁄₁₆" **Height:** 4"
Additional Notes: 1⅝ top of figure. Custard made by Jefferson Glass Co., ca. 1916. Imprinted in bottom, "Krys-Tol".

AKA: Swirl

Color: Opaque Blue
Value: $50.00 – 75.00
Description — Top: Fire polished **Bottom:** Matte ground
Dimensions — Top: 3¹⁄₁₆" **Bottom:** 2³⁄₁₆" rim **Height:** 3⅞"
Additional Notes: 3⅜" top of figure. This is probably a European tumbler.

AKA: **Tiny Polka Dots**

Color: Canary
Value: $25.00 – 35.00
Description — Top: Fire polished **Bottom:** Unfinished
Dimensions — Top: 2¹³⁄₁₆" **Bottom:** 2⁷⁄₁₆" **Height:** 3¹³⁄₁₆"

Original Name: Polka Dot

Manufacturer: Northwood Glass Co.; Wheeling, WV **Date:** after 1903
Color: Blue
Value: $35.00 – 45.00
Description — Top: Fire polished **Bottom:** May have polished rim, see notes.
Dimensions — Top: 3⅛" **Bottom:** 2⅜" **Height:** 3¹⁵⁄₁₆"
Additional Notes: This tumbler was dug at Northwood factory site, probably unfinished, still holds paint for the decorating department. Polka dots are five rows, ten around.

AKA: **14 Panels**

Manufacturer: Northwood Glass Co.; Wheeling, WV **Date:** after 1903
Color: Blue
Value: $35.00 – 45.00
Description — Top: Fire polished
Dimensions — Top: 2⅞" **Bottom:** 2½" **Height:** 3¹³⁄₁₆"

AKA: Internal Panels

Color: Emerald Green
Value: $35.00 – 50.00
Description — Top: Fire polished **Bottom:** Unfinished
Dimensions — Top: 2¹³⁄₁₆" **Bottom:** 2⁵⁄₁₆" **Height:** 3¹³⁄₁₆"
Decoration: Etched floral.
Additional Notes: 14-panel optic.

Original Name: No. 462, X-Ray

Manufacturer: Riverside Glass Co. **Date:** 1896
Color: Crystal, Emerald Green
Value: $60.00 – 70.00
Description — Top: Fire polished **Bottom:** Ground rim
Dimensions — Top: 2⅞" **Bottom:** 2⅝" **Height:** 3⅞"
Decoration: Gold in figure.

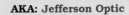

AKA: Jefferson Optic

Manufacturer: Jefferson Glass Co. **Date:** 1910
Color: Amethyst
Value: $40.00 – 50.00
Description — Top: Fire polished **Bottom:** Unfinished
Dimensions — Top: 2⅞" **Bottom:** 2³⁄₁₆" **Height:** 3¹³⁄₁₆"
Decoration: ½ flower, leaves, white enamel figure.

Original Name: No. 337 Touraine

Manufacturer: A. H. Heisey & Co. **Date:** 1902
Color: Crystal
Value: $75.00 – 100.00
Description — Top: Fire polished **Bottom:** Full ground **Bottom Figure:** Irregular 6-point star
Dimensions — Top: 3¹⁄₁₆" **Bottom:** 2⅛" **Height:** 3¹⁵⁄₁₆"
Decoration: Ruby stained, gold, engraved.
Additional Notes: Marked with the Diamond H inside bottom. The Touraine, a hotel in New York City torn down in 1929 to make room for the Empire State Building, specified this form for its barware. The shape became known industry wide as Touraine.

AKA: Internal Leaf

Color: Crystal
Value: $35.00 – 40.00
Description — Top: Fire polished Bottom: Unfinished
Dimensions — Top: 3" Bottom: 2⁵⁄₁₆" Height: 3⁵⁄₈"
Decoration: Leaf band is on inside, cut into plunger.
Additional Notes: 3¹⁄₃₂" top of figure.

AKA: Ten Panel

Color: Blue
Value: $35.00 – 40.00
Description — Top: Fire polished Bottom: Unfinished Bottom Figure: 10-point star
Dimensions — Top: 3⅛" Bottom: 2¼" Height: 4"
Decoration: Red, yellow, and blue enamel.

AKA: Picket & Band

Date: Ca. 1898
Color: Crystal
Value: $35.00 – 50.00
Description — Top: Unfinished Bottom: Unfinished
  Bottom Figure: Portrait of Admiral Dewey in bottom
  of glass
Dimension — Top: 3" Bottom: 2¼" Height: 3¾"
Additional Notes: Top made to accept tin top, rim is
  not tapered for ¼".

Portrait of Dewey

Original Name: No. 93
AKA: Ribbed Droplet Band

Manufacturer: Geo. Duncan & Sons **Date:** 1887
Color: Crystal
Value: $75.00 – 100.00
Description — Top: Fire polished **Bottom:** Ground and polished
  Bottom Figure: Rounded ribs taper to center.
Decoration: Satin on body with Amber-stained leaves and tendrils.

AKA: 16 Panels

Color: Copper Blue
Value: $30.00 – 40.00
Description — Top: Fire polished **Bottom:** Ground rim
Dimensions — Top: 2¾" **Bottom:** 2³⁄₁₆" **Height:** 4"
Decoration: Green, white, pink, brown enamel; gold.
Additional Notes: Gold on top rim, 16 internal panels.

AKA: Inside Ribbing

Color: Red
Value: $40.00 – 50.00
Description — Top: Fire polished **Bottom:** Unfinished **Bottom Figure:** Fancy
Dimensions — Top: 3⅛" **Bottom:** 2³⁄₁₆" **Height:** 4"
Decoration: Enameled floral decorations.
Additional Notes: 28 internal ribs.

Original Name: No. 1207

Manufacturer: A. J. Beatty & Sons **Date:** 1887
Color: Crystal
Value: $30.00 – 40.00
Description — Top: Fire polished **Bottom:** Full ground **Bottom Figure:** 24-point star
Dimensions — Top: 2¹¹⁄₁₆" **Bottom:** 2½" **Height:** 3¹³⁄₁₆"
Additional Notes: 3¾" top of figure.

Original Name: Gem
AKA: Nailhead

Manufacturer: Bryce, Higbee & Co. **Date:** 1885
Color: Crystal
Value: $35.00 – 50.00
Description — Top: Fire polished **Bottom:** Ground **Bottom Figure:** 15-point star
Dimensions — Top: 2¹⁵⁄₁₆" **Bottom:** 2⁷⁄₁₆" **Height:** 3⁹⁄₁₆"

Original Name: X. L. C. R.
AKA: King's Crown

Manufacturer: Adams & Co. **Date:** 1890
Color: Crystal
Value: $35.00 – 45.00
Description — Top: Fire polished **Bottom:** Unfinished **Bottom Figure:** 12-point starbu...
Dimensions — Top: 3" **Bottom:** 2" **Height:** 3¾"
Decoration: Engraved.
Additional Notes: 1¹⁵⁄₁₆" top of figure.

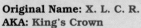

Original Name: X. L. C. R.
AKA: King's Crown

Manufacturer: Adams & Co. **Date:** 1890
Color: Crystal
Value: $50.00 – 60.00
Description — Top: Fire polished **Bottom:** Unfinished **Bottom Figure:** 12-point sunburst
Dimensions — Top: 3¹⁄₁₆" **Bottom:** 2⅛" rim **Height:** 3⅝"
Decoration: Ruby stained, engraved.
Additional Notes: 1¹⁵⁄₁₆" top of figure.

AKA: Beaded Block Band

Color: Crystal
Value: $45.00 – 55.00
Description — Top: Fire polished **Bottom Figure:** 20-point star
Dimensions — Top: 2¹⁵⁄₁₆" **Bottom:** 1⅝" rim **Height:** 3¹³⁄₁₆"
Decoration: Ruby stained.
Additional Notes: 1⁹⁄₁₆" top of figure.

Original Name: Dakota
AKA: Baby Thumbprint

Manufacturer: Ripley & Co. **Date:** Ca. 1885
Color: Crystal
Value: $50.00 – 60.00 Crystal, $75.00 – 95.00 Ruby stained
Description — Top: Fire polished **Bottom:** Ground **Bottom Figure:** Tick-Tack-Toe figure
Dimensions — Top: 3" **Bottom:** 3" **Height:** 3½"
Decoration: Ruby stained, engraved.

Original Name: Atlas
AKA: Crystal Ball, Cannonball

Manufacturer: Bryce Bros. **Date:** 1889
Color: Crystal
Value: $30.00 – 40.00
Description — Top: Fire polished **Bottom:** Ground and polished
   Bottom Figure: 14-point star, 2 miter circles
Dimensions — Top: 2¹¹⁄₁₆" **Bottom:** 3" over balls **Height:** 3⅝"

Original Name: No. 15057 Colorado

Manufacturer: United States Glass Co. **Date:** 1898
Color: Crystal, Dewey Blue, Emerald Green
Value: $40.00 – 50.00
Description — Top: Fire polished **Bottom:** Full ground **Bottom Figure:** 22-point star
Dimensions — Top: 3³⁄₁₆" **Bottom:** 2¹¹⁄₁₆" **Height:** 3½"
Decoration: Gold.
Additional Notes: Note ground bottom compare with Jewel, below.

Original Name: Jewel
AKA: Lacy Medallion

Manufacturer: United States Glass Co.
     Date: 1899
Color: Crystal
Value: $40.00 – 50.00
Description — Top: Fire polished
     Bottom: Unfinished
     Bottom Figure: 22-point star
Dimensions — Top: 3³⁄₁₆" **Bottom:** 2⅝"
     Height: 3½"
Decoration: Ruby stained.
Additional Notes: 1¹¹⁄₁₆" top of figure.
     Note snap rim on bottom; this is the
     difference between Jewel and
     Colorado.

Original Name: No. 197

Manufacturer: A. H. Heisey & Co. **Date:** Ca. 1913
Color: Crystal
Value: $40.00 – 70.00
Description — Top: Fire polished **Bottom:** Full ground **Bottom Figure:** 18-point star
Dimensions — Top: 2⅝" **Bottom:** 2⅝" **Height:** 3½"
Additional Notes: ⁷⁄₁₆" top of figure. Diamond H inside. Made for use in tumble-up.

Original Name: No. 361
AKA: Angular Criss-Cross

Manufacturer: A. H. Heisey & Co. **Date:** 1909, Flamingo after 1925
Color: Crystal, Flamingo
Value: $75.00 – 85.00
Description — Top: Fire polished **Bottom:** Ground and polished
   Bottom Figure: Diamond H in center
Dimensions — Top: 3¼" **Bottom:** 2⁹⁄₁₆" over figure **Height:** 3¾"
Additional Notes: 2⅞" top of figure.

Iridescent

Iridescent glass was created in an attempt to immitate the look of the centuries-old surface of buried glassware. Soon, others who found an easy, less expensive way to produce the same effect copied these original artists. Today, there are far more people collecting carnival glass than were ever collecting Tiffany's Favrile or Steuben's Aurene. This may be due to the wide availability of the carnival glass and the difficulty of accumulating the latter two.

Pricing of carnival tumblers is heavily dependant upon color and condition. Any imperfection, whether damage or a manufacturing flaw, makes the tumbler undesirable. Color is extremely important; a tumbler in a rare color may have a value ten times or more that of one found in a more available color.

Original Name: Kew Blas
AKA: Pinched

Manufacturer: Union Glass Works; Somerville, MA. **Date:** Ca. 1900
Color: Gold Iridescent
Value: $350.00 – 450.00
Description — Top: Fire polished **Bottom:** Unfinished
  Bottom Figure: Polished pontil
Dimensions — Top: 2¾" **Bottom:** 2½" on diagonal **Height:** 3½"
Additional Notes: "Kew Blas" on pontil.

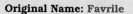

AKA: Aurene

Manufacturer: Steuben Glass Works **Date:** Ca. 1900
Color: Gold Aurene
Value: $250.00 – 350.00
Description — Top: Fire polished **Bottom:** Unfinished
  Bottom Figure: Polished pontil
Dimensions — Top: 3⅛" **Bottom:** 2⅛" **Height:** 3¾"
Additional Notes: "Aurene" engraved in pontil.

Original Name: Favrile

Manufacturer: L. C. Tiffany & Co. **Date:** Ca. 1900
Color: Gold Iridized
Value: $300.00 – 400.00
Description — Top: Fire polished **Bottom:** Unfinished
  Bottom Figure: Ground pontil
Dimensions — Top: 3 1/16" **Bottom:** 2⅞" **Height:** 4"
Additional Notes: Engraved "L. C. Tiffany — Favrile" around pontil.

Manufacturer: Possibly Loetz
Color: Iridescent Marigold
Value: $300.00 – 400.00
Description — Top: Fire polished **Bottom:** Unfinished
   Bottom Figure: Swirls go to polished pontil.
Dimensions — Top: 3⅛" **Bottom:** 2⅞" **Height:** 4⅛"
Decoration: Iridized inside and out.
Additional Notes: 16 swirled ribs.

AKA: Pseudo Steuben

Date: Ca. 1960
Inner Color: Salmon Pink **Intermediate Color:** White **Outer Color:** Selenium Red
Value: $45.00 – 80.00
Description — Top: Flat ground
Dimensions — Top: 2¾" **Bottom:** 2⁷⁄₁₆" **Height:** 3⁹⁄₁₆"
Decoration: Iridized (washes off).
Additional Notes: Found with fake Steuben mark etched inside bottom. Relatively modern.

AKA: Maple Leaf

Manufacturer: Northwood Glass Co., Dugan Glass Co. **Date:** Ca. 1913
Color: Amethyst
Value: $60.00 – 75.00
Description — Top: Fire polished **Bottom Figure:** 24-point star
Dimensions — Top: 3¼" **Bottom:** 2⅝" **Height:** 4"
Additional Notes: 3⁷⁄₁₆" top of figure. Shards have been found at Indiana PA, the site of
   Northwood/National/Dugan. At this time, there is no way to determine which company
   originated the pattern. This tumbler may also be a product of L.G. Wright, ca. 1960.

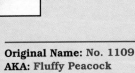

Original Name: No. 1109
AKA: Fluffy Peacock

Manufacturer: Fenton Art Glass Co. **Date:** 1910
Color: Amethyst
Value: $80.00 – 95.00
Description — Top: Fire polished **Bottom:** Unfinished
Dimensions — Top: 2¹⁵⁄₁₆" **Bottom:** 2⅜" **Height:** 4¹⁄₁₆"

AKA: Paneled Dandelion

Manufacturer: Fenton Art Glass Co. **Date:** Ca. 1910
Color: Amethyst
Value: $50.00 – 65.00
Description — Top: Fire polished **Bottom:** Flat ground
Dimensions — Top: 3¹⁄₁₆" **Bottom:** 2" across flats **Height:** 4¹⁄₁₆"

AKA: Stork & Rushes

Manufacturer: Dugan Glass Co. **Date:** Ca. 1912
Color: Blue
Value: $50.00 – 65.00
Description — Top: Fire polished **Bottom:** Unfinished
Dimensions — Top: 2⅞" **Bottom:** 2⁷⁄₁₆" **Height:** 3¹⁵⁄₁₆"
Additional Notes: Variation, beaded bands replaced with lattice band. The variation is more difficult to find. This tumbler was reproduced by the L. G. Wright Glass Co., from original Dugan molds.

AKA: Peacock at the Fountain

Manufacturer: Dugan Glass Co. **Date:** Ca. 1912
Color: Blue
Value: $80.00 – 100.00
Description — Top: Fire polished **Bottom:** Unfinished
Dimensions — Top: 2⅞" **Bottom:** 2⅜" **Height:** 4"
Additional Notes: Northwood also made the pattern, usually marked.

AKA: Rambler Rose

Manufacturer: Dugan Glass Co. **Date:** Ca. 1914
Color: Amethyst, Marigold, Blue
Value: $35.00 – 50.00 Blue
Description — Top: Fire polished **Bottom:** Unfinished
Additional Notes: L. G. Wright reproduced this in Amethyst in 1977.

AKA: Singing Birds

Manufacturer: Northwood Glass Co.; Wheeling, WV **Date:** Ca. 1912
Color: Green
Value: $65.00 – 80.00
Description — Top: Fire polished **Bottom Figure:** 24-point star
Dimensions — Top: 3¹⁄₁₆" **Bottom:** 2¹¹⁄₁₆" **Height:** 4⅛"

AKA: Acorn Burrs

Manufacturer: Northwood Glass Co.; Wheeling, WV **Date:** Ca. 1912
Color: Amethyst
Value: $80.00 – 95.00
Description — Top: Fire polished
Dimensions — Top: 3⅛" **Bottom:** 2½" **Height:** 4³⁄₁₆"
Additional Notes: Signed with an *N* in circle.

AKA: Grape & Leaves, Vineyard

Manufacturer: Dugan Glass Co. **Date:** Ca. 1912
Color: Amethyst
Value: $45.00 – 70.00
Description — Top: Imperfectly fire polished
Dimensions — Top: 2¾" **Bottom:** 2⁹⁄₁₆" **Height:** 3¹³⁄₁₆"

Marigold

AKA: Plain with Knurled Ring

Color: Blue
Value: $35.00 – 50.00
Description — Top: Fire polished **Bottom:** Ground
Dimensions — Top: 3¹⁄₁₆" **Bottom:** 2⅛" **Height:** 3¹³⁄₁₆"
Decoration: Enamel flowers.
Additional Notes: 20 panels.

Manufacturer: Northwood Glass Co. **Date:** Ca. 1914
Color: Pale Blue
Value: $30.00 – 45.00
Description — Top: Fire polished **Bottom:** Ground
Dimensions — Top: 2⅞" **Bottom:** 2⅜" **Height:** 3¾"
Decoration: Large enamel flowers.

AKA: 22 Panels

Color: Marigold
Value: $35.00 – 50.00
Description — Top: Imperfectly fire polished **Bottom:** Unfinished
Dimensions — Top: 2¾" **Bottom:** 2³⁄₁₆" **Height:** 3¾"

Original Name: No. 409
AKA: Crab Claw

Manufacturer: Imperial Glass Corp. **Date:** 1912
Color: Marigold
Value: $40.00 – 55.00
Description — Top: Fire polished **Bottom:** Ground **Bottom Figure:** Hobstar
Dimensions — Top: 3³⁄₁₆" **Bottom:** 2⁵⁄₁₆" **Height:** 4¼"

Original Name: No. 402½
AKA: Fashion

Manufacturer: Imperial Glass Corp. **Date:** Ca. 1910
Color: Marigold
Value: $40.00 – 55.00
Description — Top: Fire polished **Bottom:** Unfinished **Bottom Figure:** Hobstar
Dimensions — Top: 3⁵⁄₁₆" **Bottom:** 2⁷⁄₁₆" **Height:** 4¼"

AKA: Roses with Internal Ribs

Color: Marigold
Value: $40.00 – 55.00
Description — Top: Fire polished **Bottom:** Unfinished **Bottom Figure:** 24-point star
Dimensions — Top: 3⁵⁄₁₆" **Bottom:** 2⅝" **Height:** 4⁵⁄₁₆"
Additional Notes: Strong internal ribs.

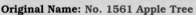

Original Name: No. 1562 Blueberry

Manufacturer: Fenton Art Glass Co. **Date:** 1912
Color: White
Value: $40.00 – 65.00
Description — Top: Fire polished **Bottom:** Unfinished
Dimensions — Top: 2¹⁵⁄₁₆" **Bottom:** 2⁷⁄₁₆" **Height:** 4⅛"

Original Name: No. 1561 Apple Tree

Manufacturer: Fenton Art Glass Co. **Date:** 1912 originally, reissued in 1997.
Color: Gold Pearl, colored glass, iridized
Value: Not established
Description — Top: Fire polished **Bottom:** Unfinished **Bottom Figure:** Fenton logo with *9* and copyright
Dimensions — Top: 2⅞" **Bottom:** 2⅜" **Height:** 4"
Decoration: Light iridescence.
Additional Notes: 3⁵⁄₁₆" top of file.

134

AKA: Floral & Grapes

Manufacturer: Dugan Glass Co. **Date:** 1914
Color: White
Value: $50.00 – 70.00
Description — Top: Fire polished **Bottom:** Unfinished **Bottom Figure:** The numer *11*
Dimensions — Top: 2¾" **Bottom:** 2⅝" **Height:** 3¹⁵⁄₁₆"

AKA: Holly

Color: Blue
Value: $40.00 – 55.00
Description — Top: Imperfectly fire polished **Bottom:** Unfinished **Bottom Figure:** Holly wreath
Dimensions — Top: 2⅞" **Bottom:** 2⁹⁄₁₆" **Height:** 3⅞"
Additional Notes: Closely resembles National's Holly Amber, may be a product of the late twentieth century.

Original Name: No. 1563
AKA: Lattice & Grape

Manufacturer: Fenton Art Glass Co. **Date:** 1912
Color: Marigold
Value: $35.00 – 50.00
Description — Top: Fire polished
Additional Notes: This tumbler is iridized on the inside, not the outside.

AKA: Frolicking Bears

Manufacturer: United States Glass Co. **Date:** Ca. 1906
Color: Crystal
Value: Auction price, $1,050.00
Description — Top: Fire polished
Additional Notes: This is one of a very few that were not iridized, hence the price.

Photo courtesy of William McGuffin, Green Valley Auctions, Inc.

135

Blown Tumblers

Manufacturing blown tumblers allows glassworkers a great deal of flexibility. The process begins when a small gob of glass is gathered on a blowpipe. A quick hard puff of air by the gatherer starts a bubble. Additional layers of glass are gathered, if the blower so wishes. Frit (powdered glass) may be added, and the gather may be put in a spot or an optic mold to give pattern to the finished product. A final gather of crystal or colored glass may be added. Then, the piece is blown into its final mold. This mold may be smooth or patterned. In any case, the inside and the outside of the glass are roughly parallel. Bumps on the outside have corresponding hollows on the inside. Once the glass has cooled, a matter of 30 seconds or less, the mold is opened and the part of the bubble outside of the mold (the overblow) is broken off, separating the tumbler from the blowpipe. If the tumbler comes from the mold in its final form, the top surface is then ground and polished and, if it is needed, chamfered. If there is more work to be done, such as flaring, interior plating (for multiple colors), striking (for Amberina or Peachblow), or perhaps the sealing of the edges of an air trap, the tumbler is stuck up on a punty rod before the overblow is broken off. In this manner, the top edge becomes fire polished. Some authors have intimated that all blown tumblers should be fire polished and that finding one ground indicates that it has been repaired. This is not necessarily so. If the tumbler was stuck up (some sort of pontil mark will remain), it probably had a Fire polished top edge. If it was not stuck up, it probably had a ground and polished rim.

Single-Color Transparent and Opaque

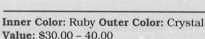

AKA: Crackle

Inner Color: Ruby **Outer Color:** Crystal
Value: $40.00 – 70.00
Description — Top: Ground and polished, chamfered inside
  Bottom: Unfinished
Dimensions — Top: 2¹³⁄₁₆" **Bottom:** 2⁹⁄₁₆" **Height:** 3¹³⁄₁₆"

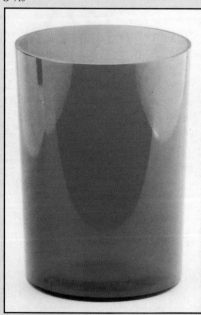

Inner Color: Ruby **Outer Color:** Crystal
Value: $30.00 – 40.00
Description — Top: Fire polished **Bottom:** Unfinished
Dimensions — Top: 2¹¹⁄₁₆" **Bottom:** 2⁷⁄₁₆" **Height:** 3¹¹⁄₁₆"

Inner Color: Ruby **Outer Color:** Crystal
Value: $75.00 – 100.00
Dimensions — Top: 2½" **Bottom:** 2½" **Height:** 3¾"
Decoration: Gold-colored applied metal mounting.

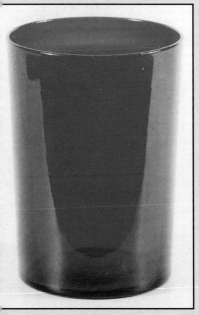

Date: After ca. 1915
Color: Selenium Ruby
Value: $30.00 – 40.00
Description — Top: Ground, chamfered inside, gold on surface **Bottom:** Unfinished
Dimensions — Top: 2⅞" **Bottom:** 2⁷⁄₁₆"
    Height: 3¹¹⁄₁₆"
Additional Notes: Blown into four part iron mold.

Color: Ruby, deep
Value: $40.00 – 70.00

Manufacturer: National Glass Co., McKee Bros. Glass Works **Date:** 1903
Color: Custard
Value: $35.00 – 50.00
Description — Top: Fire polished
    Bottom: Unfinished **Bottom Figure:** Circle McK mark
Dimensions — Top: 2¹¹⁄₁₆" **Bottom:** 2⁷⁄₁₆"
    Height: 3¹³⁄₁₆"
Additional Notes: This tumbler is pressed, but appears blown. It is shown here for comparison.

Inner Color: Lavender **Outer Color:** Opal
Value: $20.00 – 35.00
Description — Top: Fire polished
    Bottom: Unfinished
Dimensions — Top: 2⅞" **Bottom:** 2¹¹⁄₁₆"
    Height: 3¹³⁄₁₆"
Decoration: Fired-on brushed yellow enamel.

Color: Aqua
Value: $40.00 – 70.00
Description — Top: Fire polished **Bottom:** Unfinished
Dimensions — Top: 2¹¹⁄₁₆" **Bottom:** 2½" **Height:** 3¾"
Additional Notes: Light weight.

AKA: Three Feet

Color: Opaque Gray, Fireglow
Value: $55.00 – 75.00
Description — Top: Ground and polished, chamfered inside and out **Bottom Figure:** Feet are ground.
Dimensions — Top: 2¾" **Bottom:** 2⅝" body **Height:** 4¹⁄₁₆"
Decoration: Heavy multicolored enamel, gold on rim.
Additional Notes: Probably European, dresser sets of this pattern exist.

The tumblers in this section, with a couple of exceptions, are not transparent. Most are opaque, but they all share the distinction of shading from one color to another. Some are uniform throughout; others are cased or plated.

Original Name: Burmese

Manufacturer: Mt.Washington Glass Co. **Date:** 1886
Color: Custard shading to Salmon
Value: $175.00 – 250.00
Description — Top: Fire polished **Bottom Figure:** Large ground pontil
Dimensions — Top: 2¾" **Bottom:** 2⅜" **Height:** 3¹¹⁄₁₆"
Decoration: Known in satin.

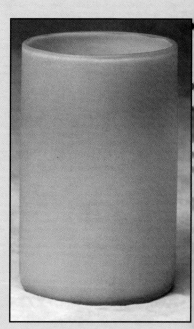

AKA: Burmese

Inner Color: Yellow shading to Salmon **Outer Color:** Transparent, not opaque glass
Value: $30.00 – 50.00
Description — Top: Fire polished **Bottom Figure:** Sharp pontil
Dimensions — Top: 2¾" **Bottom:** 2¾" **Height:** 4⁵⁄₁₆"
Decoration: Frosted inside and out.
Additional Notes: It is the author's opinion that this is a recent product, mid-twentieth century.

Original Name: No. 236
AKA: Wheeling Peach Blow

Manufacturer: Hobbs, Brockunier & Co. **Date:** 1886
Inner Color: Opal **Outer Color:** Yellow shading to Red
Value: $175.00 – 225.00
Description — Top: Ground, chamfered outside **Bottom Figure:** Large ground pontil
Dimensions — Top: 2¹³⁄₁₆" **Bottom:** 2⅜" **Height:** 3½"
Decoration: May have satin finish.

AKA: Peach Blow

Manufacturer: Wright/Diana **Date:** Ca. 1950
Inner Color: Opal **Outer Color:** Pale Yellow shading to Salmon
Value: $125.00 – 175.00
Description — Top: Ground and polished, not flat, faceted **Bottom Figure:** Small, sharp pontil
Dimensions — Top: 2¾" **Bottom:** 2⅝" **Height:** 3⅝"
Additional Notes: Made for L. G. Wright by Sam Diana of Venetian Art Glass Co., Rochester, PA.

AKA: Reverse Amberina

Manufacturer: Possibly Imperial Glass Co. **Date:** Ca. 1960s
Color: Selenium Amberina, Red shading to Yellow shading to Clear
Value: $80.00 – 120.00
Description — Top: Ground and polished, chamfered outside
Dimensions — Top: 2¹⁵⁄₁₆" **Bottom:** 2⁹⁄₁₆" **Height:** 3¹³⁄₁₆"
Additional Notes: Reacts orange to black light.

Original Name: Wild Rose
AKA: New England Peach Blow

Manufacturer: New England Glass Co. **Date:** 1886
Color: Opal shading to Rose
Value: $250.00 – 300.00
Description — Top: Fire polished **Bottom Figure:** Concave ground pontil
Dimensions — Top: 2⁹⁄₁₆" **Bottom:** 2⅜" **Height:** 3¹¹⁄₁₆"
Decoration: Satin.

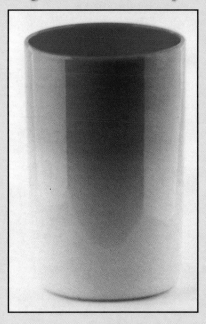

Original Name: Wild Rose
AKA: New England Peach Blow

Manufacturer: New England Glass Co. **Date:** 1886
Color: Opal shading to Rose
Value: $250.00 – 300.00
Description — Top: Fire polished **Bottom Figure:** Concave ground pontil
Dimensions — Top: 2⁹⁄₁₆" **Bottom:** 2⅜" **Height:** 3¹³⁄₁₆"

Original Name: Wild Rose
AKA: New England Peach Blow

Manufacturer: New England Glass Co. **Date:** 1886
Color: Opal shading to Rose
Value: $350.00 – 400.00
Description — Top: Fire polished **Bottom Figure:** Polished pontil
Dimensions — Top: 2¹¹⁄₁₆" **Bottom:** 2⅜" **Height:** 3¹³⁄₁₆"
Decoration: Gold enamel "Gerturde," "Centennial Exposition, Cin. 1888."

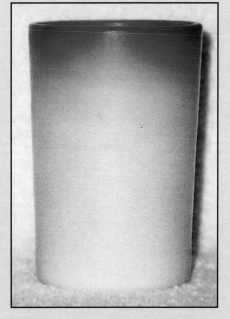

AKA: Peach Blow

Manufacturer: Gunderson Glass Co. **Date:** 1950s
Color: Opal shading to Rose
Value: $125.00 – 175.00
Description — Top: Fire polished **Bottom Figure:** Rough pontil
Dimensions — Top: 2¾" **Bottom:** 2⁷⁄₁₆" **Height:** 4"
Additional Notes: Satin finish.

Date: 1890s
Color: Pink shading to Opal
Value: $45.00 – 80.00
Description — Top: Ground and polished
Dimensions — Top: 2¾" **Bottom:** 2⅛" rim **Height:** 3¹¹⁄₁₆"
Additional Notes: Several companies made this color; Challinor, Taylor and Buckeye are two. This is a pressed tumbler.

Inner Color: Opal **Outer Color:** Ruby shading to Crystal
Value: $200.00 – 250.00
Description — Top: Ground **Bottom Figure:** *18* in gold
Dimensions — Top: 2¹³⁄₁₆" **Bottom:** 2¹¹⁄₁₆" **Height:** 4
Decoration: Enamel flowers, stems, and leaves.

Inner Color: Opal **Outer Color:** Ruby shading to Crystal
Value: $175.00 – 225.00
Description — Top: Ground **Bottom:** Ground flat
Dimensions — Top: 2⅝" **Bottom:** 2⁷⁄₁₆" **Height:** 3¾"
Decoration: Satin finish, gold rim, enamel flowers and leaves.

Inner Color: Blue **Intermediate Color:** Opal **Outer Color:** Ruby shading to Crystal
Value: $175.00 – 225.00
Description — Top: Ground
Dimensions — Top: 3" **Bottom:** 2¹¹⁄₁₆" **Height:** 4"

Inner Color: Opal **Outer Color:** Shaded Blue
Value: $120.00 – 175.00
Description — Top: Ground and polished, chamfered
   inside
Dimensions — Top: 2¹¹⁄₁₆" **Bottom:** 2⁵⁄₁₆" **Height:** 3¹¹⁄₁₆"

141

AKA: Mary Gregory

Color: Crystal
Value: $65.00 – 75.00 each
Description — Top: Ground
Dimensions — Top: 2¾" **Bottom:** 2⁷⁄₁₆" **Height:** 3⅝"
Decoration: Mary Gregory decoration, enamel.
Additional Notes: This decoration originated in the 1880s and ha[s]
   continued in popularity to the present time.

Color: Crystal
Value: $50.00 – 70.00
Description — Top: Flat ground, trace of gold **Bottom:** Unfinished **Bottom Figure:** Full flat
   ground
Dimensions — Top: 2⅞" **Bottom:** 2¾" **Height:** 3⅞"
Decoration: Satin, gold and white enamel, three glued-on jewels, gold-inscribed "Aus Albendorf."
Additional Notes: German or Austrian manufacture.

AKA: Lily-of-the-Valley

Color: Crystal
Value: $25.00 – 30.00
Description — Top: Fire polished
Dimensions — Top: 2¾" **Bottom:** 2½"
   Height: 3¹³⁄₁₆"
Decoration: Cranberry, green wash, white enamel.

Color: Canary
Value: $45.00 – 55.00
Description — Top: Fire polished
Dimensions — Top: 2¹¹⁄₁₆" **Bottom:** 2⅜" **Height:** 3⅞"
Decoration: Cut design, etched and gilded top band, gold on top.

AKA: Ruby with Frit

Inner Color: Ruby **Outer Color:** Crystal
Value: $40.00 – 50.00
Description — Top: Ground **Bottom Figure:** Polished pontil
Dimensions — Top: 2½" **Bottom:** 2¼" **Height:** 3½"
Decoration: Gold tracery, glued and fired frit design.

Manufacturer: Model Flint Glass Co. **Date:** Ca. 1901
Inner Color: Opal **Intermediate Color:** Pink **Outer Color:** Opal frit
Value: $200.00 – 300.00
Description — Top: Ground
Dimensions — Top: 2¹³⁄₁₆" **Bottom:** 2⁹⁄₁₆" **Height:** 3⅞"
Additional Notes: Opal frit on outer surface, expanded to give crackled effect.

AKA: Niagara Falls

Color: Ruby
Value: $75.00 - 85.00
Description — Top: Fire polished
Dimensions — Top: 2⁷⁄₁₆" **Bottom:** 2⁵⁄₁₆" **Height:** 3¾"
Decoration: Decal of Niagara Falls, gold, white enamel.

AKA: Engraved Souvenir

Color: Crystal
Value: $60.00 – 70.00
Decoration: Ruby stained.
Additional Notes: Dated "Aug. 18, 1894, Atlantic City."

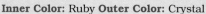

AKA: Etched Windmill

Color: Crystal
Value: $60.00 – 70.00
Decoration: Ruby stained, etched windmill.

Inner Color: Ruby **Outer Color:** Crystal
Value: $40.00 – 50.00
Description — Top: Flat ground, chamfered outside
Dimensions — Top: 2⅞" **Bottom:** 2⁵⁄₁₆"
  Height: 3⅞"
Decoration: Gold, pink, and white enamel.

Color: Crystal
Value: $45.00 – 55.00
Description — Top: Fire polished
Dimensions — Top: 3¹⁄₁₆" **Bottom:** 2⁵⁄₁₆"
  Height: 3¹⁵⁄₁₆"
Decoration: Pink wash, applied berries, natural color enamel leaves.
Additional Notes: Eight optics.

Color: Crystal
Value: $55.00 – 65.00
Description — Top: Fire polished
Dimensions — Top: 2⅞" **Bottom:** 2⁷⁄₁₆"
  Height: 3¾"
Decoration: Pink and yellow wash. Enamel elk in natural colors.

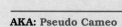

AKA: Pseudo Cameo

Color: Brownish Amber
Value: $60.00 – 70.00
Description — Top: Full ground, chamfered outside
Dimensions — Top: 2¾" **Bottom:** 2⁵⁄₁₆"
  Height: 3⅝"
Decoration: Satin, enamel bird and leaves.
Additional Notes: This type tumbler has been found with a stamped signature on the bottom reading "Florentine Art Cameo" and "Art Cameo." These wares were imported from central Europe into England by a firm named Silver-Fleming.

144

AKA: Pseudo Cameo

Inner Color: Deep Blue
Value: $60.00 – 70.00
Description — Top: Cracked off, glazed **Bottom Figure:** Ground pontil
Dimensions — Top: 2¾" **Height:** 3½"
Decoration: Heavy white enamel.

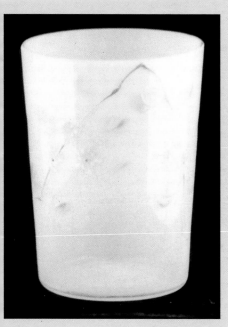

Manufacturer: Webb
Inner Color: Opaline **Outer Color:** Pale Pink
Value: $35.00 – 45.00
Description — Top: Flat ground, chamfered inside and out
Dimensions — Top: 2¹³⁄₁₆" **Bottom:** 2⅜" **Height:** 3¹¹⁄₁₆"
Decoration: Enamel.

AKA: Gold Sponge

Color: Opal
Value: $25.00 – 35.00
Description — Top: Full ground **Bottom Figure:** Tooled concave
Dimensions — Top: 2⅞" **Bottom:** 2⁷⁄₁₆" **Height:** 3¹³⁄₁₆"
Decoration: Yellow, pink, yellow wash, gold sponge figures.

AKA: Delft

Color: Opal
Value: $50.00 – 75.00
Description — Top: Ground and polished
Dimensions — Top: 2⅝" **Bottom:** 2⁵⁄₁₆" **Height:** 4¹⁄₁₆"
Decoration: Delft-type blue enamel.
Additional Notes: Delft designs were applied by several companies.

Color: Custard/Ivory
Value: $50.00 – 60.00
Description — Top: Flat ground with gold traces
Dimensions — Top: 2¹³⁄₁₆" **Bottom:** 2⁷⁄₁₆" **Height:** 3⅝"
Decoration: Satin, gold floral decoration.

Color: Ivory
Value: $55.00 – 65.00
Description — Top: Full ground
Dimensions — Top: 2¾" **Bottom:** 2⅜" **Height:** 4"
Decoration: Enamel and gold lily, gold butterfly.

Color: Ivory
Value: $45.00 – 55.00
Description — Top: Full ground
Dimensions — Top: 2¹¹⁄₁₆" **Bottom:** 3⁵⁄₁₆" **Height:** 3⅝"
Decoration: Enamel flowers.

Color: Opal
Value: $30.00 – 40.00
Description — Top: Flat ground, chamfered inside, gold on surface
  Bottom: Flat ground
Dimensions — Top: 2¾" **Bottom:** 2¼" **Height:** 3¾"
Decoration: Pink wash with floral enamel.

Inner Color: Pink **Outer Color:** Custard
Value: $60.00 – 70.00
Description — Top: Full ground
Dimensions — Top: 2¹³⁄₁₆" **Bottom:** 2⁹⁄₁₆" **Height:** 3¹³⁄₁₆"
Decoration: Red and brown enamel flowers and leaves.

Color: Opal
Value: $60.00 – 70.00
Description — Top: Ground and polished, traces of gold **Bottom Figure:** Flat ground
Dimensions — Top: 2¹¹⁄₁₆" **Bottom:** 2¼" **Height:** 3¾"
Decoration: Pink wash, natural leaves and flowers.

Color: Opal
Value: $25.00 – 35.00
Description — Top: Ground, chamfered outside
Dimensions — Top: 2¾" **Bottom:** 2⅜" **Height:** 3¹¹⁄₁₆"
Decoration: Deep red enamel bamboo.

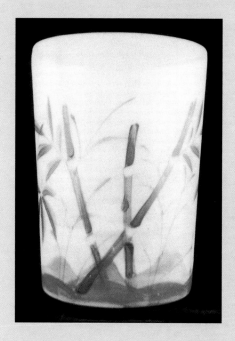

Color: Opal
Value: $60.00 – 70.00
Description — Top: Ground and polished
Dimensions — Top: 2¾" **Bottom:** 2⅜" **Height:** 3¹¹⁄₁₆"
Decoration: Satin, enamel, glass beads (coralene).
Additional Notes: Fiery opalescent.

Color: Opal
Value: $60.00 – 75.00
Description — Top: Ground and polished, chamfered inside and out
Dimensions — Top: 2¾" **Bottom:** 2⅜" **Height:** 3¾"
Decoration: Satin, enamel, coralene leaves.

Inner Color: Pink **Outer Color:** Opal
Value: $45.00 – 55.00
Description — Top: Ground and polished
Dimensions — Top: 2¾" **Bottom:** 2⅜" **Height:** 3¹¹⁄₁₆"
Decoration: Blue and white enamel, gold.
Additional Notes: Traces of gold on top.

Inner Color: Yellow **Outer Color:** Opal
Value: $45.00 – 55.00
Description — Top: Ground and polished
Dimensions — Top: 2¾" **Bottom:** 2⅜" **Height:** 3⅞"
Decoration: Blue and white enamel, gold.
Additional Notes: Trace of gold on top, yellow reacts orange under black light.

Inner Color: Ruby **Intermediate Color:** Opal **Outer Color:** Yellow
Value: $50.00 – 70.00
Description — Top: Ground, chamfered inside and out
Dimensions — Top: 2¹³⁄₁₆" **Bottom:** 2⁷⁄₁₆" **Height:** 3⅝"
Decoration: Enamel flowers.

AKA: Fireglow

Manufacturer: Thomas Webb & Sons.
Color: Brownish, very opalescent
Value: $100.00 – 120.00
Description — Top: Matte ground
Dimensions — Top: 2¾" **Bottom:** 2⅜" **Height:** 3⅝"
Decoration: Satin inside and out, enamel decoration.

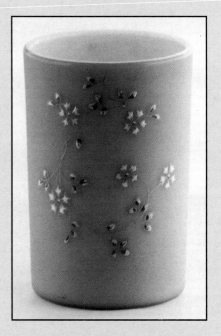

Manufacturer: Thomas Webb & Sons.
Inner Color: Opal **Outer Color:** Apricot shading to Pink
Value: $200.00 – 250.00
Description — Top: Polished **Bottom:** Ground, full-ground pontil
Dimensions — Top: 2¹³⁄₁₆" **Bottom:** 2⁹⁄₁₆" **Height:** 4"
Decoration: Enamel flowers.

AKA: Coralene

Color: Blue
Value: $500.00 – 700.00
Description — Top: Fire polished **Bottom:** Ground and polished
   Bottom Figure: Polished pontil
Dimensions — Top: 2¾" **Bottom:** 2" **Height:** 4¾"
Decoration: Coralene flowers and leaves.
Additional Notes: Crystal rigaree around base, signed "Patent."

← **AKA:** Blurina

Inner Color: Inverted Rubina **Outer Color:** Blue
Value: $250.00 – 350.00
Description — Top: Fire polished **Bottom:** Ground and polished
  Bottom Figure: Polished pontil
Dimensions — Top: 2¹¹⁄₁₆" **Bottom:** 2⁵⁄₁₆" **Height:** 3⅞"
Decoration: Enamel flowers and leaves.

Inner Color: Opaline **Outer Color:** Blue →
Value: $125.00 – 175.00
Description — Top: Ground and polished **Bottom Figure:** Sharp pontil
Dimensions — Top: 2¾" **Bottom:** 2¾" **Height:** 3⅞"
Decoration: Enameled bird, flowers, coralene leaves.

← **AKA:** Yellow Flower

Manufacturer: Moser
Inner Color: Ruby **Outer Color:** Crystal
Value: $150.00 – 200.00
Description — Top: Ground and polished
Dimensions — Top: 2¹⁵⁄₁₆" **Bottom:** 2¾" **Height:** 3⅞"
Decoration: Gold, yellow, and blue enamel floral.

Manufacturer: Moser →
Color: Green
Value: $150.00 – 250.00
Description — Top: Ground and polished
Dimensions — Top: 2¹¹⁄₁₆" **Bottom:** 2¼" **Height:** 3⅞"
Decoration: Green enamel, gold, platinum, butterflies.

Manufacturer: Moser
Inner Color: Lavender shading to Crystal **Outer Color:** Crystal
Value: $125.00 – 175.00
Description — Top: Ground and polished
Dimensions — Top: 2⅞" **Bottom:** 2⁷⁄₁₆" **Height:** 3⅞"
Decoration: Gold, yellow/gold enamel.

Manufacturer: Moser
Color: Blue
Value: $125.00 – 175.00
Description — Top: Ground
Dimensions — Top: 2¹³⁄₁₆" **Bottom:** 2⁵⁄₁₆" **Height:** 4"
Decoration: Rust, blue, and white enamel flowers and leaves.

Manufacturer: Moser
Color: Amber
Value: $300.00 – 350.00
Description — Top: Ground **Bottom Figure:** 6-pointed gold star
Dimensions — Top: 2⁹⁄₁₆" **Bottom:** 1⅝" **Height:** 2⅞"
Decoration: Gold, applied acorns, enamel oak leaves, bees, dragonfly.
Additional Notes: Narrow optic.

Inner Color: Ruby **Outer Color:** Opal
Value: $175.00 – 225.00
Description — Top: Ground
Dimensions — Top: 2¹³⁄₁₆" **Bottom:** 2⅜" **Height:** 3¹¹⁄₁₆"
Decoration: Multicolored hand-painted bird and leaves.

Inner Color: Ruby **Outer Color:** Crystal
Value: $175.00 – 225.00
Description — Top: Ground
Dimensions — Top: 2¾" **Bottom:** 2⅜" **Height:** 3¹¹⁄₁₆"
Decoration: Coralene beads in seaweed design.

Original Name: Montana

Manufacturer: D. C. Ripley & Co. **Date:** Ca. 1888
Color: Crystal
Value: $40.00 – 70.00
Description — Top: Fire polished
Dimensions — Top: 2½" **Bottom:** 2½" **Height:** 3¹⁵⁄₁₆"
Decoration: Engraved bird and lilies-of-the-valley.

Original Name: Pomona
AKA: Blueberries

Manufacturer: New England Glass Co. **Date:** 1885
Color: Crystal
Value: $90.00 – 150.00
Description — Top: Fire polished **Bottom:** Unfinished **Bottom Figure:** Ground pontil
Dimensions — Top: 2⅝" **Bottom:** 2⅜" **Height:** 3¾"
Decoration: Etched decoration, metallic stains, gold luster on top band.
Additional Notes: There were several imitators that used inexpensive etching techniques.

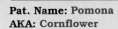

Pat. Name: Pomona
AKA: Cornflower

Manufacturer: New England Glass Co. **Date:** 1885
Color: Crystal
Value: $90.00 – 150.00
Description — Top: Fire polished **Bottom:** Unfinished **Bottom Figure:** Ground pontil
Dimensions — Top: 2⁹⁄₁₆" **Bottom:** 2⅜" **Height:** 3¾"
Decoration: Etched decoration, metallic stains, gold luster on top band.

Original Name: Pomona

Manufacturer: New England Glass Co. **Date:** 1885
Color: Crystal
Value: $90.00 – 150.00
Decoration: Etched design, large flower.

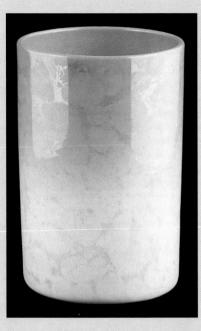

Original Name: Agata

Manufacturer: New England Glass Co. **Date:** 1887
Color: Custard shading to Pink
Value: $400.00 – 600.00
Description — Top: Fire polished **Bottom:** Unfinished **Bottom Figure:** Large ground pontil
Dimensions — Top: 2⁹⁄₁₆" **Bottom:** 2⅜" **Height:** 3¹¹⁄₁₆"
Decoration: Metallic stain.
Additional Notes: One sold at auction in 2003 for $1,050.00; it had excellent staining.

AKA: Green Opaque

Manufacturer: New England Glass Co. **Date:** 1885
Color: Opaque Green
Value: Seller's choice
Description — Top: Ground
Dimensions — Top: 2½" **Bottom:** 2¼" **Height:** 3½"
Decoration: Metallic stain, gold.

Color: Crystal
Value: $25.00 – 35.00
Description — Top: Fire polished **Bottom:** Unfinished
Dimensions — Top: 2¹¹⁄₁₆" **Bottom:** 2⅜" **Height:** 3½"
Decoration: Yellow enamel, gold, resembles oil on water.
Additional Notes: Probably from the mid-twentieth century.

153

The manufacture of Polka Dot wares involves two molds. The first, a spot mold, leaves the gather with a pattern of bumps on the outside. The gather is then warmed-in and blown into the final mold. The gather expands, transferring the bumps to the inside, where they form a spot optic. Occasionally, the warming-in is incomplete and ripples can be seen on the outer surface. These ripples are remnants of the bumps. This treatment was developed about 1884 and is now often called "inverted thumbprint" out of ignorance of the original name. The AKA name in this chapter is used to indicate the number of dots on the tumbler, e.g., the first listing indicates five rows of polka dots ten dots around.

←

Original Name: Polka Dot
AKA: 5 row, 10 around

Inner Color: Ruby **Outer Color:** Crystal
Value: $45.00 – 55.00
Description — Top: Ground
Dimensions — Top: 2¾" **Bottom:** 2⅜" **Height:** 3¾"
Additional Notes: One row PD on bottom.

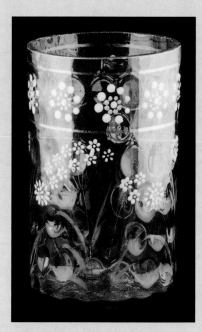

→

Original Name: Polka Dot
AKA: 7 row

Color: Olive
Value: $45.00 – 55.00
Description — Top: 2⅝" **Bottom:** 2⁹⁄₁₆" **Height:** 4⅛"
Dimensions — Top: Flat ground
Decoration: Blue and white enamel with gold.

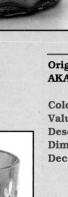

←

Original Name: Polka Dot
AKA: 6 row, 12 around

Inner Color: Ruby **Outer Color:** Crystal
Value: $55.00 – 65.00
Description — Top: Ground and polished, chamfer inside and out
Dimensions — Top: 2¹¹⁄₁₆" **Bottom:** 2⅜" **Height:** 3⅞"
Decoration: Gold on top rim; yellow, brown, blue, green, and white enamel.

Original Name: Polka Dot
AKA: 7 row, 16 around

Inner Color: Ruby **Outer Color:** Crystal
Value: $75.00 – 100.00
Description — Top: Flat ground, chamfered inside and out
Dimensions — Top: 2¹¹⁄₁₆" **Bottom:** 2³⁄₁₆" **Height:** 3¾"
Decoration: Enamel lily-of-the-valley; brown, orange, green, white, gray; gold on top rim.
Additional Notes: Not Polka Dot; the bumps are concave.

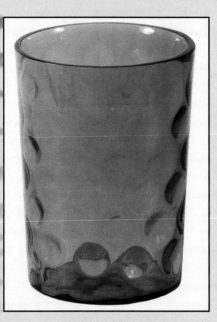

Original Name: Polka Dot
AKA: 7 row, 10 around

Inner Color: Ruby **Outer Color:** Crystal
Value: $45.00 – 55.00
Description — Top: Polished
Dimensions — Top: 2¹³⁄₁₆" **Bottom:** 2⁷⁄₁₆" **Height:** 3¹¹⁄₁₆"

Original Name: No. 290 Polka Dot
AKA: 3 row, 10 around

Manufacturer: Hobbs, Brockunier & Co. **Date:** 1885
Color: Ruby Sapphire, Ruby Amber, Amber, Rubina, Canary, Ruby, Marine Green,
   Sapphire, Crystal
Value: $45.00 – 60.00
Description — Top: Ground and polished **Bottom:** Unfinished
Dimensions — Top: 2¹³⁄₁₆" **Bottom:** 2⁹⁄₁₆" **Height:** 3¹¹⁄₁₆"
Decoration: Engraved number *3*.

AKA: Circle Optic

Color: Green
Value: $45.00 – 60.00
Description — Top: Ground and polished **Bottom:** Unfinished
Dimensions — Top: 2¹¹⁄₁₆" **Bottom:** 2⁹⁄₁₆" **Height:** 3¹³⁄₁₆"
Decoration: Enamel daisies.
Additional Notes: The optic is composed of circles instead of dots.

Original Name: Polka Dot
AKA: 4 row, 9 around

Inner Color: Selenium Ruby **Outer Color:** Crystal
Value: $30.00 – 40.00
Description — Top: Ground and polished, chamfered inside and out
  Bottom Figure: Full concave grind
Dimensions — Top: 2⅞" **Bottom:** 2⅝" **Height:** 3¾"
Additional Notes: Possibly mid-twentieth century.

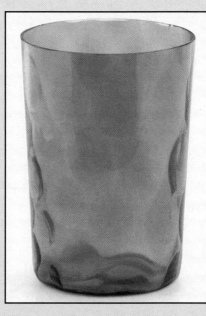

Original Name: Polka Dot
AKA: 4 row, 10 around

Inner Color: Ruby **Outer Color:** Crystal
Value: $45.00 – 55.00
Description — Top: Ground, chamfered inside
Dimensions — Top: 2¹¹⁄₁₆" **Bottom:** 2⅜" **Height:** 3½"

Original Name: Polka Dot
AKA: 6 row, 16 around

Color: Crystal
Value: $50.00 – 65.00
Description — Top: Flat ground, chamfered inside and out
Dimensions — Top: 2¹³⁄₁₆" **Bottom:** 2⅜" **Height:** 3⅝"
Decoration: Diagonal amber stain stripes, frosted between.

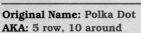

Original Name: Polka Dot
AKA: 5 row, 10 around

Color: Amber
Value: $35.00 – 50.00
Decoration: Blue, white, and yellow enamel.
Dimensions — Top: 2¹³⁄₁₆" **Bottom:** 2⁹⁄₁₆ **Height:** 3¹³⁄₁₆"
Additional Notes: Not a true Polka Dot; each dot is a ring.

Original Name: Polka Dot
AKA: 5 row, 12 around

Manufacturer: Geo. Duncan & Sons **Date:** 1884
Color: Canary
Value: $45.00 – 60.00
Description — Top: Polished, chamfered inside and out
Dimensions — Top: 2¹³⁄₁₆" **Bottom:** 2⁷⁄₁₆" **Height:** 3¹⁵⁄₁₆"

Original Name: Polka Dot
AKA: 5 row, 12 around

Manufacturer: Geo. Duncan & Sons **Date:** 1884
Color: Amber
Value: $30.00 – 40.00
Description — Top: Polished, chamfered inside and out **Bottom:** Unfinished
Dimensions — Top: 2¾" **Bottom:** 2⅜" **Height:** 3¾"

Original Name: Polka Dot
AKA: 5 row, 9 around

Color: Amber
Value: $15.00 – 20.00
Description — Top: Ground, chamfered inside and out
Dimensions — Top: 2⅞" **Bottom:** 2⁹⁄₁₆" **Height:** 3⅝"
Additional Notes: Shape of bottom indicates recent
   manufacture. See L. G. Wright in Appendix A.

Original Name: Polka Dot
AKA: 5 row, 10 around

Color: Blue
Value: $25.00 – 35.00
Description — Top: Fire polished **Bottom:** Unfinished
Dimensions — Top: 2⅞" **Bottom:** 2⁷⁄₁₆" **Height:** 3⅝"
Additional Notes: This is a pressed tumbler.

Original Name: Polka Dot
AKA: 8 row, 15 around

Color: Crystal
Value: $35.00 – 45.00
Description — Top: Ground and polished **Bottom:** Unfinished
Dimensions — Top: 2⅝" **Bottom:** 2¼" **Height:** 4⅛"
Decoration: Gold, blue, and white enamel.

Original Name: Polka Dot
AKA: 7½ row, 15 around

Color: Blue
Value: $30.00 – 40.00
Description — Top: Ground and polished, chamfered inside and out
Dimensions — Top: 2¹¹⁄₁₆" **Bottom:** 2¼" **Height:** 3¹⁵⁄₁₆"
Additional Notes: The vertical lines in the picture are on a piece of paper inside the tumbler.

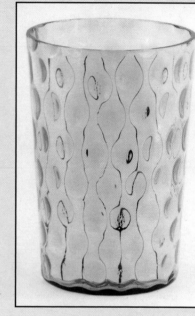

AKA: 7 row, 16 around

Color: Blue
Value: $75.00 – 100.00
Description — Top: Ground, chamfered outside **Bottom:** Unfinished
Dimensions — Top: 2¾" **Bottom:** 2⅜" **Height:** 3¹¹⁄₁₆"
Decoration: Satin, coraline seaweed.

Original Name: Polka Dot
AKA: 4 row, 9 around

Manufacturer: Possibly Central Glass Co. **Date:** Ca. 1884
Inner Color: Blue **Outer Color:** Crystal
Value: $35.00 - 45.00
Description — Top: Ground and polished, chamfered inside and out **Bottom Figure:** Full concave grind
Dimensions — Top: 2⅞" **Bottom:** 2⅝" **Height:** 3⅞"
Additional Notes: There is some question about the age of this tumbler. Many others similar to it have been seen recently, as if they were recent imports. In most cases, only ruby was cased inside crystal.

158

Multicolored Non-opalescent

The shading of color in a tumbler can be achieved in different ways. Heat-sensitive glass (glass containing gold or selenium), when reheated, turns red where the heat was applied after it had cooled a bit. New England Glass Co. named this Amberina.

Another means of shading color is to insert a bubble of two-toned glass inside an already formed tumbler. The glass in this chapter colored this way is called ruby amber, ruby sapphire, etc. There are two reasons glass was processed this way; the first was to get around a patent. New England held the patent on Amberina and prosecuted those who infringed upon it. The second reason was that it cost less to color glass this way. You will see a distinct (well, more distinct than that in Amberina) line between the two colors in these plated pieces.

A third process, die-away, involves the progressive thinning of a color over a crystal or an opal layer.

AKA: Wide Optic Twelve Panel

Inner Color: Amberina
Value: $75.00 – 100.00
Description — Top: Fire polished **Bottom Figure:** Large ground pontil
Dimensions — Top: 2⅝" **Bottom:** 2⅜" **Height:** 3¹¹⁄₁₆"
Additional Notes: Twelve interior panels, flint or lead glass.

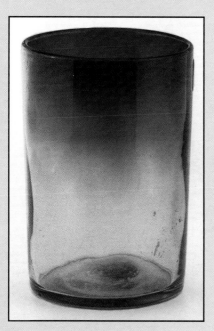

AKA: Diamond Optic

Inner Color: Amberina
Value: $75.00 – 100.00
Description — Top: Fire polished **Bottom Figure:** Sharp pontil
Dimensions — Top: 2⅞" **Bottom:** 2⅝" **Height:** 3¾"
Additional Notes: There is a bit of struck color in pontil.

Color: Amberina
Value: $75.00 – 100.00
Additional Notes: Diamond optic.

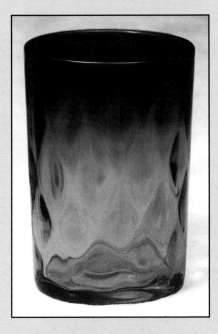

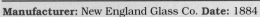

Manufacturer: New England Glass Co. Date: 1884
Color: Amberina
Value: $75.00 – 100.00
Description — Top: Fire polished Bottom Figure: Ground pontil
Dimensions — Top: 2¾" Bottom: 2½" Height: 3¾"
Additional Notes: Diamond optic.

AKA: Plated Amberina

Manufacturer: New England Glass Co. Date: 1886
Inner Color: Opal Outer Color: Amberina
Value: Seller's Choice
Description — Top: Fire polished Bottom Figure: Ground pontil
Dimensions — Top: 2½" Bottom: 2⅜" Height: 3¹¹⁄₁₆"
Additional Notes: Nine vertical ribs.

AKA: Liberté

Inner Color: Blue on bottom, Crystal in middle, Ruby on top
    Outer Color: Crystal
Value: Seller's choice
Description — Top: Ground and polished Bottom: Full flat ground
Dimensions — Top: 2¾" Bottom: 2⅜" Height: 3⁹⁄₁₆"
Additional Notes: Swirl optic.

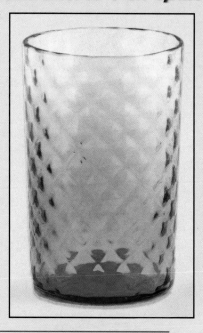

AKA: Diamond Optic

Color: Reverse Ruby Amber
Value: $75.00 – 100.00
Description — Top: Ground
Dimensions — Top: 2¹³⁄₁₆" **Bottom:** 2½" **Height:** 4⅛"
Additional Notes: Strong diamond optic.

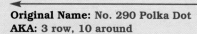

Original Name: No. 290 Polka Dot
AKA: 3 row, 10 around

Manufacturer: Hobbs, Brockunier & Co. **Date:** 1884
Color: Crystal, Ruby Sapphire, Ruby Amber, Amber, Rubina, Canary,
  Ruby, Marine Green, Sapphire
Value: $70.00 – 90.00 Ruby Amber, $250.00 – 300.00 Ruby Sapphire
Description — Top: Ground and polished
Dimensions — Top: 2¹³⁄₁₆" **Bottom:** 2⁹⁄₁₆" **Height:** 3¹¹⁄₁₆"
Decoration: Engraved number 3.

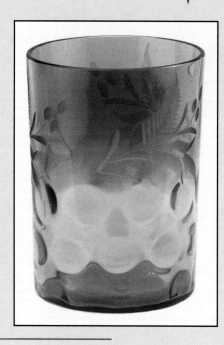

AKA: Polka Dot, 6 row

Color: Rubina Verde
Value: $100.00 – 125.00
Description — Top: Ground and polished, chamfered outside
Dimensions — Top: 2¹³⁄₁₆" **Bottom:** 2⅝" **Height:** 3¹³⁄₁₆"

AKA: Polka Dot, 8 row, 20 around

Color: Reverse Ruby Amber
Value: $75.00 – 85.00
Description — Top: Ground and polished, chamfered inside and out
Dimensions — Top: 2¹³⁄₁₆" **Bottom:** 2⁹⁄₁₆" **Height:** 3¹¹⁄₁₆"
Additional Notes: Is not a struck color; note division between colors.

AKA: 6 row, 12 around

Color: Ruby Amber
Value: $75.00 – 85.00
Description — Top: Ground and polished
Additional Notes: Is not a struck color; note division between colors.

AKA: 6 row, 12 around

Color: Ruby Amber
Value: $75.00 – 85.00
Description — Top: Ground and polished
Additional Notes: Is not a struck color.

Original Name: No. 406 Granite

Manufacturer: Northwood Glass Co., Elwood City, PA **Date:** 1893
Inner Color: Blue **Intermediate Color:** Opal frit **Outer Color:** Blue
Value: $55.00 – 65.00
Description — Top: Ground and polished **Bottom:** Unfinished
Dimensions — Top: 2¾" **Bottom:** 2½" **Height:** 3¹³⁄₁₆"
Additional Notes: Twenty strong narrow interior ribs.

Original Name: No. 406 Granite
AKA: Ruby

Manufacturer: Northwood Glass Co.; Elwood City, PA **Date:** 1893
Inner Color: Crystal **Intermediate Color:** Pink, Opal frit **Outer Color**: Crystal
Value: $65.00
Description — Top: Ground and polished, chamfered inside **Bottom:** Unfinished
Dimensions — Top: 2¾" **Bottom:** 2⁷⁄₁₆" **Height:** 3¹³⁄₁₆"
Additional Notes: 20 strong narrow ribs inside.

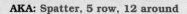

AKA: Spatter, 4 row, 12 around

Inner Color: Crystal **Intermediate Color:** Green, Opal flakes **Outer Color:** Crystal
Value: $35.00 – 45.00
Description — Top: Fire polished
Dimensions — Top: 2¾" **Bottom:** 2⅜" **Height:** 3¹¹⁄₁₆"

AKA: Spatter, 5 row, 12 around

Inner Color: Crystal **Intermediate Color:** Blue, Opal frit **Outer Color:** Crystal
Value: $45.00 – 70.00
Description — Top: Polished
Dimensions — Top: 2¾" **Bottom:** 2⅜" **Height:** 3¹¹⁄₁₆"

AKA: Spatter

Inner Color: Crystal with Opal, Ruby frit **Intermediate Color:** Yellow frit
   Outer Color: Crystal
Value: $40.00 – 50.00
Description — Top: Ground
Dimensions — Top: 2⅝" **Bottom:** 2⅜" **Height:** 3¹¹⁄₁₆"

AKA: Spatter

Color: Ruby and Opal spatter
Value: $65.00 – 75.00
Description — Top: Ground, chamfered inside and out
Dimensions — Top: 2¾" **Bottom:** 2⁷⁄₁₆" **Height:** 3¹³⁄₁₆"
Decoration: Satin. gold and enamel floral.

AKA: Spatter

Inner Color: Crystal **Intermediate Color:** Ruby, Opal frit **Outer Color:** Crystal
Value: $55.00 – 65.00
Description — Top: Ground and polished
Dimensions — Top: 2¾" **Bottom:** 2⁷⁄₁₆" **Height:** 3¾"

AKA: Tortoise Shell

Manufacturer: Phœnix Glass Co. **Date:** 1886
Inner Color: Crystal **Intermediate Color:** Ruby, Opal frit **Outer Color:** Crystal
Value: $75.00 – 95.00
Description — Top: Ground and polished, chamfered inside and out
Dimensions — Top: 2¾" **Bottom:** 2⅜" **Height:** 3¹⁵⁄₁₆"

AKA: Tortoise Shell, 4½ row

Manufacturer: Phœnix Glass Co. **Date:** 1886
Inner Color: Crystal **Intermediate Color:** Ruby, Opal frit **Outer Color:** Crystal
Value: $100.00 – 125.00
Description — Top: Ground and polished, chamfered inside
Dimensions — Top: 2¹¹⁄₁₆" **Bottom:** 3⅜" **Height:** 3¹¹⁄₁₆"
Decoration: Heavy natural color enamel morning glories.

AKA: Orange Swirl

Inner Color: Whitish **Intermediate Color:** Orange **Outer Color:** Crystal
Value: $45.00 – 55.00
Description — Top: Ground, facets, chamfered inside and out **Bottom:** Unfinished
Dimensions — Top: 2¾" **Bottom:** 2¼" **Height:** 3¾"

AKA: Smooth Swirl

Inner Color: Opal **Intermediate Color:** Swirled shades of Amber **Outer Color:** Pale Amber
Value: $55.00 – 65.00
Description — Top: Ground and polished, chamfered inside and out
Dimensions — Top: 2¾" **Bottom:** 2⁵⁄₁₆" **Height:** 3¾"

AKA: Spatter

Inner Color: Crystal **Intermediate Color:** Ruby, Opal frit **Outer Color:** Crystal
Value: $65.00 – 80.00
Description — Top: Ground **Bottom:** Polished
Dimensions — Top: 2¾" **Bottom:** 2¼" **Height:** 3¾"

AKA: Spatter, 5 row, 16 around

Inner Color: Crystal **Intermediate Color:** Ruby, Opal frit **Outer Color:** Crystal
Value: $45.00 – 70.00
Description — Top: Ground and polished, chamfered inside and out
Dimensions — Top: 2¹¹⁄₁₆" **Bottom:** 2⁵⁄₁₆" **Height:** 3⅞"

AKA: Spatter

Inner Color: Crystal **Intermediate Color:** Green, Opal frit **Outer Color:** Crystal
Value: $40.00 – 50.00
Description — Top: Ground
Dimensions — Top: 2¾" **Bottom:** 2½" **Height:** 3½"

AKA: Spatter/Spangle, 4 row, 12 around

Inner Color: Crystal with Ruby and Opal frit **Intermediate Color:** Mica **Outer Color:** Amber
Value: $45.00 – 70.00
Description — Top: Ground and polished
Dimensions — Top: 2¾" **Bottom:** 3⅜" **Height:** 3¾"

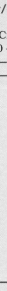

AKA: Spatter/Spangle

Inner Color: Crystal **Intermediate Color:** Mica, Ruby, White frit **Outer Color:** Crystal
Value: $75.00 – 90.00
Description — Top: Ground and polished, chamfered inside and out
Dimensions — Top: 2¾" **Bottom:** 2⅜" **Height:** 3¾"

AKA: Spangle

Inner Color: Ruby, Opal frit, mica **Intermediate Color:** Crystal **Outer Color:** Amber, Opal frit
Value: $75.00 – 90.00
Description — Top: Ground and polished, chamfered outside
Dimensions — Top: 2¾" **Bottom:** 2⅜" **Height:** 3¾"

AKA: Spatter/Spangle

Inner Color: Crystal **Intermediate Color:** Mica, Amber, Opal **Outer Color:** Crystal
Value: $55.00 – 70.00
Description — Top: Ground and polished
Dimensions — Top: 2¾" **Bottom:** 2⅜" **Height:** 3⁹⁄₁₆"

AKA: Spatter/Spangle

Inner Color: Opal **Intermediate Color:** Ruby frit, mica **Outer Color:** Crystal
Value: $75.00 – 90.00
Description — Top: Flat ground
Dimensions — Top: 2⅝" **Bottom:** 2⁵⁄₁₆" **Height:** 3¹¹⁄₁₆"

AKA: Rainbow, Spatter/Spangle

Inner Color: Opal **Intermediate Color:** Multicolor frit and mica **Outer Color:** Crystal
Value: $200.00 – 300.00
Description — Top: Flat ground, chamfered inside
Dimensions — Top: 2⅝" **Bottom:** 2⅜" **Height:** 3⅝"

AKA: Rainbow

Inner Color: Crystal **Intermediate Color:** Ruby, Blue stripes **Outer Color:** Amber
Value: $200.00 – 300.00
Description — Top: Ground **Bottom Figure:** Ruby, blue stripes go to center.
Dimensions — Top: 2¾" **Bottom:** 2⅜" **Height:** 3½"

AKA: Deep Rubina, Spatter/Spangle

Inner Color: Opal **Intermediate Color:** Ruby, Opal frit, mica **Outer Color:** Crystal
Value: $90.00 – 110.00
Description — Top: Ground **Bottom Figure:** Polished pontil
Dimensions — Top: 2½" **Bottom:** 2¼" **Height:** 3¾"

AKA: Spangle

Inner Color: Opaque Pink **Intermediate Layer:** Mica **Outer Color:** Amber
Value: $75.00 – 90.00
Description — Top: Repaired
Dimensions — Top: 2¹¹⁄₁₆" **Bottom:** 2⅜" **Height:** 3¾"

AKA: Spangle

Inner Color: Opaline Blue **Intermediate Layer:** Mica **Outer Color:** Crystal
Value: $70.00 – 85.00
Description — Top: Ground and polished, chamfered inside and out
Dimensions — Top: 2⅝" **Bottom:** 2⁵⁄₁₆" **Height:** 3¾"
Additional Notes: Ten optic panels.

AKA: Spangle

Inner Color: Opal **Intermediate Color:** Lemon Yellow, mica over Yellow
    Outer Color: Crystal
Value: $100.00 – 125.00
Description — Top: Ground and polished, chamfered inside and out
    Bottom Figure: Full concave grind
Dimensions — Top: 2⅞" **Bottom:** 2⁹⁄₁₆" **Height:** 3⅞"
Additional Notes: This tumbler is bright yellow. Full ground bottom indicates
    possible European origin.

AKA: Spangle

Inner Color: Opaque Green **Intermediate Layer:** Mica **Outer Color:** Crystal
Value: $70.00 – 85.00
Description — Top: Ground and polished
Dimensions — Top: 2¹¹⁄₁₆" **Bottom:** 2⁵⁄₁₆" **Height:** 3¹¹⁄₁₆"

AKA: Reverse Rubina

Inner Color: Deep Ruby **Intermediate Color:** Crystal, Opal spatter, mica
   Outer Color: Crystal
Value: $150.00 – 200.00
Description — Top: Ground and polished, chamfered inside and out
Dimensions — Top: 2⅞" **Bottom:** 2⁵⁄₁₆" **Height:** 3⁹⁄₁₆"
Additional Notes: Ruby bubble was blown and burst inside finished tumbler.

Original Name: Polka Dot
AKA: PD6½ row

Inner Color: Inverted Rubina **Intermediate Color:** Opal spatter, mica **Outer Color:** Crystal
Value: $90.00 – 110.00
Description — Top: Ground and polished
Dimensions — Top: 2¹³⁄₁₆" **Bottom:** 2⅜" **Height:** 3¾"

Original Name: Polka Dot
AKA: Reverse Rubina

Inner Color: Deep Ruby, Inverted Rubina **Intermediate Color:** Opal spatter, mica
   Outer Color: Crystal
Value: $90.00 – 110.00
Description — Top: Ground, not polished, chamfered inside and out
Dimensions — Top: 2⅞" **Bottom:** 2⁵⁄₁₆" **Height:** 3⁹⁄₁₆"

Original Name: Polka Dot
AKA: PD 7 row

Date: 1888
Color: Amber shading upward to Blue
Value: $90.00 – 100.00
Description — Top: Flat ground
Dimensions — Top: 2¹¹⁄₁₆" **Bottom:** 2⅜" **Height:** 3¾"
Additional Notes: This tumbler appears in a distributor's catalog ca. 1888 as imported. In 2003, one sold at auction for $250.00.

Original Name: Polka Dot
AKA: 6½ row, 16 around

Date: 1888
Color: Amber shading upward to Blue
Value: $90.00 – 110.00
Description — Top: Ground and polished
Dimensions — Top: 2¾" **Bottom:** 2⅜" **Height:** 3¾"

AKA: Honeycomb

Inner Color: Amethyst **Outer Color:** Crystal
Value: $75.00 – 125.00
Description — Top: Fire polished **Bottom:** Ground flat
Dimensions — Top: 3" **Bottom:** 2⅜" **Height:** 3¹³⁄₁₆"
Additional Notes: Six horizontal rows of honeycombs.

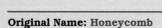

Original Name: Honeycomb

Color: Blue fading to Crystal
Value: $125.00 – 150.00
Description — Top: Ground
Dimensions — Top: 2⅞" **Bottom:** 2⅜" **Height:** 3⅞"

Other Optics

AKA: Cased Amber Vertical Rib

Inner Color: Opal **Outer Color:** Amber
Value: $45.00 – 60.00
Description — Top: Ground and polished, chamfered inside **Bottom:** Full ground
Dimensions — Top: 2¹⁵⁄₁₆" **Bottom:** 2⅛" **Height:** 4¼"
Additional Notes: 12 ribs.

AKA: Eight Panel Optic

Manufacturer: Possibly Monet & Stumpf, French
Inner Color: Shaded Amber **Outer Color:** Canary
Value: $70.00 – 85.00
Description — Top: Ground and polished, chamfered inside and out **Bottom:** Unfinished
Dimensions — Top: 2¾" **Bottom:** 2⅜" **Height:** 3¾"

AKA: Ten Panel

Color: Green
Value: $20.00 – 30.00
Description — Top: Flat ground
Dimensions — Top: 2⅜" **Bottom:** 2⁵⁄₁₆" **Height:** 4"
Decoration: Gold floral design.

AKA: Ten Panel

Manufacturer: Possibly Jefferson
Color: Amethyst
Value: $20.00 – 30.00
Description — Top: Fire polished **Bottom:** Ground
Dimensions — Top: 2⅞" **Bottom:** 2½" **Height:** 3¹⁵⁄₁₆"
Additional Notes: Ten interior panels.

AKA: Dimples

Inner Color: Pink **Outer Color:** Crystal
Value: $50.00 – 70.00
Description — Top: Ground and polished, chamfered inside **Bottom:** Unfinished
    Bottom Figure: 16-petal flower
Dimensions — Top: 2⅞" **Bottom:** 2⁷⁄₁₆" **Height:** 3⅝"
Decoration: Gold and white enamel flowers.
Additional Notes: Similar in color and optic to a pitcher ascribed to Stevens & Williams.

AKA: Fish Scale

Color: Pale Blue
Value: $30.00 – 50.00
Description — Top: Fire polished
Dimensions — Top: 2¾" **Bottom:** 2½" **Height:** 3⅞"
Additional Notes: The optic has the appearance of fish scales.

AKA: Eight Panel

Manufacturer: Possibly Monet & Stumpf, French
Inner Color: Pink Opalescent **Outer Color:** Crystal
Value: $75.00 – 100.00
Description — Top: Polished **Bottom:** Unfinished
Dimensions — Top: 2¹³⁄₁₆" **Bottom:** 2⅜" **Height:** 3¾"
Decoration: Gold, colored enamel.

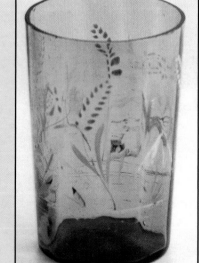

AKA: Ten Panel

Color: Olive Green
Value: $20.00 – 30.00
Description — Top: Ground and polished **Bottom:** Unfinished
Dimensions — Top: 2¹¹⁄₁₆" **Bottom:** 2⁵⁄₁₆" **Height:** 4"
Decoration: White enamel, wash, gold.
Additional Notes: All optic panels are not equal, gold on top rim.

Ribs & Swirls

AKA: **Swirled Stripes**

Inner Color: Rubina **Outer Color:** Crystal with Yellow and Opal stripe
Value: $250.00 – 300.00
Description — Top: Ground **Bottom:** Unfinished
Dimensions — Top: 2¹³⁄₁₆" **Bottom:** 2³⁄₁₆" **Height:** 4⅛"
Decoration: Gold on top. Gold and enamel décor.

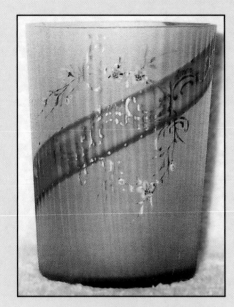

AKA: **Swirled Stripes**

Inner Color: Crystal **Outer Color:** Ruby swirled strip
Value: $250.00 – 300.00
Description — Top: Ground and polished **Bottom:** Unfinished **Bottom Figure:** Ribs extend to center.
Dimensions — Top: 2¾" **Bottom:** 2³⁄₁₆" **Height:** 3⅝"
Decoration: Satin, yellow, orange flowers, gold tracery.
Additional Notes: 65 ribs.

AKA: **Complex Swirl**

Color: Crystal
Value: $50.00 – 65.00
Description — Top: Ground and polished **Bottom:** Unfinished **Bottom Figure:** Figure continues to center.
Dimensions — Top: 2¹¹⁄₁₆" **Bottom:** 2⁷⁄₁₆" **Height:** 3⅞"
Decoration: Gold tracery and white 5-petal flowers.

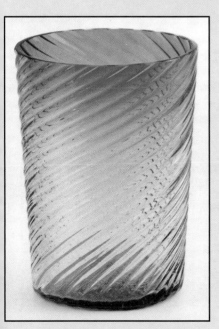

AKA: **Fine Rib Swirl**

Color: Rubina
Value: $75.00 – 100.00
Description — Top: Polished **Bottom:** Unfinished **Bottom Figure:** Pattern to center
Dimensions — Top: 2¾" **Bottom:** 2⁵⁄₁₆" **Height:** 3¹¹⁄₁₆"

AKA: Two-part Swirl

Inner Color: Ruby **Outer Color:** Crystal
Value: $75.00 – 100.00
Description — Top: Ground and polished **Bottom:** Unfinished
Dimensions — Top: $2^{11}/_{16}$" **Bottom:** $2^{5}/_{16}$" **Height:** $3^{13}/_{16}$"
Decoration: Traces of gold in swirls.

AKA: Tight Swirl

Inner Color: Lavender **Outer Color:** Opaline
Value: $75.00 – 100.00
Description — Top: Ground, chamfered outside **Bottom:** Unfinished
Dimensions — Top: $2^{11}/_{16}$" **Bottom:** $2^{5}/_{16}$" **Height:** $3^{3}/_{4}$"
Decoration: Gold and enamels.

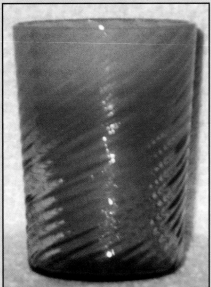
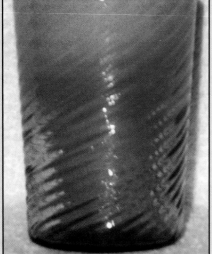

AKA: Tight Swirl

Inner Color: Yellow to Crystal **Outer Color:** Amethyst
Value: $75.00 – 125.00
Description — Top: Ground **Bottom Figure:** Swirls to center
Dimensions — Top: $2^{3}/_{4}$" **Bottom:** $2^{5}/_{16}$" **Height:** $3^{9}/_{16}$"

AKA: Fine Swirl

Inner Color: Crystal **Intermediate Color:** Dark Ruby and Ivory **Outer Color:** Crystal
Value: $140.00 – 170.00
Description — Top: Ground and polished, chamfered inside and out
Dimensions — Top: $2^{11}/_{16}$" **Bottom:** $2^{5}/_{16}$" **Height:** $3^{3}/_{4}$"
Additional Notes: Fine patterned bubbles throughout.

AKA: Fine Rib & Herringbone

Color: Blue Opalescent
Value: $150.00 – 200.00
Description — Top: Ground
Dimensions — Top: 2¾" **Bottom:** 2⁷⁄₁₆" **Height:** 3¾"

AKA: Low Vertical Rib

Color: Opal
Value: $35.00 – 50.00
Description — Top: Stone ground **Bottom:** Unfinished
Dimensions — Top: 2¹³⁄₁₆" **Bottom:** 2⁹⁄₁₆" **Height:** 3¾"
Decoration: Upper, yellow enamel; lower, orange enamel; enamel flowers and leaves, gold on top rim.
Additional Notes: 1⅞" top of figure.

AKA: 20 Ribs

Inner Color: Crystal **Intermediate Color:** Ruby, Opal chips **Outer Color:** Crystal
Value: $60.00 – 70.00
Description — Top: Ground and polished, chamfered inside and out **Bottom:** Unfinished
Dimensions — Top: 2¹¹⁄₁₆" **Bottom:** 2¼" **Height:** 3⅞"
Additional Notes: Satin finish, 3" top of figure.

Manufacturer: Possibly Northwood
Inner Color: Crystal **Intermediate Color:** Ruby and opal frit **Outer Color:** Crystal
Value: $60.00 – 70.00
Dimensions — Top: 2¾" **Bottom:** 2½" **Height:** 3¾"
Description — Top: Ground and polished **Bottom:** Unfinished
Additional Notes: Color very reminiscent of other Northwood pieces.

AKA: 24 Ribs

Inner Color: Opal **Intermediate Color:** Pink **Outer Color:** Crystal.
Value: $150.00 – 200.00
Description — Top: Fire polished **Bottom Figure:** Ground pontil
Dimensions — Top: 2⅝" **Bottom:** 1⅞" **Height:** 3⅜"
Decoration: Satin finish.
Additional Notes: 2⅞" top of figure, 24 vertical ribs.

Original Name: No. 528
AKA: Reverse Swirl

Manufacturer: Buckeye Glass Co. **Date:** 1888
Color: Opal shading to Rose
Value: $50.00 – 60.00
Description — Top: Ground and polished, chamfered inside and out
  Bottom: Unfinished
Dimensions — Top: 2⁹⁄₁₆" **Bottom:** 2¼" rim **Height:** 3¾"
Additional Notes: 3⁵⁄₁₆" top of figure.

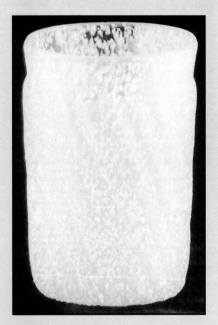

AKA: Reverse Swirl

Manufacturer: Model Flint Glass Co.; Albany, IN
Inner Color: Crystal **Outer Color:** Canary Opalescent
Value: $60.00 – 70.00
Description — Top: Matte ground **Bottom:** Unfinished
Dimensions — Top: 2⁹⁄₁₆" **Bottom:** 2¼" **Height:** 3¾"

AKA: Narrow Swirl with Rim

Inner Color: Crystal **Intermediate Color:** Various combinations of frit **Outer Color:** Crystal
Value: $50.00 – 60.00
Description — Top: Flat ground, chamfered inside and out **Bottom:** Unfinished
Dimension — Top: 2¹¹⁄₁₆" **Bottom:** 2⁹⁄₁₆" **Height:** 3⅝"
Additional Notes: 3" top of figure, 24 ribs.

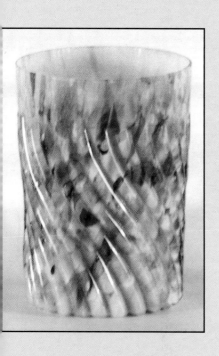

AKA: Narrow Swirl with Rim

Inner Color: Opal Outer Color: Amber
Value: $45.00 – 55.00
Description — Top: Ground Bottom: Ground pontil
Dimensions — Top: 2¾" Bottom: 2½" Height: 3¾"
Additional Notes: 3" top of figure.

No. 1839
AKA: Narrow Swirl with Rim

Inner Color: Opal Intermediate Color: Brown trailings and Mica Outer Color: Crystal
Value: $100.00 – 125.00
Description — Top: Ground and polished, chamfered inside and out Bottom: Unfinished
Dimensions — Top: 2¾" Bottom: 2⅝" Height: 3⅝"
Additional Notes: 3-part mold, 24 ribs.

AKA: Narrow Swirl with Rim

Inner Color: Tan Intermediate Color: Orange/Blue frit Outer Color: Crystal
Value: $70.00 – 80.00
Description — Top: Flat ground, chamfered inside and out Bottom: Unfinished
Dimensions — Top: 2¹³⁄₁₆" Bottom: 2½" Height: 3¾"
Additional Notes: 3" top of figure, 24 ribs, 4-part mold. "Made in Czechoslovakia" etched on bottom.

Original Name: No. 207
AKA: Satina Swirl

Manufacturer: Hobbs, Brockunier & Co. Date: 1887
Inner Color: Alabaster Intermediate Color: Pink Outer Color: Crystal
Value: $90.00 – 110.00
Description — Top: Ground and polished, chamfered outside Bottom Figure: Figure to center
Dimensions — Top: 2¾" Bottom: 2½" Height: 3¹³⁄₁₆"
Decoration: May be frosted.
Additional Notes: May be right or left hand swirl; Amber, Ruby, Canary, possibly others.

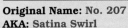

No. 1129d
AKA: Fine Rib Swirl

Color: Orange, Yellow, Crystal overshot
Value: $100.00 – 125.00
Description — Top: Ground and polished, chamfered inside and out **Bottom:** Unfinished
Dimensions — Top: 2⅝" **Bottom:** 2⅜" **Height:** 3¹¹⁄₁₆"

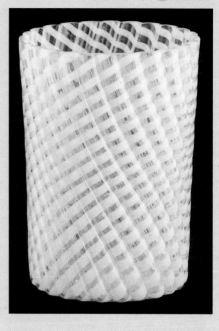

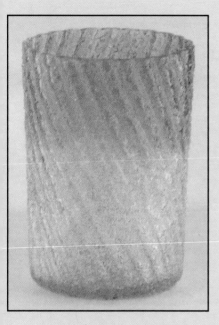

Value: $150.00 – 200.00

Value: $100.00 – 125.00

AKA: Fine Rib Swirl

Manufacturer: Probably European
Color: Solid Yellow, Opal spatter, Crystal with stain,
Amber with Opal stripes, various other treatments
Value: $70.00 – 85.00
Description — Top: Ground and polished **Bottom:** Unfinished
Dimensions — Top: 2¹³⁄₁₆" **Bottom:** 2⁷⁄₁₆" **Height:** 3⅝"
Additional Notes: 24 ribs, may have opalescent stripes.

Value: $80.00 – 110.00

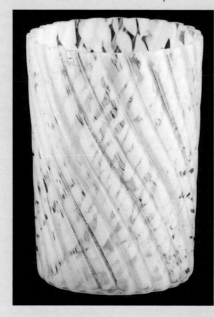

Value: $50.00 – 60.00

Value: $70.00 – 85.00

179

AKA: Fine Rib Swirl

Color: Dull Turquoise spatter
Value: $70.00 – 85.00
Description — Top: Ground, chamfered inside and out **Bottom:** Unfinished
Dimensions — Top: 2¾" **Bottom:** 2⁷⁄₁₆" **Height:** 3¹¹⁄₁₆"
Additional Notes: 24 ribs.

AKA: Fine Rib Swirl

Inner Color: Rubina **Outer Color:** Blue
Value: $250.00 – 300.00
Description — Top: Ground
Dimensions — Top: 2¹⁵⁄₁₆" **Bottom:** 2⅜" **Height:** 3⅝"
Additional Notes: 24 ribs.

AKA: Swirl with Medallion

Manufacturer: Probably European
Color: Rainbow spatter
Value: $100.00 – 150.00
Description — Top: Ground and polished, chamfered inside and out **Bottom:** Unfinished
Dimensions — Top: 2¹¹⁄₁₆" **Bottom:** 2½" **Height:** 3¹³⁄₁₆"
Additional Notes: 24 swirls, seems to match a pitcher attributed to S & W.

AKA: Swirl with Medallion

Color: Yellow
Value: $100.00 – 150.00
Description — Top: Ground
Dimensions — Top: 2¾" **Bottom:** 2⁷⁄₁₆" **Height:** 3¹³⁄₁₆"
Additional Notes: 24 swirls, 4 medallions have 16 petals each.

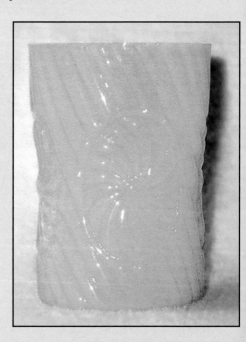

AKA: Swirl

Manufacturer: Hobbs, Brockunier & Co. **Date:** 1886
Inner Color: Alabaster **Outer Color:** Amber
Value: $45.00 – 55.00
Description — Top: Ground and polished, chamfered outside **Bottom:** Unfinished
 Bottom Figure: Swirl
Dimensions — Top: 2¹¹⁄₁₆" **Bottom:** 2½" **Height:** 3¹³⁄₁₆"

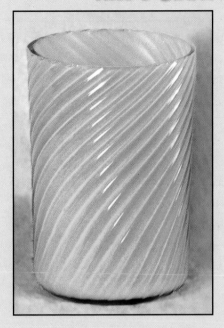

AKA: Swirl & Bread

Color: Translucent Yellow
Value: $85.00 – 100.00
Description — Top: Ground and polished **Bottom:** Unfinished
Dimensions — Top: 2¾" **Bottom:** 2⁵⁄₁₆" **Height:** 3¾"

AKA: Swirl & Bead

Color: Pink Opaline
Value: $85.00 – 100.00
Description — Top: Ground and polished, chamfered inside and out **Bottom:** Unfinished **Dimensions — Top:** 2¾" **Bottom:** 2⁵⁄₁₆" **Height:** 3¾"

AKA: Swirl & Bead

Color: Blue and Opal spatter
Value: $75.00 – 90.00
Dimensions — Top: 2⅝" **Bottom:** 2¼" **Height:** 3¹¹⁄₁₆"
Description — Top: Ground and polished, chamfered inside and out **Bottom:** Unfinished
Decoration: Gold.

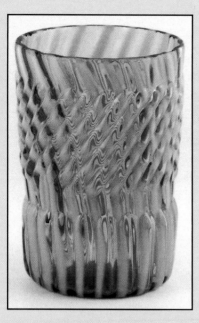

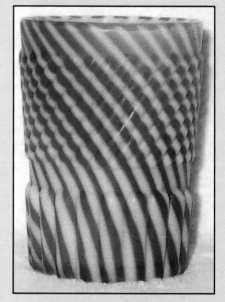

AKA: Chrysanthemum Base Swirl

Manufacturer: Northwood at Martin's Ferry, OH **Date:** 1889
Color: Blue Opalescent
Value: $95.00 – 110.00
Description — Top: Stone ground **Bottom:** Unfinished
Dimensions — Top: 2¹¹⁄₁₆" **Bottom:** 2⁷⁄₁₆" **Height:** 3¹¹⁄₁₆"

AKA: Chrysanthemum Base Swirl

Manufacturer: Northwood at Martin's Ferry, OH **Date:** 1889
Inner Color: Ruby **Outer Color:** Opalescent Crystal
Value: $125.00 – 175.00
Description — Top: Ground and polished **Bottom Figure:** Swirl continues to center.
Dimensions — Top: 2¹¹⁄₁₆" **Bottom:** 2⅜" **Height:** 3¹¹⁄₁₆"
Decoration: Satin finish.

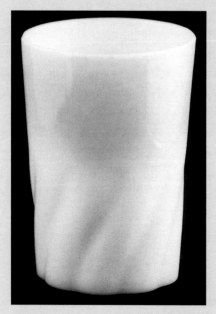

AKA: Lower Half Swirl

Manufacturer: Possibly Buckeye Glass
Color: White shading to Pink
Value: $45.00 – 65.00
Description — Top: Repaired **Bottom:** Unfinished
Dimensions — Top: 2¾" **Bottom:** 2⁵⁄₁₆" **Height:** 3¾"
Decoration: May have gold/enamel decoration.
Additional Notes: 2¹⁄₁₆" top of figure, nine swirls.

AKA: Parian Swirl

Manufacturer: Northwood; Ellwood City,s PA **Date:** 1895
Inner Color: Ruby **Outer Color:** Crystal
Value: $125.00 – 175.00
Description — Top: Ground **Bottom:** Unfinished
Dimensions — Top: 2½" **Bottom:** 2½" **Height:** 3¾"
Decoration: Satin inside and out; blue, white, red, and yellow enamel.
Additional Notes: Eight swirled ribs.

AKA: Ten Swirl

Date: 1886
Color: Light Amethyst
Value: $60.00 – 75.00
Description — Top: Ground rough **Bottom:** Unfinished
Dimensions — Top: 2¾" **Bottom:** 2⅜" **Height:** 3¾"
Decoration: Gold on top rim, gold and gray enamel flowers and leaves.
Additional Notes: This tumbler, Ten Swirl, is often associated with a pitcher that is seen in an importer's ad from 1886.

AKA: Ten Swirl

Color: Crystal
Value: $45.00 – 55.00
Description — Top: Polished **Bottom:** Unfinished
Dimensions — Top: 2⅞" **Bottom:** 2⅜" **Height:** 3⁹⁄₁₆"
Decoration: Amber stain, white enamel outlining swirls.

AKA: Ten Swirl

Inner Color: Opal **Intermediate Color:** Peach stripe **Outer Color:** Crystal
Value: $90.00 – 110.00
Description — Top: Ground **Bottom Figure:** Polished pontil
Dimensions — Top: 2¾" **Bottom:** 2½" **Height:** 3¾"
Decoration: Colored enamel floral.

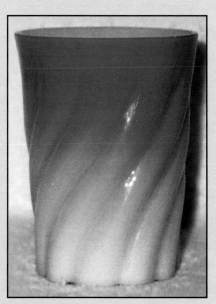

AKA: Ten Swirl

Inner Color: Opal **Outer Color:** Ruby shading to Crystal
Value: $100.00 – 150.00
Description — Top: Ground
Dimensions — Top: 2⅞" **Bottom:** 2⁵⁄₁₆" **Height:** 3¹¹⁄₁₆"

AKA: Ten Swirl

Inner Color: Pink Intermediate Color: Mica inclusions Outer Color: Crystal
Value: $45.00 – 70.00
Description — Top: Ground and polished Bottom: Unfinished
Dimensions — Top: 2¹³⁄₁₆" Bottom: 2⁵⁄₁₆" Height: 3⅝"

Original Name: No. 326
AKA: Francis

Manufacturer: Hobbs, Brockunier & Co. Date: 1886
Color: Crystal
Value: $50.00 – 65.00
Description — Top: Ground and polished, chamfered inside and out
    Bottom: Unfinished
Dimensions — Top: 2⅞" Bottom: 2⁷⁄₁₆" Height: 3⅝"
Decoration: Amber stain, satin on ribs.
Additional Notes: 12 ribs.

AKA: Eight Swirl

Color: Amethyst, Opaline
Value: $75.00 – 125.00
Description — Top: Ground Bottom: Unfinished
Dimensions — Top: 2¹³⁄₁₆" Bottom: 2⅜" Height: 3⅞"
Decoration: Gold and white enameled flowers.
Additional Notes: Eight optic swirls.

Flowers & Leaves

AKA: Grape & Leaf, Vintage

Manufacturer: Northwood Glass Co.; Indiana, PA **Date:** Ca. 1897
Color: Opal
Value: $45.00 – 55.00
Description — Top: Flat ground **Bottom:** Unfinished
Dimensions — Top: 2¹¹⁄₁₆" **Bottom:** 2½" **Height:** 3⅞"
Decoration: Gold, pink, green enamel.
Additional Notes: Known as Vintage in carnival colors. Was probably continued by Dugan.

Original Name: No. 315 Royal Oak

Manufacturer: Northwood at Martin's Ferry, OH
   Date: 1891
Inner Color: Rubina **Outer Color:** Crystal
Value: $75.00 – 95.00
Description — Top: Ground and polished
   Bottom: Unfinished
Dimensions — Top: 2½" **Bottom:** 2½" **Height:** 3¾"
Decoration: Satin, leaves are bright.

Original Name: Royal Ivy

Manufacturer: Northwood Glass Co. at Martin's Ferry, OH **Date:** 1890
Inner Color: Ruby **Outer Color:** Crystal
Value: $125.00 – 145.00 due to strong Ruby color.
Description — Top: Ground and polished, chamfered inside and out
   Bottom: Unfinished
Dimensions — Top: 2⅝" **Bottom:** 2⁷⁄₁₆" **Height:** 3¾"
Decoration: Satin, leaves and top rim are bright.
Additional Notes: 3⅜" top of figure.

Original Name: Maize

Manufacturer: W. L. Libbey & Son Co.
   Date: 1889
Color: Custard
Value: $120.00 – 140.00
Description — Top: Flat ground
   Bottom: Unfinished
Dimensions — Top: 2⁷⁄₁₆" **Bottom:** 1⅞" **Height:** 4"
Decoration: Leaves decorated with yellow, green,
   or blue enamel and gold.
Additional Notes: Reproduced by Fenton/Wright
   in cased glass. Between 1966 and 1968, 568
   Amber overlay and 557 pink overlay tumblers
   were made.

AKA: Cosmos

Manufacturer: Consolidated
Color: Opal
Value: $75.00 – 95.00
Description — Top: Ground and polished **Bottom:** Unfinished
Dimensions — Top: 2¹³⁄₁₆" **Bottom:** 2½" **Height:** 3¹¹⁄₁₆"
Decoration: Pink, yellow, and blue enamel; gold.
Additional Notes: 3⁵⁄₁₆" top of figure, four lobes.

Color: Pink spatter/spangle
Value: $95.00 – 115.00

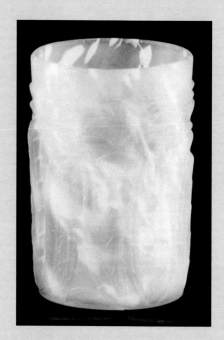

Color: Rainbow Satin
Value: $130.000 – 150.00

Color: Rainbow
Value: $125.00 – 140.00

AKA: Leaf Mold

Manufacturer: Northwood at Martin's Ferry, OH **Date:** 1891
Inner Color: Pink/Opal **Intermediate Layer:** Mica **Outer Color:** Canary
  Other Color: Opal, Ruby frit, mica inside with Crystal outside, others
Value: $95.00 – 150.00
Description — Top: Ground and polished **Bottom:** Unfinished
Dimensions — Top: 2⅝" **Bottom:** 2⁷⁄₁₆" **Height:** 3¹³⁄₁₆"

Original Name: No. 263
AKA: Leaf Umbrella

Manufacturer: Northwood at Martin's Ferry, OH **Date:** 1889
Inner Color: Opal **Outer Color:** Blue **Other Colors:** Ruby, Canary
spatter, Rose Du Bary (Opaque Pink)
Value: $75.00 – 100.00
Description — Top: Ground and polished, chamfered inside and out
Bottom: Unfinished
Dimensions — Top: $2^{11}/_{16}$" **Bottom:** $2^{5}/_{16}$" **Height:** $3^{3}/_{4}$"
Additional Notes: $3^{1}/_{4}$" top of figure.

Original Name: No. 263
AKA: Leaf Umbrella

Manufacturer: Northwood at Martin's Ferry, OH **Date:** 1889
Inner Color: Ruby **Intermediate Color:** Blue and Opal frit **Outer Color:** Crystal
Value: $135.00 – 150.00
Description — Top: Ground and polished **Bottom:** Unfinished
Additional Notes: This color may have been originally called Ruby Agate.

Original Name: No. 263
AKA: Leaf Umbrella

Manufacturer: Northwood at Martin's Ferry, OH **Date:** 1889
Inner Color: Alabaster **Outer Color:** Blue
Value: $75.00 – 100.00
Description — Top: Ground and polished, chamfered inside and out
Bottom: Unfinished
Dimensions — Top: $2^{11}/_{16}$" **Bottom:** $2^{5}/_{16}$" **Height:** $3^{3}/_{4}$"
Decoration: Irregular satin.

AKA: Flower & Pleat

Color: Crystal
Value: $35.00 – 50.00
Description — Top: Fire polished **Bottom:** Unfinished
Dimensions — Top: $2^{1}/_{2}$" **Bottom:** $2^{7}/_{16}$" **Height:** $3^{3}/_{4}$"
Decoration: Satin.

Bulges & Billows

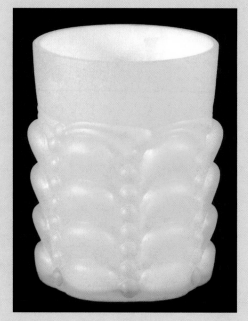

AKA: Guttate, Large

Manufacturer: Consolidated Lamp & Glass Co. **Date:** 1894
Inner Color: Opal **Outer Color:** Yellow
Value: $95.00 – 115.00
Description — Top: Ground **Bottom:** Unfinished
Dimensions — Top: 2⅞" **Bottom:** 2¾" over figure **Height:** 3⅝"
Decoration: Satin

AKA: Guttate, Small

Manufacturer: Consolidated Lamp & Glass Co. **Date:** 1894
Color: White, also cased Pink over Opal
Value: $65.00 – 80.00
Description — Top: Ground and polished **Bottom:** Unfinished
Dimensions — Top: 2¾" **Bottom:** 2½" **Height:** 3¹¹⁄₁₆"
Decoration: Blue enamel.

AKA: Guttate, Small

Manufacturer: Consolidated Lamp & Glass Co.
    Date: 1894
Color: Opal with Amber frit
Value: $45.00 – 70.00
Description — Top: Polished **Bottom:** Unfinished
Dimensions — Top: 2¹³⁄₁₆" **Bottom:** 2⁷⁄₁₆"
    Height: 3⅝"
Additional Notes: 3¼" top of figure.

Color: Blue enamel, floral
Value: $55.00 – 65.00

Original Name: Quilt

Manufacturer: Consolidated Lamp & Glass Co. **Date:** 1894
Inner Color: Opal shading to pink **Outer Color:** Crystal
Value: $60.00 – 75.00
Description — Top: Polished **Bottom:** Unfinished
Dimensions — Top: 2¾" **Bottom:** 2½" **Height:** 3⁹⁄₁₆"
Decoration: Satin.

Original Name: Quilt

Manufacturer: Consolidated Lamp & Glass Co. **Date:** 1894
Inner Color: Opal **Outer Color:** Pink
Value: $60.00 – 75.00
Description — Top: Fire polished
Dimensions — Top: 2¾" **Bottom:** 2½" **Height:** 3½"

AKA: Cone

Manufacturer: Consolidated Lamp & Glass Co.
  Date: 1894
Inner Color: Opaque Pink, Yellow, Light Blue
  Outer Color: Crystal
Value: $70.00 – 90.00
Description — Top: Ground and polished
  Bottom: Unfinished
Dimensions — Top: 2¾" **Bottom:** 2⁵⁄₁₆"
  Height: 3¹³⁄₁₆"

AKA: Bulging Loops

Manufacturer: Consolidated Lamp & Glass Co. **Date:** 1894
Inner Color: Opal **Outer Color:** Yellow
Value: $95.00 – 115.00
Description — Top: Ground and polished **Bottom:** Unfinished
Dimensions — Top: 2¹³⁄₁₆" **Bottom:** 2½" **Height:** 3¾"

AKA: Torquay

Manufacturer: Consolidated Lamp & Glass Co. **Date:** 1894
Inner Color: Selenium/Cadmium Ruby **Outer Color:** Crystal
Value: $95.00 – 130.00
Description — Top: Ground and polished, chamfered inside and out
   Bottom: Unfinished
Dimensions — Top: 2¹⁵⁄₁₆" **Bottom:** 2½" over ribs **Height:** 3¾"
Decoration: Satin outside.
Additional Notes: Pattern consists of alternating high and low ribs, eight repeats.

Original Name: Plume

Manufacturer: Adams & Co. **Date:** Ca. 1880s
Color: Crystal
Value: $35.00 – 50.00
Description — Top: Flat ground **Bottom:** Unfinished
Dimensions — Top: 2¹¹⁄₁₆" **Bottom:** 3⅛" widest part **Height:** 3⅞"
Decoration: Engraved leaf.
Additional Notes: This tumbler is blown; most of the pattern is pressed. See page 98.

AKA: Leaf Medallion

Manufacturer: West Virginia Glass Co.
Color: Blue shading to Crystal, Amethyst, Green
Value: $65.00 – 85.00
Description — Top: Ground and polished, chamfered outside
   Bottom: Unfinished
Dimensions — Top: 2¹³⁄₁₆" **Bottom:** 2⅝" **Height:** 3⅞"

Inner Color: Ruby **Outer Color:** Crystal
Value: $110.00 – 130.00
Description — Top: Flat ground, chamfered inside and out
   Bottom: Unfinished
Dimensions — Top: 2¾" **Bottom:** 2⁷⁄₁₆" **Height:** 3¾"
Decoration: White wash on vertical panels, gold in all design.
Additional Notes: Eight repeats.

Original Name: Ruba Rombic

Manufacturer: Consolidated Lamp & Glass Co./ Reuben Haley **Date:** 1928
Color: Smoke
Value: $120.00 – 175.00
Description — Top: Ground and polished **Bottom:** Ground and polished

Original Name: Florette

Manufacturer: Consolidated Lamp & Glass Co. **Date:** 1895
Color: Crystal, Light Blue Opaque, Rainbow colors
Value: $85.00 – 110.00
Description — Top: Ground and polished **Bottom:** Unfinished
Dimensions — Top: 2⅞" **Bottom:** 2⅜" over figure **Height:** 3¹³⁄₁₆"
Decoration: Gold, Ruby stain.
Additional Notes: 3⁵⁄₁₆" top of figure. Be aware that there were two molds used for this tumbler. This tumbler has eight "cushions" around.

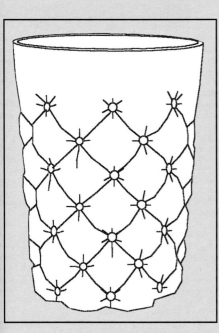

AKA: Cushions

Color: Rainbow
Value: $450.00 – 600.00
Decoration: Gold, enamel.
Additional Notes: Appears to have seven "cushions" around; blue tumbler shown above has eight. Be aware that there were two molds used for this tumbler. This one may have been imported.

Threaded

→ **AKA:** Threaded

Color: Opal and Ruby
Value: $175.00 – 200.00
Description — Top: Ground **Bottom:** Unfinished
Dimensions — Top: 2⅞" **Bottom:** 2⁵⁄₁₆" **Height:** 3¹³⁄₁₆"
Decoration: Blue and green enamel, gold.

Original Name: Venetian →

Manufacturer: Hobbs, Brockunier & Co. **Date:** 1886
Inner Color: Crystal **Intermediate Color:** White looping **Outer Color:** Ruby threading
Value: $250.00 – 300.00
Description — Top: Flat ground, chamfered outside **Bottom Figure:** Loops and threading
continue to center.
Dimensions — Top: 2¹¹⁄₁₆" **Bottom:** 2⁵⁄₁₆" **Height:** 3⅝"
Additional Notes: Known with blue threading.

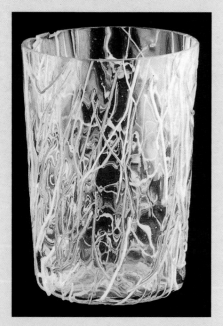

→ **AKA:** Peloton

Color: Crystal
Value: $175.00 – 200.00
Description — Top: Ground and polished, chamfered inside and out
Bottom: Unfinished
Dimensions — Top: 2¹¹⁄₁₆" **Bottom:** 2⁵⁄₁₆" **Height:** 3¹¹⁄₁₆"
Additional Notes: Multicolored threads have been applied randomly all over body.

Miscellaneous Patterns

AKA: Pseudo Crackle

Color: Olive Green
Value: $35.00 – 50.00
Description — Top: Ground and polished **Bottom:** Unfinished
Dimensions — Top: 2¹³⁄₁₆" **Bottom:** 2⅜" **Height:** 3¹⁵⁄₁₆"
Decoration: Blue, white, and yellow enamel with gold.
Additional Notes: Surface has raised crackle-type lines.

AKA: Pseudo Crackle

Color: Rubina
Value: $90.00 – 140.00
Description — Top: Ground
Dimensions — Top: 2¹³⁄₁₆" **Bottom:** 2⅜" **Height:** 3¾"
Decoration: Enamel flower, gold leaves.

AKA: Drape

Manufacturer: Phoenix Glass Co. **Date:** 1886
Inner Color: Opal **Outer Color:** Rubina
Other Colors: Rubina, Blue, Orange, Ruby Amber, others
Value: $150.00 – 225.00
Description — Top: Ground and polished, chamfered inside and out **Bottom:** Unfinished
Bottom Figure: Drape pattern continues into bottom.
Dimensions — Top: 2¹³⁄₁₆" **Bottom:** 2⁹⁄₁₆" **Height:** 3¾"
Additional Notes: Also exists in Ruby Opalescent, eight and ten drapes around tumbler.
Incorrectly known as Wheeling Drape.

AKA: Drape

Manufacturer: Phoenix Glass Co. **Date:** 1886
Inner Color: Opal **Intermediate Color:** Ruby upper portion **Outer Color:** Amber
Value: $150.00 - 225.00
Description — Top: Ground and polished **Bottom Figure:** Drape pattern continues into bottom.
Dimensions — Top: 2¾" **Bottom:** 2⁷⁄₁₆" **Height:** 3¾"
Additional Notes: Ten drapes around tumbler. Incorrectly known as Wheeling Drape.

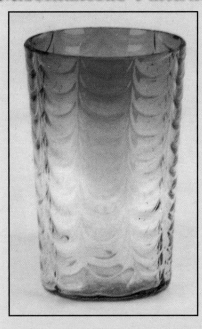

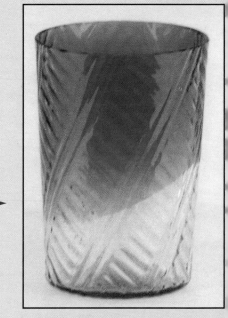

AKA: Drape

Manufacturer: Phoenix Glass Co.
Inner Color: Rubina **Outer Color:** Amber
Value: $150.00 – 225.00
Description — Top: Ground and polished, chamfered inside and out
Dimensions — Top: 2¾" **Bottom:** 2¼" **Height:** 4³⁄₁₆"
Additional Notes: Ten drapes around tumbler. Incorrectly known as Wheeling Drape.

AKA: Alternating Diagonals

Inner Color: Rubina **Outer Color:** Amber
Value: $125.00 – 175.00
Description — Top: Ground and polished, chamfered inside and out
   Bottom: Unfinished
Dimensions — Top: 2¹¹⁄₁₆" **Bottom:** 2¼" **Height:** 3¾"

Original Name: Muranese
AKA: Sunglow

Manufacturer: New Martinsville Glass Co. **Date:** 1902
Inner Color: Salmon **Intermediate Color:** Yellow **Outer Color:** Crystal
Value: $400.00 – 500.00
Description — Top: Ground and polished **Bottom Figure:** Ribs meet in center to form star
Dimensions — Top: 2¾" **Bottom:** 2⅜" **Height:** 3¾"
Additional Notes: 20 vertical ribs.

Original Name: Muranese
AKA: Sunglow

Manufacturer: New Martinsville Glass Co. **Date:** 1902
Inner Color: Salmon **Intermediate Color:** Yellow **Outer Color:** Crystal
Value: $400.00 – 500.00
Description — Top: Ground and polished **Bottom Figure:** Ribs meet in center.
Dimensions — Top: 2¾" **Bottom:** 2⅜" **Height:** 3¹³⁄₁₆"
Additional Notes: Sand inclusions inside tumbler, 20 vertical ribs.

AKA: Strong Diamond

Color: Rubina
Value: $80.00 – 120.00
Description — Top: Polished **Bottom:** Unfinished **Bottom Figure:** Pattern continued to center.
Dimensions — Top: 3" **Bottom:** 2½" **Height:** 3¹¹⁄₁₆"

AKA: Small Diamond Optic

Manufacturer: Stevens & Williams
Inner Color: Crystal **Outer Color:** Two Ruby stripes with Opal bands
Value: $100.00 – 150.00
Description — Top: Ground and polished
Dimensions — Top: 2¾" **Bottom:** 2⅜" **Height:** 3¾"
Additional Notes: Note strong diamond optic.

AKA: Rib & Swirl

Color: Ruby Amber
Value: $125.00 – 175.00
Description — Top: Ground
Dimensions — Top: 2¹¹⁄₁₆" **Bottom:** 2⁵⁄₁₆" **Height:** 3¾"
Additional Notes: Vertical ribs between diamond quilted swirls.

Original Name: Silver Filigree
AKA: Flourish, Cornflower

Manufacturer: Dugan Glass Co. **Date:** Ca. 1907
Color: Emerald Green, possibly blue, others
Value: $45.00 – 55.00
Decoration: Gold on figure.

195

Original Name: No. 2 Filigree Art Ware

Manufacturer: Dugan Glass Co. **Date:** Ca. 1907
Color: Green, Blue, Ruby, Ivory
Value: $45.00 – 55.00
Description — Top: Flat ground
Dimensions — Top: 2¹⁵/₁₆" **Bottom:** 2½" **Height:** 3¹⁵/₁₆"
Decoration: Gold, silver.

AKA: Filagree

Color: Green
Value: $45.00 – 55.00
Description — Top: Flat ground
Decoration: Silver.

Original Name: No. 151
AKA: Filigree

Manufacturer: Indiana Glass Co. **Date:** 1912
Color: Crystal
Value: $35.00 – 45.00
Dimensions — Top: 2¹¹/₁₆" **Bottom:** 2⅜" **Height:** 4⅛"
Description — Top: Fire polished **Bottom:** Rough, stuck-up **Bottom Figure:** 6-point uneven sta
Decoration: Platinum on figure.
Additional Notes: This is a pressed pattern.

AKA: Herringbone

Color: Shaded Aqua
Value: $80.00 – 120.00
Description — Top: Ground and polished, chamfered inside and out
   Bottom Figure: Herringbone continues to center, forms star figure.
Dimensions — Top: 2¹¹⁄₁₆" **Bottom:** 2⁵⁄₁₆" **Height:** 3¹³⁄₁₆"
Decoration: Frosted, gold alternating on figure.

Original Name: No. 25
AKA: Four Pinch

Manufacturer: Challinor, Taylor & Co.
Color: Opal
Value: $60.00 – 70.00
Description — Top: Ground and polished **Bottom:** Unfinished
Dimensions — Top: 2¾" **Bottom:** 2⅛" **Height:** 3⅝"
Decoration: Blue and yellow wash, green, brown enamel leaves and vines.

AKA: Windows

Inner Color: Crystal **Intermediate Color:** Opal **Outer Color:** Die-away Blue
Value: $150.00 – 200.00
Description — Top: Ground and polished
Dimensions — Top: 3¹⁄₁₆" **Bottom:** 2½" **Height:** 3¾"
Additional Notes: Pattern 5½" vertical, 10" around.

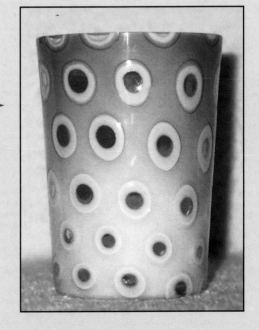

Air Trap

The process of making Air Trap (mother-of-pearl) glass involves dipping the started bubble (usually opal) in a mold that leaves closely spaced designs on the surface of the glass. A second gather of crystal is applied on top of the first, and the tumbler is expanded in the mold. The second gather traps little bubbles of air between the ribs, and as the glass is expanded, these bubbles become the pattern of the piece. The bubbles may be diamond shaped, or may form a teardrop, honeycomb, or some other design. Usually, the piece is lightly frosted, which gives a pearly luster to the glass. Occasionally, the second gather is eliminated, leaving the piece with strong ribs on the surface. When these are frosted, the style is called "cut velvet." It was originally called just "velvet."

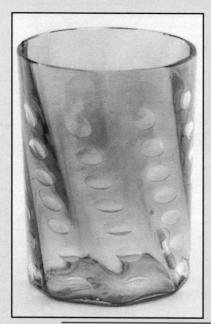

Original Name: No. 336
AKA: Air Trap Swirl

Manufacturer: Hobbs Glass Co. **Date:** 1889
Inner Color: Ruby **Outer Color:** Crystal
Value: Seller's choice
Description — Top: Ground and polished, chamfered inside and out
 Bottom Figure: Flat ground
Dimensions — Top: 2¹³⁄₁₆" **Bottom:** 2⁹⁄₁₆" **Height:** 3¹¹⁄₁₆"
Additional Notes: Eight diagonal ribs, seven horizontal rows of bubbles.

AKA: Air Trap

Inner Color: Pale Cranberry **Intermediate Color:** Crystal with mica **Outer Color:** Amber
Value: $125.00 – 200.00
Description — Top: Ground and polished, chamfered inside and out
 Bottom Figure: Ground pontil
Dimensions — Top: 2¹¹⁄₁₆" **Bottom:** 2⁵⁄₁₆" **Height:** 3¹⁵⁄₁₆"
Additional Notes: Mica is in the air cavities.

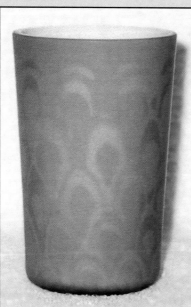

AKA: Mother-of-Pearl Peacock

Inner Color: Opal **Outer Color:** Orange/Bronze/Apricot
Value: $225.00 – 275.00
Description — Top: Ground **Bottom Figure:** Figure continues onto bottom.
Dimensions — Top: 2¾" **Bottom:** 2½" **Height:** 4"
Decoration: Satin finish.

AKA: Mother-of-Pearl Raindrop

Color: Rubina
Value: $125.00 – 150.00
Description — Top: Fire polished **Bottom:** Ground pontil
Dimensions — Top: 2¾" **Bottom:** 2½" **Height:** 3⁹⁄₁₆"
Decoration: Satin.

AKA: Oval to Round, Mother-of-Pearl

Manufacturer: Phoenix Glass Co. **Date:** Ca. 1886
Inner Color: Opal **Intermediate Color:** Blue **Outer Color:** Crystal
Value: $90.00 – 115.00
Description – Top Rim: Fire polished **Bottom:** Unfinished **Bottom Figure:** Ground pontil
Dimensions — Top: 2¹¹⁄₁₆" **Bottom:** 2½" **Height:** 3⁹⁄₁₆"
Decoration: Satin, floral, leaves, butterflies in enamel.

AKA: Tricorn Mother-of-Pearl

Color: Yellow
Value: $200.00 – 250.00
Description — Top: Fire polished, tricornered **Bottom:** Ground pontil
Dimensions — Bottom: 2⅜" **Height:** 3¹³⁄₁₆"
Decoration: Shiny finish.

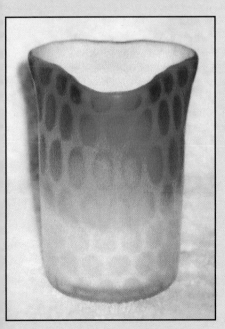

AKA: Tricorn Mother-of-Pearl

Inner Color: Opal **Outer Color:** Blue shading to Crystal.
Value: $200.00 – 250.00
Description — Top: Fire polished, tricornered **Bottom Figure:** Ground pontil
Dimensions — Bottom: 2⅜" **Height:** 3¾"
Decoration: Satin finish.

AKA: Tricorn Mother-of-Pearl Raindrop

Inner Color: Opal **Intermediate Color:** Bands of Pink and Blue
Value: $250.00 – 300.00
Description — Top: Ground, tricornered
Dimensions — Bottom: 2⁵⁄₁₆" **Height:** 4"

AKA: Mother-of-Pearl Rainbow

Inner Color: Opal **Intermediate Color:** Bands of Red, Yellow, and Blue **Outer Color:** Crystal
Value: $450.00 – $500.00
Description — Top: Fire polished **Bottom Figure:** Polished pontil
Dimensions — Top: 2¾" **Bottom:** 2⁵⁄₁₆" **Height:** 3¼"
Decoration: Enamel floral decoration.

AKA: Mother-of-Pearl Diamond Quilted

Inner Color: White **Outer Color:** Rubina
Value: $115.00 – 135.00
Description — Top: Fire polished
  Bottom Figure: Ground punty
Dimensions — Top: 2⅞" **Bottom:** 2½"
  Height: 3⅞"
Decoration: Satin.

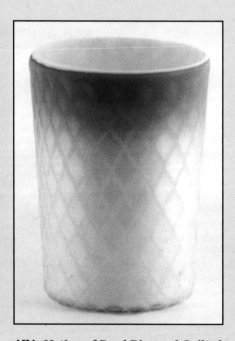

AKA: Mother-of-Pearl Diamond Quilted

Color: Rubina
Value: $115.00 – 135.00
Description — Top: Fire polished
  Bottom: Stone ground pontil
Dimensions — Top: 2¹³⁄₁₆" **Bottom:** 2⅜"
  Height: 3¾"

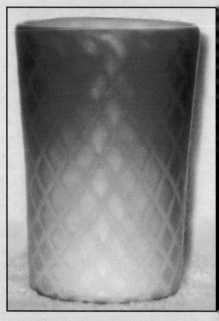

AKA: Mother-of-Pearl Diamond Quilted

Inner Color: Opal **Outer Color:** Rubina
Value: $115.00 – 135.00
Description — Top: Fire polished
  Bottom Figure: Polished pontil
Dimensions — Top: 2¾" **Bottom:** 2⁹⁄₁₆"
  Height: 3¹⁵⁄₁₆"
Decoration: Satin finish.

AKA: Mother-of-Pearl Diamond Quilted

Inner Color: White **Outer Color:** Yellow shaded to White
Value: $115.00 – 135.00
Description — Top: Fire polished **Bottom Figure:** Ground punty
Dimensions — Top: 2⅞" **Bottom:** 2½" **Height:** 3⅞"
Decoration: Satin.

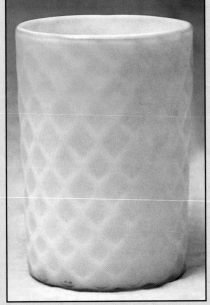

AKA: Mother-of-Pearl Diamond Quilted

Inner Color: Opal **Intermediate Color:** Yellow shaded to White **Outer Color:** Crystal
Value: $115.00 – 135.00
Description — Top: Fire polished **Bottom Figure:** Concave ground
Dimensions — Top: 2¹³⁄₁₆" **Bottom:** 2½" **Height:** 3⅞"
Decoration: Satin.

AKA: Mother-of-Pearl Diamond Quilted

Inner Color: Opal **Outer Color:** Blue shading to Clear
Value: $75.00 – 100.00
Description — Top: Fire polished **Bottom Figure:** Ground pontil
Dimensions — Top: 2⅞" **Bottom:** 2⁹⁄₁₆" **Height:** 4"

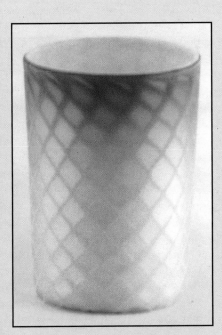

AKA: Mother-of-Pearl Diamond Quilted

Color: Blue
Value: $100.00 – 125.00
Description — Top: Fire polished **Bottom:** Ground pontil
Dimensions — Top: 2⅞" **Bottom:** 2½" **Height:** 3¹⁵⁄₁₆"

AKA: Mother-of-Pearl Elongated Diamonds

Inner Color: Opal **Outer Color:** Crystal
Value: $75.00 – 100.00
Description — Top: Fire polished **Bottom:** Ground pontil
Dimensions — Top: 2¾" **Bottom:** 2⅜" **Height:** 3¾"
Decoration: Gold spatter in swirl.

AKA: Mother-of-Pearl Diamond Quilted

Manufacturer: Phoenix Glass Co. **Date:** Ca. 1886
Color: Yellow
Value: $125.00 – 140.00
Description — Top: Fire polished **Bottom:** Ground pontil
Dimensions — Top: 2⅞" **Bottom:** 2⁹⁄₁₆" **Height:** 4"
Decoration: Enamel leaves.

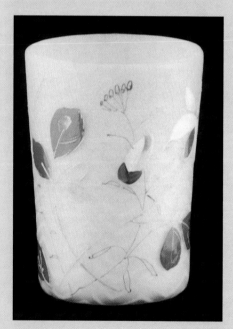

AKA: Mother-of-Pearl Herringbone

Manufacturer: Phoenix Glass Co. **Date:** Ca. 1886
Color: Yellow
Value: $125.00 – 150.00
Description — Top: Fire polished **Bottom:** Ground pontil
Dimensions — Top: 2¹³⁄₁₆" **Bottom:** 2⁷⁄₁₆" **Height:** 3¾"
Decoration: Enamel floral.

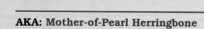

AKA: Mother-of-Pearl Herringbone

Inner Color: White **Outer Color:** Butterscotch/Amber
Value: $100.00 – 120.00
Description — Top: Fire polished **Bottom Figure:** Stone
ground pontil, 8-point star, figure continues to center.
Dimensions — Top: 2¹³⁄₁₆" **Bottom:** 2⁷⁄₁₆" **Height:** 3¾"

AKA: Mother-of-Pearl Herringbone

Inner Color: Opal **Outer Color:** Rubina
Value: $125.00 – 150.00
Description — Top: Fire polished **Bottom Figure:** Polished pontil
Dimensions — Top: 2¾" **Bottom:** 2⅝" **Height:** 3¹¹⁄₁₆"
Decoration: Satin finish.

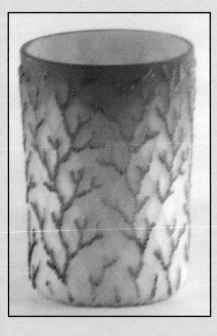

AKA: Mother-of-Pearl Coraline

Color: Burnt Apricot
Value: $150.00 – 170.00
Description — Top: Fire polished **Bottom:** Ground pontil
Dimensions — Top: 2¾" **Bottom:** 2½" **Height:** 3¹³⁄₁₆"
Decoration: Coraline in seaweed design.

AKA: Cut Velvet

Inner Color: Opal **Outer Color:** Ruby
Value: $225.00 – 275.00
Description — Top: Ground **Bottom Figure:** Figure forms flower with 16 petals.
Dimensions — Top: 2¹³⁄₁₆" **Bottom:** 2¾" **Height:** 3¾"
Decoration: Coralene beads in seaweed design.

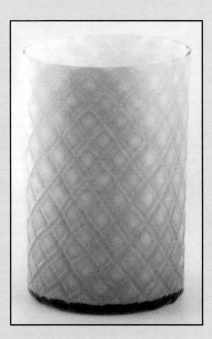

AKA: Glossy Cut Velvet

Inner Color: Opal **Outer Color:** Amber
Value: $75.00 – 100.00
Description — Top: Ground and polished, chamfered inside
   Bottom: 16-point star
Dimensions — Top: 2¾" **Bottom:** 2⁹⁄₁₆" **Height:** 3¹⁵⁄₁₆"

AKA: Glossy Cut Velvet

Inner Color: Opal **Outer Color:** Blue
Value: $120.00 – 140.00
Description — Top: Flat ground
Dimensions — Top: 2¾" **Bottom:** 2½" **Height:** 3⅞"
Decoration: Gold on top surface, enamel floral.

AKA: Glossy Cut Velvet

Inner Color: Ruby **Intermediate Color:** Opal (vertical panels) **Outer Color:** Crystal
Value: $150.00 – 200.00
Description — Top: Ground and polished **Bottom Figure:** Multi-petaled flower
Dimensions — Top: 2¹¹⁄₁₆" **Bottom:** 2⁵⁄₁₆" **Height:** 3¾"
Additional Notes: Surface is heavily diamond embossed, precursor to Air trap. The design is composed of alternating ruby and opal canes laid together, warmed-in, and expanded to form the tumbler.

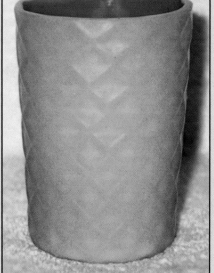

AKA: Cut Velvet

Inner Color: Ruby **Intermediate Color:** Opal **Outer Color:** Yellow
Value: $100.00 – 150.00
Description — Top: Ground and polished **Bottom:** Pattern continues onto bottom.
  Bottom Figure: 12-point design
Dimensions — Top: 2⅝" **Bottom:** 2⁵⁄₁₆" **Height:** 3⅝"
Decoration: Satin finish.

AKA: Glossy Cut Velvet

Inner Color: Opal **Outer Color:** Ruby
Value: $125.00 – 150.00
Description — Top: Ground and polished, chamfered inside and out
Dimensions — Top: 2¾" **Bottom:** 2⁵⁄₁₆" **Height:** 3¾"

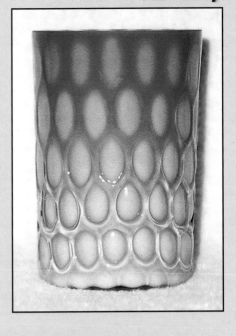

AKA: Honeycomb

Manufacturer: Phoenix Glass Co. **Date:** 1886
Inner Color: Opal **Intermediate Color:** Pink **Outer Color:** Crystal
Value: $130.00 – 160.00
Description — Top: Ground and polished **Bottom Figure:** Pattern continues halfway across.
Dimensions — Top: 2¹³⁄₁₆" **Bottom:** 2⁹⁄₁₆" **Height:** 4¹⁄₁₆"

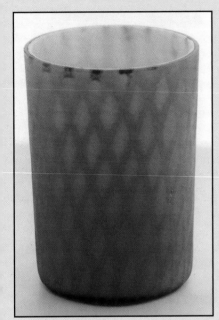

AKA: Mother-of-Pearl Diamond Quilted

Inner Color: Opal **Intermediate Color:** Ruby **Outer Color:** Crystal
Value: $85.00 – 110.00
Description — Top: Ground, chamfered inside
Dimensions — Top: 2¹³⁄₁₆" **Bottom:** 2⁹⁄₁₆" **Height:** 3¹³⁄₁₆"
Decoration: Satin.
Additional Notes: May be mid-twentieth century.

AKA: Mother-of-Pearl Diamond Quilted

Color: Rubina
Value: $85.00 – 110.00
Dimensions — Top: 2¹¹⁄₁₆" **Bottom:** 2⅜" **Height:** 3¹³⁄₁₆"
Decoration: Satin.

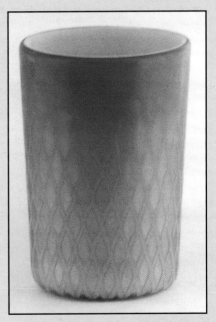

AKA: Mother-of-Pearl Diamond Quilted

Inner Color: Opal **Intermediate Color:** Ruby **Outer Color:** Crystal
Value: $85.00 – 110.00
Description — Top: Fire polished **Bottom:** Unfinished
Dimensions — Top: 2½" **Bottom:** 2¼" **Height:** 3¾"

←————————————————

AKA: Air Trap

Date: Ca. 1973
Inner Color: Pale Rubina **Outer Color:** Crystal
Value: $50.00 – 60.00
Description — Top: Fire polished **Bottom Figure:** Imperfectly ground pontil
Dimensions — Top: 2⅞" **Bottom:** 2⅝" **Height:** 3¹¹⁄₁₆"
Decoration: Frosted inside and out.
Additional Notes: This tumbler matches a pitcher advertised in 1973.

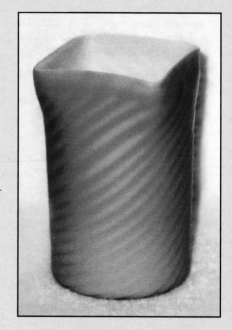

————————————————→

AKA: Mother-of-Pearl Swirl

Inner Color: Opal **Outer Color:** Blue
Value: $150.00 – 250.00
Description — Top: Fire polished **Bottom Figure:** Polished pontil
Dimensions — Top: 2¼" across flats **Bottom:** 2⅜" **Height:** 3¾"

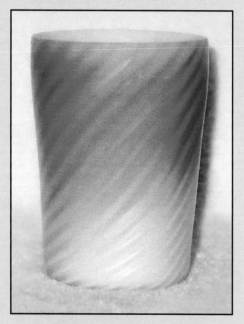

←————————————————

AKA: Mother-of-Pearl Swirl

Inner Color: Opal **Outer Color:** Blue shading to crystal.
Value: $125.00 – 175.00
Description — Top: Fire polished **Bottom:** Polished pontil
   Bottom Figure: Swirl goes to center.
Dimensions — Top: 2¹¹⁄₁₆" **Bottom:** 2⁷⁄₁₆" **Height:** 3⁹⁄₁₆"
Decoration: Satin finish.

————————————————→

AKA: Mother-of-Pearl Swirl

Inner Color: Opal **Outer Color:** Yellow
Value: $200.00 – 250.00
Description — Top: Ground **Bottom:** Ground pontil
   Bottom Figure: Swirls continue to center.
Dimensions — Top: 2¹³⁄₁₆" **Bottom:** 2½" **Height:** 3¹³⁄₁₆"
Decoration: Satin finish.

Cut to Clear

These tumblers were made by blowing a bubble of clear glass and gathering colored glass over it before forming the glass into tumbler shape. It was annealed and then cut. The design was cut through the outer layer or layers, exposing the clear inner layer. It's an old technique that has recently been revived by importers.

AKA: Blue Cut to Clear

Inner Color: Crystal **Outer Color:** Blue
Value: $50.00 – 70.00
Description — Top: Fire polished **Bottom:** Concave ground
Dimensions — Top: 2⅞" **Bottom:** 2¾" **Height:** 3¹¹⁄₁₆"
Decoration: 19 bottom flutes.

AKA: Opal Cut to Clear

Inner Color: Crystal **Outer Color:** Opal
Value: $35.00 – 45.00
Description — Top: Flat ground, chamfered inside and out **Bottom:** Flat and concave ground
Dimensions — Top: 2⅞" **Bottom:** 2½" **Height:** 3¹⁵⁄₁₆"
Decoration: 14 bottom flutes.

AKA: Cut to Clear, Irish Cross

Inner Color: Crystal **Intermediate Color:** Opal **Outer Color:** Opaque Green
Value: $100.00 – 125.00
Description — Top: Sterling band **Bottom Figure:** Cut ogee star
Dimensions — Top: 2¹⁵⁄₁₆" **Bottom:** 2⁹⁄₁₆" **Height:** 3¹³⁄₁₆"
Decoration: Pattern of crosses cut into clear inner layer.

Cut to Clear

AKA: Ruby Cut to Clear

Inner Color: Crystal **Outer Color:** Ruby
Value: $60.00 – 80.00
Description — Top: Ground and polished, chamfered inside and out
Dimensions — Top: 3¹⁄₁₆" Other dimensions not available

AKA: Amber Stained Cut to Clear

Color: Crystal
Value: $45.00 – 55.00
Description — Top: Flat ground, chamfered inside and out
   Bottom: Concave ground
Dimensions — Top: 2⅞" **Bottom:** 2⅝" **Height:** 3⅞"
Decoration: Amber stain, 18 top flutes, 14 bottom flutes.

AKA: Rosebush, Cameo

Manufacturer: Val St. Lambert, Belgium
Inner Color: Crystal **Outer Color:** Ruby
Value: $140.00 – 170.00
Description — Top: Ground and polished **Bottom Figure:** 24-point cut star
Dimensions — Top: 2¾" **Bottom:** 2⁷⁄₁₆" **Height:** 3½"
Decoration: Etched in relief and etched through Ruby to Clear, cameo style.

Opalescent

The process of manufacturing opalescent glass involves putting a chemical (bone ash) into the batch. The mold must contain cavities that will allow the glass to form prominences. Once the glass is out of the mold, cool air is blown over the piece. The blown tumbler is warmed-in (reheated), and blown into its final mold, taking the shape intended. It is then placed in the lehr to anneal. The outside is generally smooth, and the design is generally white, showing up nicely against the clear or colored background. Only ruby glass need be plated over with opalescent; all other colors can become opalescent using only one layer of glass.

Original Name: No. 293
AKA: Stars & Stripes

Manufacturer: Beaumont Glass Co. **Date:** 1900
Color: Crystal Opalescent
Value: $125.00 – 200.00
Description — Top: Ground and polished
Dimensions — Top: 2¹³⁄₁₆" **Bottom:** 2½"
  Height: 3¾"
Additional Notes: Bottom has an outer ring, ⁵⁄₁₆" wide, and a concave center; compare to the two tumblers below. Hobbs Glass Co.'s tumblers were flat on the bottom.

AKA: Stars & Stripes

Manufacturer: L. G. Wright/Fenton
  Date: 1940 – 1965
Inner Color: Ruby **Outer Color:** Crystal Opalescent
Value: $75.00 – 95.00
Description — Top: Ground **Bottom:** Unfinished
  Bottom Figure: Entire bottom is concave.
Dimensions — Top: 2⅞" **Bottom:** 2⅝"
  Height: 3⅝"
Additional Notes: 14 stripes and three rows of 12 stars, common to all varieties. Note that two stripes connected at bottom, common to L. G. Wright/Fenton production.

AKA: Stars & Stripes

Manufacturer: L. G. Wright/Fenton
  Date: Ca. 1940 – 1965
Color: Blue Opalescent
Value: $45.00 – 60.00
Description — Top: Ground and polished, chamfered inside and out
  Bottom: Unfinished
  Bottom Figure: Entire bottom is concave.
Dimensions — Top: 2⅞" **Bottom:** 2⁹⁄₁₆"
  Height: 3¹¹⁄₁₆"
Additional Notes: Watch for the two connected stripes.

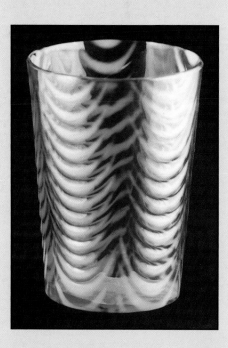

Original Name: No. 528 Venetian

Manufacturer: Buckeye Glass Co.
  Date: 1888
Color: Blue Opalescent
Value: $45.00 – 70.00
Description — Top: Ground and polished, chamfered outside **Bottom:** Unfinished
Dimensions — Top: 2⅞" **Bottom:** 2⁵⁄₁₆"
  Height: 3⅞"

Original Name: Floradine
AKA: Onyx

Manufacturer: Dalzell, Gilmore & Leighton **Date:** 1889
Inner Color: Ruby **Outer Color:** Crystal Opalescent
Value: Seller's choice
Description — Top: Ground bottom
Decoration: Glossy (unfrosted) finish.

Original Name: Floradine
AKA: Onyx

Manufacturer: Dalzell, Gilmore & Leighton **Date:** 1889
Inner Color: Ruby **Outer Color:** Crystal Opalescent
Value: Seller's choice
Description — Top: Ground
Decoration: Satin finish.
Additional Notes: These three tumblers seem to have been made using the same spot mold.

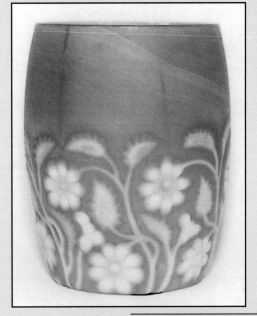

Original Name: Floradine
AKA: Onyx

Manufacturer: Dalzell, Gilmore & Leighton **Date:** 1889
Inner Color: Ruby **Outer Color:** Crystal Opalescent
Value: Seller's choice
Description — Top: Ground
Decoration: Satin finish.
Additional Notes: Note that all three Floradine tumblers have slightly differing pattern heights.

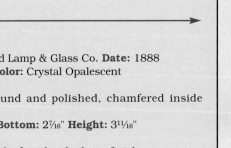

AKA: Criss-Cross

Manufacturer: Consolidated Lamp & Glass Co. **Date:** 1888
Inner Color: Ruby **Outer Color:** Crystal Opalescent
Value: $250.00 – 350.00
Description — Top: Ground and polished, chamfered inside and out
Dimensions — Top: 2¹³⁄₁₆" **Bottom:** 2⁷⁄₁₆" **Height:** 3¹¹⁄₁₆"
Decoration: Satin.
Additional Notes: May also be found with glossy finish.

Swirled Opalescent

These swirl opalescent tumblers were blown into two molds. The first mold imparted vertical ribs. After the bubble of glass was removed from the rib mold, it had cool air blown over it. When warmed-in, it was twisted by holding the bottom with a tool and turning the blowpipe. It was then blown into the final mold, which expanded the glass and pushed the thinner areas to the outside, leaving the ribs on the inside. The direction of twist may have been a whim of the blower, or may have been by design. These tumblers seem to twist both ways.

Original Name: No. 325
AKA: Opalescent Swirl

Manufacturer: Hobbs Glass Co. **Date:** 1888
Inner Color: Ruby **Outer Color:** Crystal Opalescent
Value: $45.00 – 70.00
Description — Top: Ground, chamfered inside and out
Dimensions — Top: 2⅞" **Bottom:** 2⁹⁄₁₆" **Height:** 3¹¹⁄₁₆ "
Decoration: Satin, shiny.

Original Name: No. 325
AKA: Opalescent Swirl

Manufacturer: Hobbs Glass Co. **Date:** 1888
Inner Color: Ruby **Outer Color:** Crystal Opalescent
Value: $90.00 – 110.00
Description — Top: Ground and polished, chamfered inside and out
   Bottom: Polished pontil
Dimensions — Top: 2¾" **Bottom:** 2½" **Height:** 3¾"
Decoration: Satin, may also be found glossy.

Original Name: No. 325
AKA: Swirl

Manufacturer: Hobbs Glass Co. **Date:** 1888
Color: Blue Opalescent
Value: $45.00 – 70.00
Description — Top: Ground and polished, chamfered inside and out
Dimensions — Top: 2⅞" **Bottom:** 2⅝" **Height:** 3¾"
Decoration: Satin, may also be found glossy.

Original Name: No. 325
AKA: Opalescent Swirl

Manufacturer: Hobbs Glass Co. **Date:** 1888
Color: Crystal Opalescent
Value: $55.00 – 65.00
Description — Top: Ground, chamfered outside
Dimensions — Top: 2⅞" **Bottom:** 2⁷⁄₁₆" **Height:** 3¾"
Decoration: Satin, may also be found glossy.

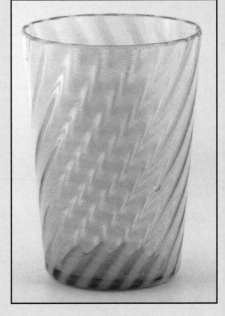

AKA: Swirl

Color: Light Green Opalescent
Value: $55.00 – 65.00
Description — Top: Ground, chamfered
Dimensions — Top: 2¹⁵⁄₁₆" **Bottom:** 2¼" **Height:** 3¹⁵⁄₁₆"

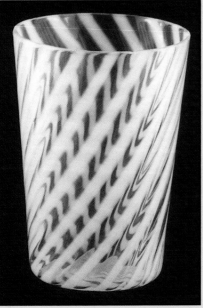

AKA: Swirl

Color: Canary Opalescent
Value: $65.00 – 75.00
Description — Top: Ground, chamfered **Bottom:** Unfinished
Dimensions — Top: 2¹¹⁄₁₆" **Bottom:** 2¼" **Height:** 4"

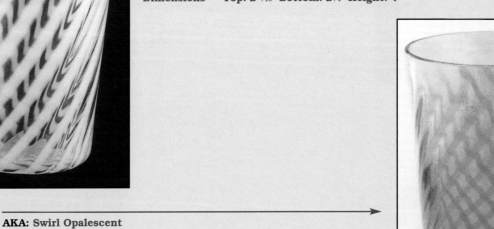
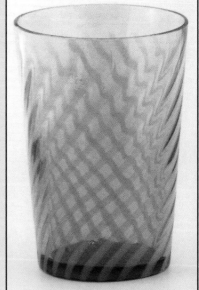

AKA: Swirl Opalescent

Color: Blue Opalescent
Value: $70.00 – 85.00
Description — Top: Ground, chamfered inside and out
   Bottom: Unfinished
Dimensions — Top: 3" **Bottom:** 2⁵⁄₁₆" **Height:** 4⅛"

AKA: Swirl

Manufacturer: Northwood Glass Co.
Color: Crystal Opalescent
Value: $50.00 – 60.00
Description — Top: Ground, chamfer inside and out **Bottom:** Unfinished
Dimensions — Top: 2¹¹⁄₁₆" **Bottom:** 2⁷⁄₁₆" **Height:** 3¹¹⁄₁₆"

AKA: Rubina Opal Swirl

Manufacturer: Northwood Glass Co.
Inner Color: Rubina **Outer Color:** Crystal Opalescent
Value: $90.00 – 110.00
Description — Top: Ground and polished, chamfer inside and out **Bottom:** Concave
Dimensions — Top: 2¹¹⁄₁₆" **Bottom:** 2⁷⁄₁₆" **Height:** 3¹¹⁄₁₆"

AKA: Swirl

Manufacturer: Northwood Glass Co.
Color: Rubina, Crystal Opalescent
Value: $90.00 – 100.00
Description — Top: Ground **Bottom:** Unfinished
Dimensions — Top: 2¾" **Bottom:** 2½" **Height:** 3¾"

AKA: Tight Swirl

Color: Crystal Opalescent
Value: $50.00 – 60.00
Description — Top: Ground **Bottom:** Unfinished
Dimensions — Top: 2¹¹⁄₁₆" **Bottom:** 2½" **Height:** 4⅛"
Decoration: Satin finish.

AKA: Opal Drape

Date: Ca. 1974
Color: Light Green, Amber, or Amethyst, all opalescent.
Value: $35.00 – 45.00
Description — Top: Fire polished **Bottom:** Unfinished
Dimensions — Top: 2¹¹⁄₁₆" **Bottom:** 2¼" **Height:** 3⁷⁄₁₆"
Additional Notes: Believed to have been imported by AA Importing, ca. 1974.

AKA: Blown Swirl

Manufacturer: Northwood Glass Co., Dugan Glass Co. **Date:** 1898
Color: Blue Opalescent
Value: $150.00 – 200.00 Blue, $250.00 – 350.00 Ruby
Description — Top: Ground
Dimensions — Top: 2¹⁵⁄₁₆" **Bottom:** 2⁵⁄₁₆" **Height:** 3⁷⁄₈"
Additional Notes: In green it is a modern tumbler.

Opalescent Miscellaneous

These tumblers are made in the same general manner as other opalescent tumblers. The difference is that their spot molds leave dimples rather than bumps. The cooling process activates a chemical that appears as whiteness surrounding transparent areas.

Original Name: No. 326
AKA: Windows Swirl

Manufacturer: Hobbs Glass Co. **Date:** 1888
Color: Blue Opalescent
Value: $85.00 – 110.00
Description — Top: Ground and polished, chamfered inside and out
   Bottom: Unfinished
Dimensions — Top: 2⅞" **Bottom:** 2⅜" **Height:** 3⅝"

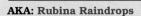

Original Name: No. 333
AKA: Windows Opalescent

Manufacturer: Hobbs Glass Co. **Date:** 1889
Inner Color: Ruby **Outer Color:** Crystal Opalescent
Value: $110.00 – 135.00
Description — Top: Ground and polished **Bottom:** Ground and polished rim and center
Dimensions — Top: 2⅞" **Bottom:** 2⁹⁄₁₆" **Height:** 3¾"

AKA: Rubina Raindrops

Inner Color: Rubina **Outer Color:** Crystal Opalescent
Value: $95.00 – 115.00
Description — Top: Ground and polished, chamfered inside and out
Bottom: Unfinished
Dimensions — Top: 2¹¹⁄₁₆" **Bottom:** 2⁷⁄₁₆" **Height:** 3¹¹⁄₁₆"

← **AKA:** Polka Dot

Inner Color: Orange fading to Crystal **Outer Color:** Crystal
Value: $95.00 – 115.00
Description — Top: Ground **Bottom Figure:** Elongated spots forming a pinwheel
Dimensions — Top: 2¾" **Bottom:** 2⅜" **Height:** 3⁹⁄₁₆"

AKA: 6 row, 17 around →

Color: Amber Opalescent
Value: $45.00 – 55.00
Description — Top: Ground and polished, chamfered inside and out **Bottom:** Full ground
Dimensions — Top: 2⅝" **Bottom:** 2⁵⁄₁₆" **Height:** 3¾"

← **AKA:** 6 row, 10 around

Color: Blue Opalescent
Value: $55.00 – 65.00
Description — Top: Repaired **Bottom:** Unfinished
Dimensions — Top: 2¹¹⁄₁₆" **Bottom:** 2¼" **Height:** 3¹¹⁄₁₆"

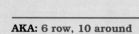

AKA: 6 row, 10 around →

Inner Color: Ruby **Outer Color:** Crystal Opalescent
Value: $90.00 – 110.00
Description — Top: Ground **Bottom Figure:** Dots to center
Dimensions — Top: 2⅞" **Bottom:** 2⁹⁄₁₆" **Height:** 3¹¹⁄₁₆"

AKA: Polka Dot, 5 row, 10 around

Color: Crystal Opalescent
Value: $35.00 – 45.00
Description — Top: Ground, chamfered outside **Bottom Figure:** PD to center
Dimensions — Top: 2¾" **Bottom:** 2⅜" **Height:** 3¹¹⁄₁₆"

AKA: Polka Dot, 6 row, 10 around

Color: Light Green Opalescent
Value: $55.00 – 65.00
Description — Top: Flat ground **Bottom:** Unfinished
Dimensions — Top: 2¹⁵⁄₁₆" **Bottom:** 2⁵⁄₁₆" **Height:** 3¹⁵⁄₁₆"

Original Name: Eye Dot

Manufacturer: Fenton Art Glass Co. **Date:** 1940 – 1960
Color: Blue Opalescent
Value: $65.00 – 75.00
Description — Top: Ground and polished, chamfered outside
   Bottom: Unfinished
Dimensions — Top: 2¹³⁄₁₆" **Bottom:** 2⁹⁄₁₆" **Height:** 3⅞"
Additional Notes: Made for L. G. Wright in Ruby & Blue Opalescent.

Original Name: Polka Dot
AKA: 6 row, 9 around

Manufacturer: West Virginia Glass Co. **Date:** Ca. 1894
Color: Blue Opalescent
Value: $75.00 – 100.00
Description — Top: Ground and polished, chamfered outside **Bottom:** Unfinished
Dimensions — Top: 2¹³⁄₁₆" **Bottom:** 2⁹⁄₁₆" **Height:** 3⅞"

Original Name: Polka Dot
AKA: 6 row, 9 around

Manufacturer: West Virginia Glass Co. **Date:** 1894
Inner Color: Ruby **Outer Color:** Crystal Opalescent.
Value: $125.00 – 160.00
Description — Top: 2¾" **Bottom:** 2½" **Bottom Figure:** 3¾"

AKA: Opal Lattice

Color: Blue Opalescent
Value: $85.00 – 110.00
Description — Top: Flat ground, chamfered outside
Dimensions — Top: 2¹³⁄₁₆" **Bottom:** 2⁷⁄₁₆" **Height:** 3¾"

AKA: Opal Lattice

Inner Color: Ruby **Outer Color:** Crystal Opalescent
Value: $110.00 – 135.00
Description — Top: Full ground, chamfered inside and out
Dimensions — Top: 2⅞" **Bottom:** 2½" **Height:** 3¾"
Decoration: Frosted.

AKA: Opal Lattice

Manufacturer: Northwood Glass Co. at Martin's Ferry, OH **Date:** 1890
Color: Canary Opalescent
Value: $100.00 – 125.00
Description — Top: Ground, chamfered inside **Bottom Figure:** 20-point opalescent star
Dimensions — Top: 2¾" **Bottom:** 2½" **Height:** 4¹⁄₁₆"
Decoration: Satin (frosted) inside and out.

Opalescent Figures

These tumblers are made in a similar manner to Polka Dot, yet the spot mold is considerably more complex. It leaves not bumps, but intricate designs which, when cooled and warmed-in, often represent natural figures.

Original Name: Coral
AKA: Seaweed

Manufacturer: Hobbs Glass Co.
  Date: 1889
Inner Color: Ruby **Outer Color:** Crystal
  Opalescent
Value: $100.00 – 150.00
Description — Top: Flat ground,
  chamfered outside **Bottom:** Unfinished
Dimensions — Top: 2⅞" **Bottom:** 2⅝"
  Height: 3⅞"

Original Name: Coral
AKA: Seaweed

Manufacturer: Hobbs Glass Co. **Date:** 1889
Inner Color: Ruby **Outer Color:** Crystal Opalescent
Value: $100.00 – 150.00
Description — Top: Ground **Bottom:** Opalescence
  continues on bottom.
Dimensions — Top: 2⅞" **Bottom:** 2⁹⁄₁₆" **Height:** 3⅞"
Decoration: Satin finish inside and out.

Color: Blue
Value: $100.00 – 135.00

AKA: Scottish Moor

Inner Color: Ruby **Outer Color:** Crystal Opalescent
Value: $75.00 – 100.00
Description — Top: Flat ground, chamfered outside **Bottom:** Unfinished
Dimensions — Top: 2¹¹⁄₁₆" **Bottom:** 2⁵⁄₁₆" **Height:** 3¾"
Decoration: Gold on top rim.
Additional Notes: Possibly of European origin; other forms
  of this pattern are not American shapes.

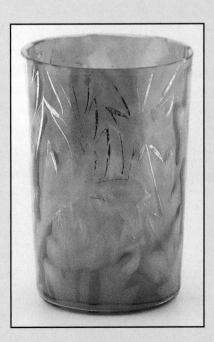

AKA: Scottish Moor

Inner Color: Orange/Apricot **Outer Layer:** Crystal Opalescent
Value: $150.00 – 200.00
Description — Top: Ground **Bottom:** Opalescence continues onto bottom.
Dimensions — Top: 2¹¹⁄₁₆" **Bottom:** 2¼" **Height:** 3¾"

Original Name: No. 182
AKA: Buttons & Braids

Manufacturer: Jefferson Glass Co. **Date:** 1905
Color: Crystal, Blue, Green, and Ruby Opalescent
Value: $75.00 – 100.00
Description — Top: Ground and polished, chamfered inside **Bottom:** Unfinished
Dimensions — Top: 2⅞" **Bottom:** 2⅝" **Height:** 3¹¹⁄₁₆"
Additional Notes: Fenton made this pattern after 1910, both pressed and blown (see page 117). Fenton's blown version has 12 buttons, Jefferson's has 15.

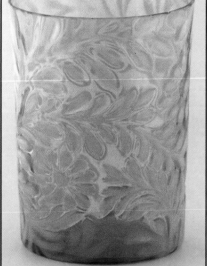

AKA: Daisy & Fern

Manufacturer: Northwood Glass Co., Elwood City, PA **Date:** 1895
Color: Blue Opalescent
Value: $65.00 – 80.00
Description — Top: Ground **Bottom:** Unfinished
Dimensions — Top: 2⅞" **Bottom:** 2⁹⁄₁₆" **Height:** 3½"
Additional Notes: Dugan Glass Co. made this pattern as late as 1917.

AKA: Daisy & Fern

Manufacturer: L. G. Wright Glass Co. **Date:** Ca. 1950
Color: Canary Opalescent
Value: $50.00 – 65.00
Description — Top: Ground, chamfered outside **Bottom:** Unfinished
Dimensions — Top: 2¹⁵⁄₁₆" **Bottom:** 2⁷⁄₁₆" **Height:** 3¾"
Additional Notes: Made for Wright by Fenton Art Glass Co.

AKA: Daisy & Fern

Manufacturer: Northwood Glass Co., Elwood City, PA **Date:** 1895
Inner Color: Crystal Opalescent
Value: $45.00 – 55.00
Description — Top: Ground, chamfered outside **Bottom:** Unfinished
Dimensions — Top: 2¹³⁄₁₆" **Bottom:** 2½" **Height:** 3¹¹⁄₁₆"

AKA: Daisy & Fern

Manufacturer: L. G. Wright **Date:** Ca. 1950 – 1970
Color: Blue Opalescent
Value: $50.00 – 65.00
Description — Top: Ground **Bottom:** Unfinished
Dimensions — Top: 2⅞" **Bottom:** 2⁹⁄₁₆" **Height:** 3¹⁵⁄₁₆"

Original Name: Fern

Manufacturer: West Virginia Glass Co. **Date:** 1894
Inner Color: Ruby **Outer Color:** Crystal Opalescent
Value: $200.00 – 240.00
Description — Top: Ground and polished, chamfered outside **Bottom:** Unfinished
Dimensions — Top: 2¹³⁄₁₆" **Bottom:** 2⁹⁄₁₆" **Height:** 3⅞"

AKA: Christmas Snowflake

Manufacturer: Northwood Glass Co. at Martins Ferry, OH **Date:** 1894
Color: Ruby Opalescent
Value: $180.00 – 230.00
Description — Top: Ground, chamfered inside and out **Bottom:** Unfinished
Dimensions — Top: 2¾" **Bottom:** 2⁷⁄₁₆" **Height:** 3¾"

AKA: Daisy in Criss-Cross

Manufacturer: Beaumont Glass Co.
  Date: 1897
Inner Color: Crystal Opalescent
Value: $75.00 – 100.00
Description — Top: Ground and polished
Dimensions — Top: 2⅞" **Bottom:** 2½"
  Height: 3¹³⁄₁₆"

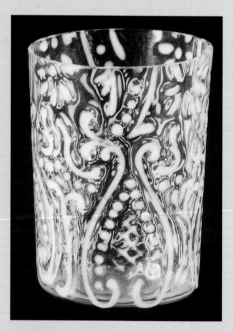

Original Name: Opaline Brocade
AKA: Spanish Lace

Manufacturer: Northwood Glass Co.;
  Indiana, PA **Date:** 1899
Color: Crystal, Ruby, and Blue Opalescent
Value: $45.00 – 65.00 Crystal Opalescent,
  other colors higher.
Description — Top: Ground and polished.
Dimensions — Top: 3" **Bottom:** 2¼" **Height:** 3⅞"

AKA: Arabian Nights

Manufacturer: Northwood Glass Co.
  Date: Ca 1895
Color: Crystal Opalescent
Value: $125.00 – 170.00
Description — Top: Ground and polished
  Bottom: Unfinished
Dimensions — Top: 2¹³⁄₁₆" **Bottom:** 2½"
  Height: 3⅝"

AKA: Arabian Nights

Manufacturer: Northwood Glass Co.
  Date: Ca. 1895
Color: Blue Opalescent
Value: $150.00 – 200.00
Description — Top: Ground and polished
  Bottom: Unfinished
Dimensions — Top: 2¾" **Bottom:** 2½"
  Height: 3½"

AKA: Arabian Nights

Inner Color: Ruby **Outer Color:** Crystal
   Opalescent
Value: $350.00 – 400.00
Description — Top: Ground and polished
   Bottom Figure: Impressed pontil
Dimensions — Top: 2¹³⁄₁₆" **Bottom:** 2½"
   Height: 3¾"

AKA: Daffodil

Manufacturer: Northwood Glass Co.;
   Wheeling, WV **Date:** 1903
Color: Crystal Opalescent
Value: $75.00 – 100.00
Description — Top: Flat ground
   Bottom: Unfinished
Dimensions — Top: 3¹¹⁄₁₆" **Bottom:** 2¼"
   Height: 4"

AKA: Poinsettia

Manufacturer: Northwood Glass Co.;
   Wheeling, WV **Date:** 1903
Inner Color: Ruby **Outer Color:** Crystal
   Opalescent
Value: $125.00 – 150.00
Description — Top: Ground, chamfered
   outside **Bottom:** Unfinished
Dimensions — Top: 3¹⁄₁₆" **Bottom:** 2¼"
   Height: 4"

AKA: Poinsettia

Manufacturer: Northwood Glass Co.; Wheeling, WV **Date:** 1903
Inner Color: Blue Opalescent
Value: $175.00 – 225.00
Description — Top: Ground, chamfered outside **Bottom:** Unfinished
Dimensions — Top: 3" **Bottom:** 2¼" **Height:** 3⅞"

AKA: Poinsettia

Manufacturer: Northwood Glass Co.; Wheeling, WV **Date:** 1903
Color: Light Green Opalescent
Value: $150.00 – 200.00
Description — Top: Ground, chamfered outside **Bottom:** Unfinished
Dimensions — Top: 3" **Bottom:** 2⁵⁄₁₆" **Height:** 4"

AKA: Poinsettia

Manufacturer: Northwood Glass Co.;
   Wheeling, WV **Date:** 1903
Color: Crystal Opalescent
Value: $75.00 – 100.00
Description — Top: Ground and polished
Dimensions — Top: 3" **Bottom:** 2¼"
   Height: 3⅞"

AKA: Floral Eyelet

Color: Blue Opalescent
Value: $225.00 – 275.00
Description — Top: Ground and polished
Dimensions — Top: 2⅝" **Bottom:** 2⅜"
   Height: 3½"

OAKA: Swirling Maze

Manufacturer: Jefferson Glass Co.
   Date: 1905
Color: Canary, Blue, and Ruby Opalescent
Value: $140.00 – 190.00,
   $200.00 – 250.00 Ruby Opalescent
Description — Top: Polished
Dimensions — Top: 2¹⁵⁄₁₆" **Bottom:** 2¼"
   Height: 4"
Additional Notes: In 2002, a blue tumbler
   sold on eBay for $135.00.

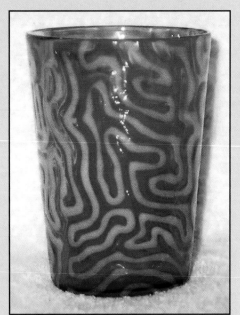

AKA: Swirling Maze

Manufacturer: Jefferson Glass Co.
Inner Color: Ruby **Outer Color:** Crystal Opalescent
Value: $200.00 – 250.00
Description — Top: Ground and polished **Bottom:** Unfinished
Dimensions — Top: 2⅞" **Bottom:** 2¼" **Height:** 4"

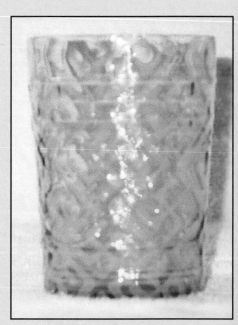

AKA: Swastika

Manufacturer: Dugan Glass Co. **Date:** Ca. 1907
Color: Green Opalescent
Value: $300.00 – 380.00
Description — Top: Ground
Dimensions — Top: 2¹⁵⁄₁₆" **Bottom:** 2½" **Height:** 3¹⁵⁄₁₆"
Additional Notes: Blown into Diamonds and Clubs mold.

Onyx

These wares were only produced for about nine months. The glass was not stable. What would be considered minor damage on other glass is accepted without discount. Major damage is balanced with availability of collectible pieces.

See Chapter 25 for Floradine, an opalescent version of this pattern.

Original Name: Oriental
AKA: Onyx

Manufacturer: Dalzell, Gilmore & Leighton Glass Co. **Date:** 1889
Color: Multiple layers, all opalescent
Value: $250.00 – 350.00
Description — Top: Ground
Additional Notes: Partial pattern.

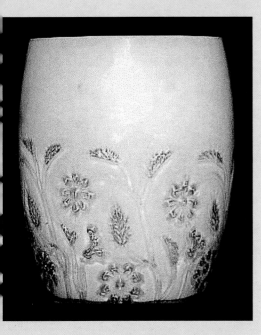

Original Name: Oriental
AKA: Onyx

Manufacturer: Dalzell, Gilmore & Leighton Glass Co. **Date:** 1889
Color: Multiple layers, all opalescent
Value: $200.00 – 250.00
Description — Top: Ground
Additional Notes: Partial pattern.

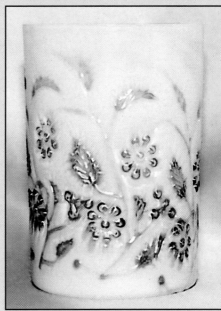

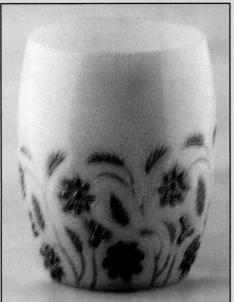

Original Name: Oriental
AKA: Onyx

Manufacturer: Dalzell, Gilmore & Leighton Glass Co. **Date:** 1889
Color: Multiple layers, all opalescent
Value: $200.00 – 250.00
Description — Top: Ground
Additional Notes: Full pattern.

Original Name: Oriental
AKA: Onyx

Manufacturer: Dalzell, Gilmore & Leighton Glass Co. **Date:** 1889
Color: Multiple layers, all opalescent
Value: $250.00 – 350.00
Description — Top: Ground
Additional Notes: Full pattern.

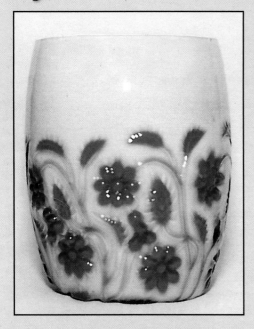

Original Name: Oriental
AKA: Onyx

Manufacturer: Dalzell, Gilmore & Leighton Glass Co. **Date:** 1889
Inner Color: Opalescent **Outer Color:** Ruby
Value: $2000.00 – 2500.00
Description — Top: Ground
Additional Notes: Partial pattern.

Original Name: Oriental
AKA: Onyx

Manufacturer: Dalzell, Gilmore & Leighton Glass Co. **Date:** 1889
Inner Color: Opalescent **Outer Color:** Bronze
Value: $2000.00 – 2500.00
Description — Top: Ground
Additional Notes: Partial pattern.

Original Name: Oriental
AKA: Onyx

Manufacturer: Dalzell, Gilmore & Leighton Glass Co. **Date:** 1889
Inner Color: Opalescent **Outer Color:** Orange
Value: $2000.00 – 2500.00
Description — Top: Ground
Additional Notes: Full pattern.

Original Name: Oriental
AKA: Onyx

Manufacturer: Dalzell, Gilmore & Leighton Glass Co. **Date:** 1889
Inner Color: Opalescent **Outer Color:** Orange
Value: $2000.00 – 2500.00
Description — Top: Ground
Additional Notes: Partial pattern.

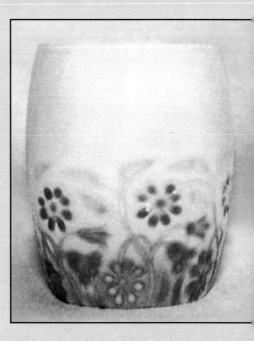

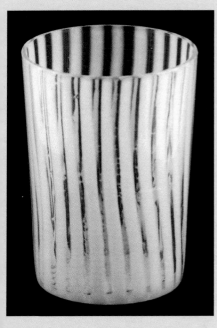

AKA: Opalescent Stripe

Color: Canary Opalescent
Value: $90.00 – 110.00
Description — Top: Flat ground, chamfered inside
Dimensions — Top: 2¾" **Bottom:** 2⅜" **Height:** 3¹¹⁄₁₆"
Additional Notes: 24 ribs.

AKA: Opalescent Stripe

Color: Crystal Opalescent
Value: $45.00 – 60.00
Description — Top: Flat ground, chamfered outside
Dimensions — Top: 2¹³⁄₁₆" **Bottom:** 2⁹⁄₁₆" **Height:** 3⅝"
Additional Notes: 20 ribs.

AKA: 4 row, 9 around

Color: Crystal
Value: $100.00 – 125.00
Decoration: Ruby stained, seven cut panels.
Additional Notes: This is NOT opalescent.

Original Name: Neapolitan

Manufacturer: Hobbs, Brockunier & Co. **Date:** 1887
Inner Color: Ruby Opalescent **Outer Color:** Crystal
Value: $200.00 – 275.00
Description — Top: Ground
Dimensions — Top: 2¾" **Bottom:** 2½" **Height:** 4"
Decoration: Satin.
Additional Notes: Vertical stripes to match pitcher.

Original Name: Neapolitan

Manufacturer: Hobbs, Brockunier & Co. **Date:** 1887
Color: Blue Opalescent
Value: $125.00 – 150.00
Description — Top: Ground and polished
Dimensions — Top: 2¾" **Bottom:** 2½" **Height:** 4"

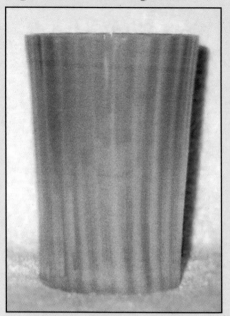

AKA: Pink Opaline

Inner Color: Rubina **Outer Color:** Crystal
Opalescent
Value: $100.00 – 150.00
Description — Top: Ground and polished
Dimensions — Top: 2¹¹⁄₁₆" **Bottom:** 2³⁄₁₆"
Height: 3⅞"

AKA: Wide Stripe

Manufacturer: Consolidated Lamp and
Glass Co.
Inner Color: Ruby **Outer Color:** Crystal
Opalescent
Value: $140.00 – 160.00
Description — Top: Ground and polished
Dimensions — Top: 2¹³⁄₁₆" **Bottom:** 2⁹⁄₁₆"
Height: 3⅝"

AKA: Opalescent Stripe

Color: Blue Opalescent
Value: $90.00 – 110.00
Description — Top: Ground and polished
Dimensions — Top: 2¹¹⁄₁₆" **Bottom:** 2⁵⁄₁₆"
Height: 3⅝"
Additional Notes: Nine vertical optics.

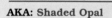

AKA: Wide Stripe

Inner Color: Ruby Amber **Outer Color:** Opalescent
Value: $200.00 – 250.00
Description — Top: Ground and polished
Dimensions — Top: 2¹⁵⁄₁₆" **Bottom:** 2⅜" **Height:** 3½"
Additional Notes: Ten opalescent stripes.

AKA: Shaded Opal

Manufacturer: Possibly Phoenix Glass Co. **Date:** 1886
Inner Color: Shaded Peach **Intermediate Color:** Crystal **Outer Color:** Opalescent Crystal
Value: $150.00 – 200.00
Description — Top: Ground and polished, chamfered inside and out
Dimensions — Top: 2¾" **Bottom:** 2⁷⁄₁₆" **Height:** 3¾"
Additional Notes: Deep crackle, expanded, ten ribs.

Etched

Both pressed and blown tumblers have been included in this section. In addition to etched, sandblasted and copper-wheel-engraved tumblers can be found here. Many people have difficulty distinguishing between the finished surfaces of the three processes. Only the very intricate designs can be etched, and gray cut and engraved designs usually show parallel striations from the cutting wheel. These striations are absent in etchings or sand blastings. Often sand blasting, which is done with a stencil, will show areas which blew past the stencil and have edges that are not distinct.

AKA: Trefoil

Color: Crystal
Value: $10.00 – 15.00
Description — Top: Ground
   Bottom: Unfinished
Dimensions — Top: 2¹¹⁄₁₆" **Bottom:** 2½"
   Height: 3⁹⁄₁₆"
Additional Notes: Basic A. B. Knight needle etching. (Knight made the machines to do needle etching.)

AKA: Trefoil

Color: Crystal
Value: $10.00 – 15.00
Description — Top: Fire polished
   Bottom: Unfinished **Bottom Figure:** Small number *3*
Dimensions — Top: 3" **Bottom:** 2¼"
   Height: 3⅝"
Additional Notes: Design was etched into plunger and is inside of tumbler. This tumbler is pressed.

AKA: Trefoil

Manufacturer: Rochester Tumbler Co.
   Date: Ca. 1915
Color: Crystal
Value: $35.00 – 50.00
Description — Top: Fire polished
   Bottom Figure: Full concave grind
Dimensions — Top: 2⅝" **Bottom:** 2½"
   Height: 3⅝"
Decoration: Needle etching, cut flutes.
Additional Notes: 30 cut flutes on bottom.

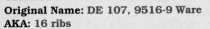

Color: Crystal
Value: $15.00 – 25.00
Description — Top: Fire polished
   Bottom: Unfinished
Dimensions — Top: 3" **Bottom:** 2⁷⁄₁₆"
   Height: 3¹¹⁄₁₆"

Original Name: DE 107, 9516-9 Ware
AKA: 16 ribs

Manufacturer: Fry Glass Co. **Date:** Ca. 1918
Color: Crystal
Value: $20.00 – 30.00
Description — Top: Fire polished
   Bottom: Unfinished
Dimensions — Top: 3" **Bottom:** 2½" **Height:** 3⅞"
Additional Notes: 16 optic ribs.

AKA: Ten Optic Flared

Color: Crystal
Value: $15.00 – 20.00
Description — Top: Fire polished
Dimensions — Top: 2¹⁵⁄₁₆" **Bottom:** 2⁷⁄₁₆"
　Height: 3¹³⁄₁₆"
Decoration: Etched design, six repeats.
Additional Notes: Ten optic panels.

AKA: Frit Decorated

Color: Crystal
Value: $15.00 – 20.00
Description — Top: Fire polished
　Bottom Figure: 5-point irregular star
Dimensions — Top: 2¾" **Bottom:** 2" rim
　Height: 3¹¹⁄₁₆"
Decoration: The decoration is of powdered
glass (frit) that was glued on in a pattern,
and then fired to fix the powder to the
glass.
Additional Notes: This is a pressed
tumbler. There are 14 interior optic
panels.

AKA: Sand Blast Clover

Color: Crystal
Value: $10.00 – 15.00
Description — Top: Fire polished
Dimensions — Top: 2¾" **Bottom:** 2½"
　Height: 3¾"
Additional Notes: This design is cut
into a steel plate; the plate becomes a
stencil through which sand is blown
by compressed air, abrading the pattern
into the glass.

← **AKA: Sand Blast Daisy**

Color: Crystal
Value: $10.00 – 15.00
Description — Top: Fire polished **Bottom:** Unfinished
Dimensions — Top: 2⅝" **Bottom:** 2⁷⁄₁₆" **Height:** 3¾"
Decoration: Four rows of daisies, ten around.

AKA: Sand Blast Flowers →

Color: Crystal
Value: $10.00 – 15.00
Description — Top: Fire polished **Bottom:** Unfinished
Dimensions — Top: 2¹¹⁄₁₆" **Bottom:** 2⁷⁄₁₆" **Height:** 3⅞"

AKA: Silkscreen Flowers

Color: Crystal
Value: $15.00 – 20.00
Description — Top: Fire polished
Dimensions — Top: 2⅝" **Bottom:** 2⁷⁄₁₆"
   Height: 3¾"
Additional Notes: This decoration is
   paint that has been applied through a
   cloth stencil.

AKA: Sandblast Ferns

Color: Crystal
Value: $15.00 – 20.00
Decoration: Sandblast decoration.

Original Name: No. 2930 Line
AKA: Pied Piper

Manufacturer: A. H. Heisey & Co.
   Date: Ca. 1922
Color: Crystal
Value: $35.00 – 50.00
Description — Top: Polished
   Bottom: Unfinished
Dimensions — Top: 2¾" **Bottom:** 2⁷⁄₁₆"
   Height: 3⅝"
Decoration: No. 439 Pied Piper etch.

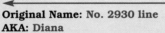

Original Name: No. 2930 line
AKA: Diana

Manufacturer: A. H. Heisey & Co. **Date:** 1925
Color: Crystal
Value: $35.00 – 50.00
Description — Top: Polished **Bottom:** Unfinished
Dimensions — Top: 2¾" **Bottom:** 2⁷⁄₁₆" **Height:** 3⅝"
Decoration: No. 442 Diana etch.

AKA: Putti

Color: Crystal
Value: $20.00 – 25.00
Description — Top: Cracked off, glazed **Bottom:** Unfinished
Dimensions — Top: 2¹¹⁄₁₆" **Bottom:** 2½" **Height:** 3⅞"
Decoration: Putti, butterflies, light etching.

AKA: Putti & Musical Instruments

Color: Crystal
Value: $20.00 – 25.00
Description — Top: Ground and polished
  Bottom: Unfinished
Dimensions — Top: 2¾" **Bottom:** 2⁵⁄₁₆"
  Height: 3¹³⁄₁₆"
Decoration: Etched putti and violin, etc.

AKA: Floral Band

Color: Crystal
Value: $15.00 – 20.00
Description — Top: Ground and polished
  Bottom: Unfinished
Dimensions — Top: 2⁷⁄₁₆" **Bottom:** 2³⁄₁₆"
  Height: 3⁹⁄₁₆"
Decoration: Etched floral band, gold
  bands.

Original Name: DE 18, 7715 Ware
AKA: Rose

Manufacturer: Fry Glass Co. **Date:** 1911
Color: Crystal
Value: $35.00 – 50.00
Description — Top: Fire polished
  Bottom: Unfinished
Dimensions — Top: 2¹¹⁄₁₆" **Bottom:** 2½"
  Height: 3¾"
Decoration: Double plate etching.
Additional Notes: Ten optics.

AKA: Flamingo Habitat

Manufacturer: Hobbs, Brockunier & Co. **Date:** 1880
Color: Crystal
Value: $40.00 – 70.00
Description — Top: Fire polished
Dimensions — Top: 2¹¹⁄₁₆" **Bottom:** 2⁷⁄₁₆" **Height:** 3¹¹⁄₁₆"
Additional Notes: Etched flamingo habitat.

AKA: Oasis

Manufacturer: Hobbs, Brockunier & Co. **Date:** 1881
Color: Crystal
Value: $40.00 – 70.00
Description — Top: Fire polished **Bottom:** Ground and polished
Dimensions — Top: 2⅞" **Bottom:** 2½" **Height:** 3⅞"
Decoration: Vapor-etched tropical scene.
Additional Notes: This tumbler is pressed.

AKA: Queen Victoria

Date: 1897
Color: Crystal
Value: $35.00 – 50.00
Description — Top: Fire polished
  Bottom: Unfinished
Dimensions — Top: 2¾" **Bottom:** 2½"
  Height: 3¹³⁄₁₆"
Decoration: Gold, vapor-etched
  Diamond Jubilee portrait.

AKA: Christopher Columbus

Date: 1893
Color: Crystal
Value: $50.00 – 75.00
Description — Top: Fire polished
Dimensions — Top: 2¹¹⁄₁₆" **Bottom:** 2⁷⁄₁₆"
  Height: 3½"
Additional Notes: Columbian Exposition.

AKA: Columbian Exposition

Date: 1893
Color: Crystal
Value: $50.00 – 75.00
Decoration: Etched design of Columbus
  landing.

AKA: Blockhouse

Color: Crystal
Value: $35.00 – 50.00
Description — Top: Fire polished
Dimensions — Top: 2¾" **Bottom:** 2⁷⁄₁₆" **Height:** 3¾"
Decoration: Vapor-etched souvenir of the Pittsburg
  Exposition shows blockhouse and commemorates
  the Pittsburg sesquicentennial, possibly 1909.
Additional Notes: For a short period of time
  around the beginning of the 1900s, the city's
  name was spelled without the final *h*.

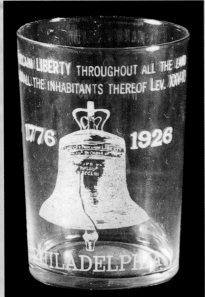

AKA: Liberty Bell

Date: 1926
Color: Crystal
Value: $25.00 – 30.00
Description — Top: Fire polished
Dimensions — Top: 2¹¹⁄₁₆" **Bottom:** 2⅜" **Height:** 3¾"
Decoration: The decoration is silk screened.
Additional Notes: Commemorates 150 years since the signing of the Declaration of Independence.

AKA: Pan Am Expo

Date: 1901
Color: Crystal
Value: $35.00 – 50.00
Description — Top: Fire polished
Dimensions — Top: 2⁵⁄₁₆" **Bottom:** 2³⁄₁₆"
   Height: 3⁹⁄₁₆"
Decoration: Gold band, souvenir for "Pan American Exposition, Buffalo, 1901."

AKA: Prayer

Color: Crystal
Value: $15.00 – 25.00
Description — Top: Fire polished
Dimensions — Top: 2¹¹⁄₁₆" **Bottom:** 2⁷⁄₁₆"
   Height: 3¹³⁄₁₆"
Decoration: Vapor etched "Now I Lay Me Down to Sleep" poem.

AKA: Home Sweet Home

Color: Crystal
Value: $15.00 - 25.00
Description — Top: Ground
Dimensions — Top: 2¾" **Bottom:** 2⅜"
   Height: 3¹¹⁄₁₆"
Decoration: Etched with poem, "Home Sweet Home."

AKA: Lord's Prayer

Color: Crystal
Value: $15.00 – 25.00
Description — Top: Fire polished
Dimensions — Top: 2¹¹⁄₁₆" **Bottom:** 2⁷⁄₁₆"
   Height: 3¹¹⁄₁₆"
Decoration: Etched with the Lord's Prayer.

AKA: Merry Christmas

Color: Crystal
Value: $15.00 – 30.00
Description — Top: Cracked off, fire polished
Dimensions — Top: 2¾" **Bottom:** 2⁷⁄₁₆"
   Height: 2⅝"

AKA: Remember the Maine

Date: 1898
Color: Crystal
Value: $35.00 – 50.00
Description — Top: Ground
Dimensions — Top: 2¹¹⁄₁₆" **Bottom:** 2⁷⁄₁₆"
   Height: 3⅞"
Decoration: Etched "Remember the Maine, Feb. 15th, 1898."

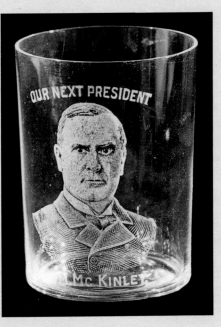

AKA: Admiral Dewey

Date: 1898
Color: Crystal
Value: $25.00 – 31.00
Description — Top: Fire polished
Dimensions — Top: 2¹³/₁₆" **Bottom:** 2⁵/₁₆"
   Height: 3⅞"
Decoration: Silkscreen picture of Admiral George Dewey.

AKA: McKinley 1

Date: 1896
Color: Crystal
Value: $45.00 – 60.00
Description — Top: Fire polished
   Bottom: Unfinished
Dimensions — Top: 2¹¹/₁₆" **Bottom:** 2½"
   Height: 3⁹/₁₆"
Decoration: "Our Next President William McKinley."

AKA: McKinley 2

Date: 1901
Color: Crystal
Value: $45.00 – 60.00
Description — Top: Fire polished
   Bottom: Unfinished
Dimensions — Top: 2¹¹/₁₆" **Bottom:** 2⁷/₁₆"
   Height: 3¹³/₁₆"
Decoration: "Our President 1897 to 1901."

AKA: Monogrammed

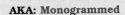

Color: Crystal
Value: $15.00 – 25.00
Description — Top: Fire polished
Dimensions — Top: 2¾" **Bottom:** 2⁷/₁₆" **Height:** 4"
Decoration: The design is copper wheel engraved.

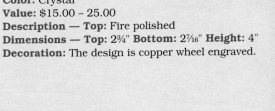

AKA: Webster Springs

Color: Crystal
Value: $25.00 – 35.00
Description — Top: Ground
Dimensions — Top: 2¾" **Bottom:** 2⁵/₁₆" **Height:** 3¹³/₁₆"
Decoration: Etched "Webster Springs Hotel, Addison, W. Va." Hotel burned in 1920s; the town has been known as Webster Springs for many years.

Appendix A

Companies That Made Glass

This list is not intended to be a complete list of glass manufacturers. These companies had an impact on the glass industry and their wares have become the heart of many collections and accumulations. The listings for which we have catalog illustrations are shown. These illustrations are not intended to be complete, but are meant to show the variety of tumblers made by the various companies. Some companies like A. J. Beatty and Rochester Tumbler made thousands of patterns and millions of tumblers. Many companies made bar tumblers as stock items because they could always be sold to hotels, restaurants, etc., even when the economy was depressed.

Adams & Co. — Founded in 1851. Produced pressed tablewares and lamps. Joined U. S. Glass in 1891.

Aetna Glass & Mfg. Co. — Established in Bellaire, Ohio, in 1879. Made primarily pressed tablewares. Noted for unusual pressed pieces. Effectively closed in 1889.

A. J. Beatty & Sons — Founded in Steubenville, Ohio, in 1862. Primary output was pressed and blown tumblers and goblets. By 1886, it was producing pressed tablewares in colors and opalescents. Moved to Tiffin, Ohio, in 1888 and joined U. S. Glass in 1891. Factory closed in the 1980s.

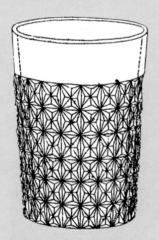
No. 560 — 6 oz.

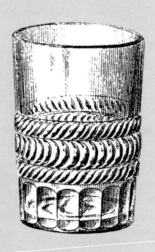
No. 1201 — 9¾ oz.

No. 1202 — 9¾ oz.

No. 1203 — 9¾ oz.

No. 1204 — 9¾ oz.

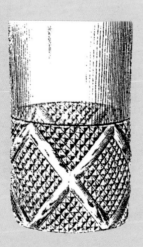
No. 1205 — 9¾ oz.

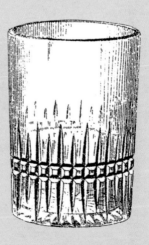
No. 1206 — 9¾ oz.

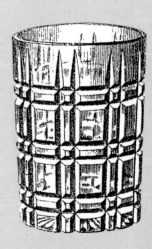
No. 1207 — 9¾ oz.

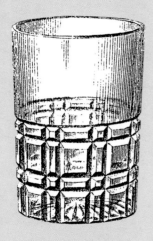

No. 1208 — 9¾ oz.

No. 1210 — 9¾ oz.

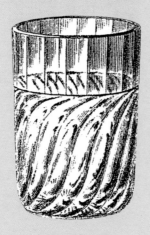

No. 1211 — 9½ oz.

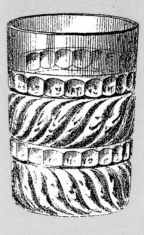

No. 1212 — 9½ oz.

No. 1213 — 8¾ oz.

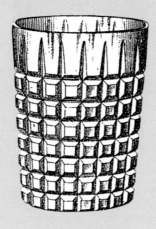

No. 1214 — 8¾ oz.

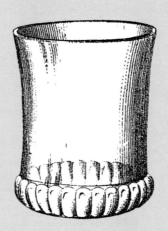

No. 1215 — 8½ oz.

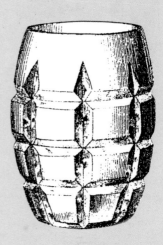

No. 1216 — 9¾ oz.

No. 1217 — 9¾ oz.

No. 1218 — 9 oz.

No. 1219 — 9¾ oz.

No. 1220 — 9¾ oz.

237

No. 27 — 9½ oz.

No. 28 — 9½ oz.

No. 29 — 9½ oz.

No. 36 — 9 oz.

No. 37 — 9 oz.

No. 74 — 10½ oz.

No. 75 — 10 oz.

No. 158 — 8 oz.

No. 159 — 8 oz.

No. 160 — 10 oz.

No. 161 — 10⅛ oz.

No. 161 — 10⅛ oz.

No. 630, Engraved No. 79

No. 630, Engraved No. 92

No. 630, Engraved No. 97

No. 630, Engraved No. 98

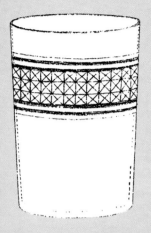

No. 630, Engraved No. 106

No. 630, Engraved No. 107

No. 637, Engraved No. 64

No. 1754, Engraved No. 41

Atterbury & Co. — Organized in 1865, in Pittsburgh's South Side. It made much opaque glass, both white and colored. Closed in 1894.

Bakewell and others. — Founded in Pittsburgh in 1808. The Bakewell family took on various partners during the operation of the glass factory. It produced both pressed and blown wares. Closed ca. 1882.

Beatty Brady Glass Co. — Organized in Dunkirk, Indiana, in 1896. Produced pressed tablewares. Joined National Glass Co. in 1899.

Beaumont Glass Co. — Organized in Martin's Ferry, Ohio, in 1896. Began as a decorating house. Made blown and pressed wares, often with decorations. Became Tygart Valley Glass in 1906.

Bellaire Goblet Co. — Founded in 1876, in Bellaire, Ohio. Moved to Findlay, Ohio, in 1888. Joined United States Glass Co. in 1892. Originally a goblet factory, it began making tableware in the late 1880s.

Boston & Sandwich Glass Co. — Founded in 1825 in Sandwich, on Cape Cod, MA. Made pressed and blown bar and tablewares; ceased production ing 1887.

Brilliant Glass Works — Organized in 1879 in La Grange, Ohio, as Novelty Glass Co. In 1881, both the plant name and the town's name were changed to Brilliant; this plant operated under several names for a total of about eight years in its 20-year life. Some pressed tablewares were produced here. The plant burned in 1897.

Bryce Bros. — Founded in about 1850, as Bryce and McKee. Reorganized in 1882 as Bryce Bros. Produced tablewares. Joined U. S. Glass Co. in 1892.

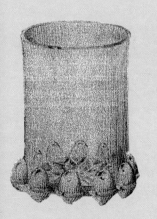

← Pint, 178

½ Pint, 179 →

← ½ Pint, 180

No. 1105 — 7 oz.   No. 1106 — 7 oz.   No. 1107 — 10 oz.   No. 1108 — 10 oz.   No. 1109 — 7 oz.

No. 1110 — 7 oz.   ½ Pint — Jersey   ½ Pint — Puritan   ½ Pint — Fashion

Atterbury & Co. — Organized in 1865, in Pittsburgh's South Side. It made much opaque glass, both whit and colored. Closed in 1894.

Bakewell and others. — Founded in Pittsburgh in 1808. The Bakewell family took on various partner during the operation of the glass factory. It produced both pressed and blown wares. Closed ca. 1882.

Buckeye Glass Co. — Founded in 1878 in Martins Ferry, Ohio. Made blown and pressed tablewares Ceased operations in about 1894.

Buckeye Tumbler Co. — Founded in Shadyside, Ohio, in about 1909. Made blown tumblers.

Cambridge Glass Co. — Founded in about 1902 by National Glass Co., in Cambridge, Ohio. Produced ba and tablewares. Ceased operations in 1954.

Bell-Shaped Tumbler   Straight Tumbler   Buzz Saw

Campbell, Jones & Co. — Founded in 1865, in Pittsburgh's South Side. It produced pressed tablewares The factory burned in 1891 and was never rebuilt.

Canton Glass Co. — Founded in 1883, in Canton, Ohio. Burned out in 1890 and moved to Marion, Indiana. Produced tablewares. Joined National Glass Co. in 1899.

No. 95 Water Set. Engraved 220. by **Canton Glass Co.**

Central Glass Co. — Founded in Wheeling, West Virginia, in 1863. Made bar and tablewares. Joined U. S. Glass Co. in 1891.

Central Glass Works. — Reorganized by Central Glass Co. management and workers in 1896. Produced pressed and blown tablewares. Absorbed by Imperial Glass in 1939.

Challinor, Taylor & Co. — Organized in 1883, in Tarentum, Pennslyvania. Challinor, Taylor & Co. began producing glass in the fall of 1884. It made pressed tablewares exclusively. Joined U. S. Glass Co. in 1891.

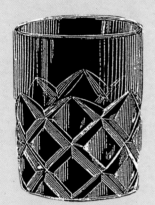

No. 10 Tumbler

No. 311

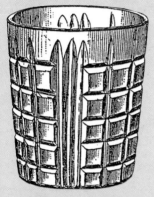

⅓ Pint Huber

9½ oz. Plain Ale

⅓ Pint Rosetta

½ Pint Star

⅓ Pint Star

Clio

No. 9

241

Columbia Glass Co. — Organized in 1886, made pressed tablewares, joined U. S. Glass Co. in 1891.

Dew Drop Tumbler
by **Columbia Glass Co.**

Consolidated Lamp and Glass Co. — Organized in Pittsburgh in 1892. In 1894, absorbed Fostoria Lamp & Shade from Ohio and moved to Coraopolis, Pennslyvania. Plant closed in 1964. Produced a great variety of pressed and blown wares and lamps.

Co-Operative Flint Glass Co. — Organized in about 1870 in Beaver Falls, Pennslyvania. Primarily produced pressed tablewares. Closed in 1937.

200 — 7½ oz. Tumbler

211 — 9 oz. Tumbler

223 — 8½ oz. Tumbler

240 — 8 oz. Tumbler

241 — 8 oz. Tumbler

242 — 8 oz. Tumbler

247 — 7¾ oz. Tumbler

247 — 8 oz. Tumbler

249 — 9 oz. Tumbler

276 — 9 oz. Tumbler

284 — 8 oz. Tumbler

287 — 8 oz. Tumbler

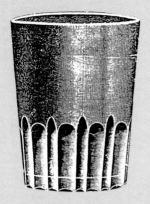

288 — 8 oz. Tumbler

289 — 8 oz. Tumbler

290 — 8 oz. Tumbler

291 — 8 oz. Tumbler

304 — 9 oz. Tumbler

309 — Tumbler

310 — Tumbler

323 — 8 oz. Tumbler

325 — 8 oz. Tumbler

367 — Tumbler

369 — 7 oz. Tumbler

375 — Tumbler

376 — Tumbler

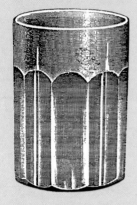

431 — Tumbler

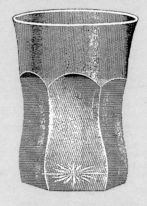

437 — 9 oz. Tumbler

1901 — 9 oz. Tumbler

1902 — Tumbler

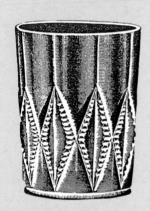

20th Century — 9 oz. Tumbler

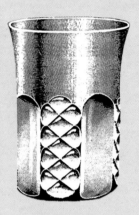

Adoria

Art Nauvo — 9 oz. Tumbler

Daisy — 8 oz. Tumbler

Forest — 8 oz. Tumbler

La France — Tumbler

Magna — 8¾ oz. Tumbler

Martha Washington

Radiant — 8 oz. Tumbler

Ray

Rex — 8 oz. Tumbler

Swan — Tumbler

Crystal Glass Co. — Founded in Bridgeport, Ohio, in 1888. Produced pressed glass tableware. Joined National Glass Co. in 1899.

Crystal Glass Co. — Founded in Pittsburgh's South Side in 1869. Produced jelly glasses and pressed wares. Went out of business in 1884.

Dalzell Bros. & Gilmore; Dalzell, Gilmore & Leighton — Founded in Wellsburg, West Virginia, in 1883, moved to Findlay, Ohio, in 1888, joined National Glass Co. in 1899. Produced pressed tablewares and lamps.

Doyle & Co. — Founded in 1866, produced pressed tablewares and jelly tumblers. Joined U. S. Glass in 1891

Dugan Glass Co.; Indiana, Pennslyvania — Acquired from National Glass Co. in 1904, produced pressed and blown tablewares. Became Diamond Glassware Co. in 1913, burned in 1931.

Geo. Duncan & Sons — Organized in 1874, in Pittsburgh's South Side. Produced pressed and blown tablewares. Joined U. S. Glass in 1891.

No. 51

No. 52

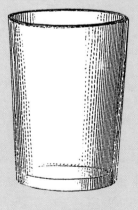

No. 53

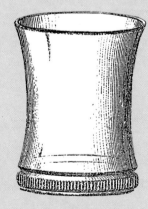

No. 89

No. 90   No. 301   No. 303   No. 304

No. 305   No. 306   No. 307   No. 308

No. 310   No. 311   No. 312   No. 313

← No. 314

No. 315 →

Geo. Duncan's Sons & Co. — Organized in Washington, Pennsylvania, by George Duncan's sons in 1892. Became Duncan & Miller Glass Co. in 1900. Produced pressed and blown tablewares. Closed in 1955.

Elson Glass Co. — Organized in 1882, in Martins Ferry, Ohio. Produced pressed colored tablewares. Plant closed in 1893.

Fairmont Glass Works, Fairmont, West Virginia — In 1905, National moved equipment here and made tumblers and stemware. Ran for a year or two.

Federal Glass Co. — Organized in 1900, in Columbus, Ohio. Began making pressed tablewares in 1906. Packers, jars, and tumblers added in 1913. Closed in 1980.

Fenton Art Glass Co. — Founded as a decorating house in 1905, in Martin's Ferry, Ohio. Moved to Williamstown, West Virginia, in 1906. Produced art and tablewares, both pressed and blown. Still in operation today (2003).

Findlay Flint Glass Co. — Organized in Findlay, Ohio, in 1888 to take advantage of free natural gas. Plant burned in 1891. Produced bar and tablewares.

Fostoria Glass Co. — Organized in Fostoria, Ohio, in 1887 (free gas). Moved to Moundsville, West Virginia, in 1891 (gas supply exhausted). Produced pressed and blown tablewares.

No. 604 Cameo
by **Fostoria Glass Co.**

Fry Glass Co. — Organized as Rochester Glass Co. in 1901. Made blown and cut glass, added heat resistant glass in 1922. Closed the plant in 1934.

Gillinder & Sons — Organized in Philadelphia in 1867. It made pressed and blown tablewares and lighting fixtures. In 1888, the company moved the pressed glass facility to Greensburg, Pennsylvania, outside of Pittsburgh. This portion of the company joined U. S. Glass in 1891. The Philadelphia branch eventually moved to Port Jervis, New York, and is still in business (2003).

Greensburg Glass Co. — Organized in Brilliant, Ohio, in 1889, and immediately moved to Greensburg, Pennslyvania. It made a limited amount of tableware and reorganized in 1892 (with new molds), as Greensburg Glass Co. Ltd. Joined National Glass Co. in 1899.

Hazel-Atlas Glass Company — Hazel and Atlas glass companies merged in 1902. Products were primarily machines made open-mouth bottles until the mid-twenties, when the company began making machine made pressed wares. The company was sold to Continental Can in 1956.

A. H. Heisey & Co. — Founded in 1896, in Newark, Ohio; produced pressed and blown table and bar wares. Closed in 1957. The author began collecting those tumblers made by Heisey. One 1913 catalog alone listed 400 tumblers. One group of tumblers, illustrated below, is a sequence from 1897. The one tumbler missing, No. 122, is a flared colonial type.

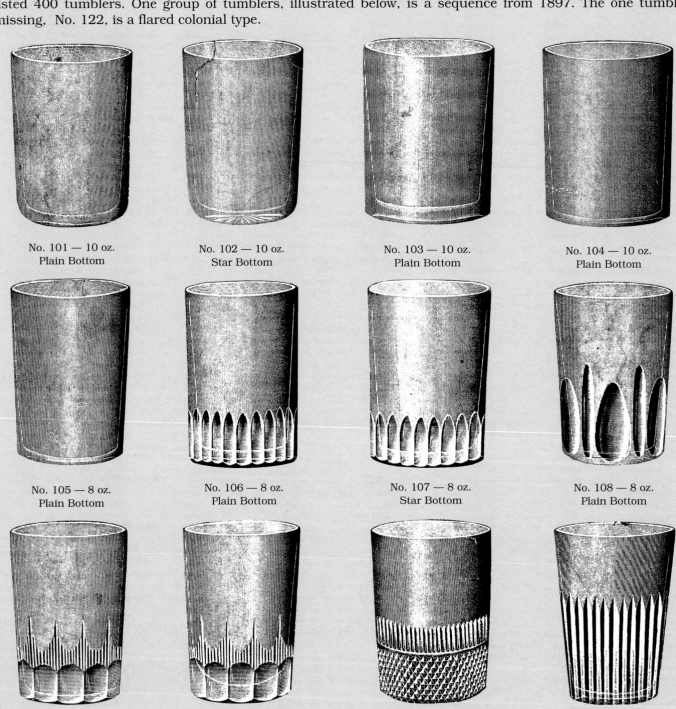

No. 101 — 10 oz. Plain Bottom

No. 102 — 10 oz. Star Bottom

No. 103 — 10 oz. Plain Bottom

No. 104 — 10 oz. Plain Bottom

No. 105 — 8 oz. Plain Bottom

No. 106 — 8 oz. Plain Bottom

No. 107 — 8 oz. Star Bottom

No. 108 — 8 oz. Plain Bottom

No. 109 — 8 oz. Plain Bottom

No. 109½ — 8 oz. Plain Bottom

No. 110 — 7 oz.

No. 111 — 8 oz.

No. 112 — 7 oz.
Plain Bottom

No. 113 — 7 oz.

No. 114 — 8 oz.

No. 115 — 8 oz.

No. 116 — 8½ oz.
Plain Bottom

No. 117 — 8½ oz.
Plain Bottom

No. 118 — 7 oz.

No. 119 — 8½ oz.

No. 120 — 8 oz. Colonial,
6 Flutes
Plain or Star Bottom

No. 121 — 7½ oz.

No. 123 — 8 oz.

No. 124 — 8 oz.

No. 125 — 8 oz.

No. 126 — 8 oz.

No. 127 — 11 oz.
Plain Bottom

No. 128 — 8 oz.

No. 129 — 8 oz.

No. 130 — 8 oz.

No. 131 — 7 oz. Colonial,
8 Flutes

No. 132 — 9 oz.

 TRADE **H** MARK. **TABLE TUMBLERS**  TRADE **H** MARK.

ALL TUMBLERS NOT OTHERWISE SPECIFIED HAVE THE USUAL STAR BOTTOM

No. 187 — 8 oz. Tumbler,
Patent No. 45605

No. 188 — 8 oz. Tumbler,
Patent No. 46320,
also made with optic

No. 189 — 9 oz. Tumbler,
Patent No. 45605

No. 190 — 8 oz. Tumbler

No. 192 — 8 oz. Tumbler,
patent applied for

No. 193 — 8 oz. Tumbler,
patent applied for

No. 194 — 8 oz. Tumbler,
patent applied for

No. 195 — 9 oz. Tumbler,
patent applied for

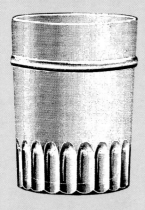

No. 196 — 8½ oz. Tumbler,
patent applied for

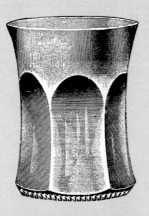

No. 300 — 7 oz. Colonial

No. 333 — 8½ oz.
Plain Bottom

No. 339 — 8 oz. Continental

No. 350 — 8 oz.

No. 351 — 8 oz. Flared

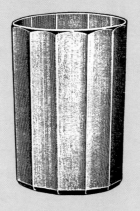

No. 353 — 8 oz. Colonial,
Plain Bottom, cut or
fire-polished top

No. 393 — 8 oz.
Plain Bottom

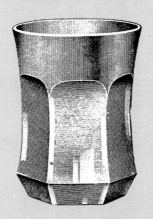

429 — 8 oz.
Patent No. 43703

A·H·HEISEY & CO·
NEWARK·OHIO

HOTEL TUMBLERS
ALL GROUND BOTTOMS
SCALE HALF SIZE

No. 106 — 8 oz.
Plain Bottom

No. 142 — 8½ oz. Optic
Plain Bottom

No. 150 — 8 oz.
Plain Bottom

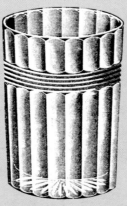

No. 153 — 8 oz.
Plain or Star Bottom

No. 154 — 8 oz.
Plain Bottom

No. 164 — 9 oz.
Plain Bottom

No. 166 — 9 oz.
Plain Bottom

No. 167 — 9 oz.
Plain Bottom

No. 168 — 9 oz.
Plain Bottom

No. 170 — 8 oz.
Plain Bottom

No. 186 — 9 oz. Colonial
Plain Bottom
Patent No. 46646

No. 191 — 10 oz.
Star Bottom

No. 201 — 8 oz.

No. 300½ — 8 oz. Colonial
Plain Bottom

No. 341 — 10 oz. Colonial
Star Bottom

HOTEL TUMBLERS
ALL GROUND BOTTOMS
SCALE HALF SIZE

No. 157— 9 oz.
Plain Bottom

No. 158 — 8½ oz.
Plain Bottom

No. 160 — 9 oz.
Plain Bottom

No. 161 — 9 oz.

No. 162 — 8 oz.
Plain Bottom

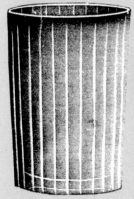

No. 170½ — 8 oz. Optic
Plain Bottom

No. 172 — 8 oz.
Plain or Star Bottom

No. 174 — 9 oz.
Plain Bottom

No. 174½ — 9 oz. Otic
Plain Bottom

No. 184 — 8 oz. Colonial
Plain Bottom
Patent No. 46646

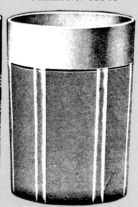

No. 341½ — 8 oz. Colonial
Star Bottom

No. 369 — 8 oz.
Plain Bottom
Also make 10 oz.

No. 369 — 10 oz. Optic
Plain Bottom
Also make 8 oz.

No. 379½ — 8 oz.
Star Bottom

No. 411 — 8 oz.
Plain Bottom

John B. Higbee Glass Co. — Founded in Bridgeville, Pennslyvania, in 1907. Produced pressed tablewares and novelties. Closed in 1918.

Hobbs, Brockunier & Co. — Founded in 1845 by Barnes and Hobbs. Made colored, etched, cut, and engraved pressed and blown table and art wares. Became Hobbs Glass Co. in 1888. Joined U. S. Glass in 1891. Factory closed in 1893.

Hocking Glass Co. — Organized in 1905, in Lancaster, Ohio. Became Anchor Hocking in 1937, continues production today (2003).

No. 3 — 7 oz.

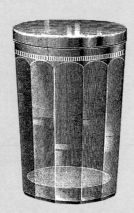

No. 5 — 6 oz.

No. 7 — 6 oz.

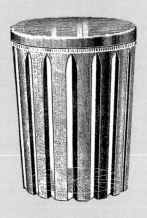

No. 8 — 8 oz.

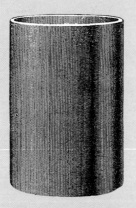

Plain Hotel Tumbler

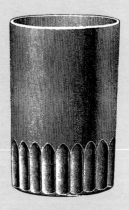

Fluted Hotel Tumbler

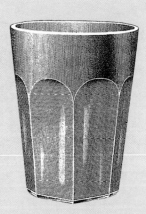

Colonial Hotel Tumbler

Huntington Glass Co. — Organized in Huntington, West Virginia, in 1892. Made blown and pressed wares. Operated sporadically until it closed in 1896.

Imperial Glass Co. — Began making glass in January 1904 in Bellaire, Ohio. Produced mostly pressed wares, although some blown wares were also made. Closed in 1984.

Keystone Tumbler Co. — Organized in 1897 in Rochester, Pennslyvania. Pressed and blown tumblers were its only products. Merged with National Glass in 1899.

Indiana Tumbler & Goblet Co. — Organized in Greentown, Indiana, in 1892. Made pressed bar goods, tablewares, and novelties in many colors. Joined National Glass in 1899.

9 Dewey Tumbler
by **Indiana Tumbler & Goblet Co.**

Jefferson Glass Co. — Organized in Steubenville, Ohio, in 1900. Produced colored and opalescent pressed glass and novelties. Phased production into lighting goods in 1920.

King, Son & Co. — Operated The Cascade Glass Works and was founded in Pittsburgh's South Side in 1869. Its primary products were pressed tablewares. The company merged with the U. S. Glass Co. in 1891.

Keystone Tumbler Co. — Organized in 1897 in Rochester, Pennslyvania. Pressed and blown tumblers were its only products. Merged with National Glass in 1899.

McKee Bros. — Originally begun in 1850, this factory (under many managements) made mostly pressed tablewares and industrial glass. The company joined National Glass in 1899. After National foundered, McKee resumed operation of the plant under the name of McKee-Jeannette Glass Co. The Jeannette Glass Co. ceased operation in 1983.

No. 508

No. 509

No. 1003

No. 1013

No. 203 Tumbler,
Etched No. 1060

No. 214 Tumbler,
Etched No. 1050

No. 1504

No. 1506

255

Artistic   Atlantic   Brunswick   Champion

Critic   Doric   Germanic   Gladiator

Masonic   Napoleon   Pilgrim   Prismatic

Teutonic

Millersburg Glass Co. — Opened in Millersburg, Ohio, in 1909. Produced primarily carnival glass. Went bankrupt in 1911; became Radium Glass Co. Closed in 1912.

Model Flint Glass Co. — Organized in 1888, in Findlay, Ohio. Primarily produced pressed tablewares. Moved to Albany Indiana in 1893. Joined National Glass Co. in 1899. Closed in 1901.

Monongah Glass Co. — Organized in Fairmont, West Virginia, in 1903 – 1904. Originally made jelly tumblers and packers' wares. Established the process for making successful vacuum-sealed glassware. Eventually also made high-grade blown wares. Closed by 1930.

No. 1260 — 9 oz.   No. 1402 — 8½ oz.   No. 1404 — 9 oz.   No. 1405 — 9 oz.

No. 1407 — 8½ oz.   No. 1470 — 8½ oz.   No. 1471 — 9 oz. Capped   No. 1472 — 8 oz. Capped

Morgantown Glass Co. (Economy Tumbler Co.) — Founded in 1900. Produced blown table, bar, and decorative wares. Purchased by the Fostoria Glass Co. in 1965. The plant was closed in 1971.

Moser is the term used to identify Karlsbader Glasindustrie Gesellschaft, Ludwig Moser & Söhne, A. G. Meierhöfen bie Karlsbad, and associated firms in central Europe.

Mosser Glass Co. — Opened in 1971 in Cambridge, Ohio. Specializes in colored, iridized, etc., pressed glass reproductions. Still in operation (2003).

Mt. Washington Glass Works (Co.) — The glass factory that became Mt. Washington was established in 1837, in South Boston, Massachusetts. Eventually, it was moved to New Bedford, Massachusetts. It produced cut glass and what is now called art glass. Became the Pairpoint Co. in 1894. It has undergone many ownership and management changes and is still operating in Sagamore, Massachusetts today (2003), alongside the Cape Cod Canal.

National Glass Company (Combine) — Nineteen tableware factories combined in 1899 and 1900 to form one company. The goal: to reduce the costs of management and enable all to stay in business. Consolidation had been working for the United States Glass Co. but National only managed about 2 years of real progress. After this there were only about three factories working; by 1907, the firm was in receivership. A list of the companies that comprised National can be found in Appendix B.

9/11 Tumbler — 8 oz.

9/16 Tumbler — 8 oz.

9/29 Tumbler — 8 oz.

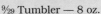
9/29 Tumbler — 8 oz.

9/102 Tumbler — 8 oz.

9/400 Tumbler — 8½ oz.

Note: These tumblers were also made by the Indiana Tumbler & Goblet Company.

New England Glass Co. — Organized in East Cambridge, Mass., in 1818. This firm changed hands many times before it moved to Toledo, Ohio, in 1888, as the W. L. Libbey & Son Co. It produced both pressed and blown tablewares and art glass.

New Martinsville Glass Co. — Organized in New Martinsville, West Virginia, in 1900. Made pressed tablewares and art glass until a flood and fire occurred in 1907; made only pressed wares after that. Became Viking Glass in 1944, closed in 1999.

Nickel Plate Glass Co. — Founded in 1888, in Fostoria, Ohio. Made pressed and blown tablewares. Joined U. S. Glass in 1891, but never operated after that.

Northwood Glass — Harry Northwood operated three glass factories between 1888 and 1899, when the then-current Northwood Glass Co. joined the National Combine. These factories made pressed and blown tablewares. In 1903, Northwood opened his fourth and last factory in Wheeling, West Virginia. This plant, primarily making pressed table and lighting goods, operated until 1924. Mr. Northwood died in 1919.

Phoenix Glass Co. — Founded in 1880, in Phillipsburg (Monaca) Pennslyvania, Phoenix's primary products have been lighting goods. Between 1884 and 1888 art glass pitchers, vases, tumblers and other blown goods were produced. Now owned by Anchor Hocking, Phoenix is still in business (2003).

Reading Glass — There seems to have been a glass company that made art glass in Berks County, Pennslyvania, in or near Reading. It may have existed between 1884 and 1886. Almost no records exist documenting its wares.

Richards and Hartley Flint Glass Co. — Organized in 1865, in Pittsburgh; moved to Tarentum, Pennslyvania, in 1883. Produced pressed tablewares. Joined U. S. Glass in 1891. The factory was closed in 1893.

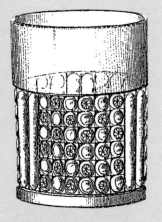

No. 25

No. 55

Mikado #99

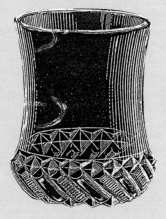

No. 190

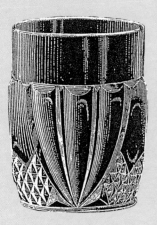

Richmond

Ripley & Co. — There were two D. C. Ripleys and three Ripley & Co. glass companies, spanning from 1865 to 1874, 1874 to 1891 (when this one joined the U. S. Glass Co.), and from 1910 to 1937. They all made pressed tablewares, and the last two also made some blown wares.

Riverside Glass Co. — Organized in 1879, in Wellsburg, West Virginia. Began producing glass in 1880. Made pressed tablewares and lamps. Joined National Glass in 1899.

Robinson Glass Co. — Organized in 1893 in Zanesville, Ohio. Made pressed bar and tablewares. Joined National Glass in 1899.

The No. 90 Handled Tumbler, by **Robinson Glass Co.**

Rochester Tumbler Co. — Organized in 1872. In 1877, this factory offered 300 different tumblers. Joined National Glass in 1899.

Royal Glass Co. — Founded in 1898, in Marietta, Ohio. Produced pressed wares. Joined National Glass Co. in 1899.

Seneca Glass Co. — Formed in 1991, in Fostoria, Ohio. Its primary products were etched, engraved, and cut lead blown tumblers and bar ware. The firm moved to Morgantown, West Virginia, in 1896. Closed in 1983.

No. 557, Engraved T

No. 557, Engraved W

No. 547, Engraved V

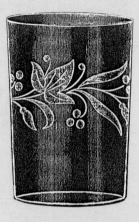
No. 557, Engraved R

No. 557, Engraved O

No. 557, Engraved Y

No. 1 Water Set, Engraved 448

No. 1 Water Set, Engraved 453

No. 1 Water Set, Engraved A

No. 1 Water Set, Engraved B

No. 1 Water Set, Engraved No. 1

No. 1 Water Set, Engraved No. 2

Water Set

Tarentum Glass Co. — Founded in 1894 in an old Richards & Hartley factory. Made pressed tablewares, lamps, and lighting fixtures. Plant burned in 1918 and never reopened.

Thompson Glass Co. — Organized in Uniontown, Pennslyvania, in 1888. Primarily produced pressed tablewares and novelties. This factory struggled with fuel supply and management problems for seven years before shutting its doors for good.

United States Glass Co. — Organized from 18 existing glass factories. Although some blown ware was produced, the primary products were pressed, table, druggists, lighting, etc., wares. Many factories were closed, and some new ones were built or acquired. In 1963, U. S. Glass Co. sold all remaining property to Tiffin Art Glass Co., which survived under several managements until the early 1980s. The tumblers illustrated here (ca. 1892) are divided into plain, fluted, figured, etc. On each tumbler will be found a number, usually at the bottom, that identifies it. For instance, "Old No. R., 169" tells us that the tumbler was made at the Tiffin plant of A. J. Beatty Glass Co. and was its number 169. Above that is the then-current system number. A list of the companies that comprised U. S. Glass can be found in Appendix B.

The following illustrations came from a catalog that contained 129 pages. These illustrations come from the most interesting 24 pages. Other pages include juice glasses, jelly tumblers, soda glasses, ale mugs, and beer mugs. In 1893, this catalog was prepared so that salesmen could offer the unsold wares of the member companies. In 1894, the glass workers struck against U. S. Glass, and for nearly four years there were almost no new wares to sell.

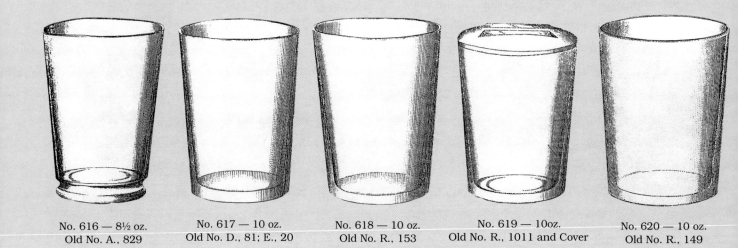

No. 616 — 8½ oz.
Old No. A., 829

No. 617 — 10 oz.
Old No. D., 81; E., 20

No. 618 — 10 oz.
Old No. R., 153

No. 619 — 10oz.
Old No. R., 1011 and Cover

No. 620 — 10 oz.
Old No. R., 149

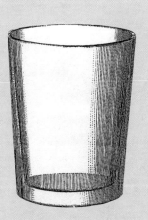

No. 621 — 10 oz.
Old No. R., 598

No. 622 — 10 oz.
Old No. R., 154

No. 623 — 12 oz.
Old No. N., 48; R., 148

No. 624 — 10½ oz.
Old No. K., 8 Plain Light

No. 625 — 7½ oz.
Old No. F., Silver Queen

No. 626 — 8 oz.
Old No. R., 584

No. 627 — 10 oz.
Old No. B., 1107;
K., 221; H., 234

No. 628 — 8¼ oz.
Old No. E., 24

No. 629 — 10 oz.
Old No. D., 52; H., 282

No. 630 — 8 oz.
Old No. O., 1022

No. 649 — 8½ oz.
Old No. L., 140

No. 650 — 7¼ oz.
Old No. R., 1213

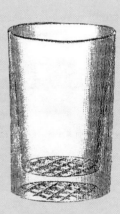

No. 651 — 8 oz.
Old No. R., 169

No. 652 — 7½ oz.
Old No. D., 311

No. 653 — 7¾ oz.
Old No. D., 305

No. 654 — 7 oz.
Old No. D., 286

No. 655 — 7¼ oz.
Old No. B., 1109

No. 656 — 9 oz.
Old No. H., 285

No. 657 — 10 oz.
Old No. A., Saxon

No. 675 — 10 oz.
Old No. R., 147

No. 676 — 10 oz.
Old No. R., 146

No. 677 — 9 oz.
Old No. O., 46

No. 678 — 10½ oz.
Old No. R., 143; K., 1 Plain

No. 680 — 11 oz.
Old No. D., ½ Pint Heavy Plain;
G., ½ Pint Heavy Bar

No. 680 — 11 oz.
Old No. D., ½ Pint
Heavy Plain; G., ½ Pint
Heavy Bar

No. 681 — 10½ oz.
Old No. R., 145

No. 682 — 10 oz.
Old No. K., 2; R., 144;
R., ½ Pint Heavy Plain

No. 684 — 12 oz.
Old No. R., 2; R.,156

No. 685 — 10½ oz.
Old No. N.,45

No. 686 — 10½ oz.
Old No. R.,164

No. 687 — 11¾ oz.
Old No. R., 141; N., 46

No. 688 — 12 oz.
Old No. D & C.,
½ Pint Heavy Plain

No. 689 — 11 oz.
Old No. R., 150

No. 690 — 11 oz.
Old No. R., 157

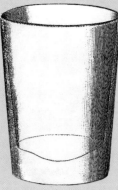

No. 691 — 13 oz.
Old No. R., 152

No. 692 — 8 oz.
Old No. R., 162

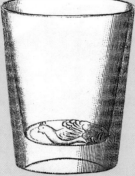

No. 713 — 8½ oz.
Old No. R., 158

No. 714 — 10½ oz.
Old No. R., 161

No. 715 — 10½ oz.
Old No. R., 163

No. 716 — 11¼ oz.
Old No. R., 173

No. 717 — 10¼ oz.
Old No. R., 175

No. 718 — 7 oz.
Old No. K., 8

No. 719 — 9 oz.
Old No. K., 9

No. 720 — 10½ oz.
Old No. D., ½ Pint Cafe;
E., 101

No. 721 — 10 oz.
Old No. R., 174

No. 722 — 11 oz.
Old No. R., 171

No. 723 — 12 oz.
Old No. R., 177

No. 724 — 11 oz.
Old No. R., 172

No. 725 — 10 oz.
Old No. R., 176

No. 726 — 8 oz.
Old No. R., 159

No. 859 — 9 oz.
Old No. N., 77

No. 740 — 9 oz.
Old No. K., 363

No. 741 — 9 oz.
Old No. O., 834

No. 742 — 8½ oz.
Old No. K., 293 — 7½ oz.

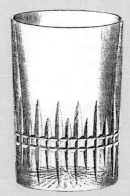

No. 745 — 9 oz.
Old No. K., 347

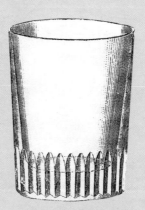

No. 746 — 9 oz.
Old No. R., 1206

No. 747 — 9 oz.
Old No. R., 120

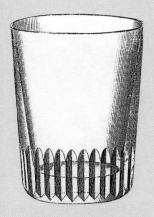

No. 748 — 9 oz.
Old Nos. R.,119; G., 89

No. 749 — 9 oz.
Old No. R., 1234

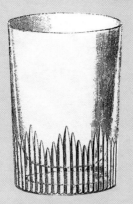

No. 750 — 8 oz.
Old No. R., 1232

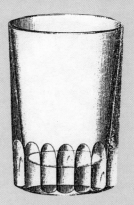

No. 751 — 7 oz.
Old No. E., 27

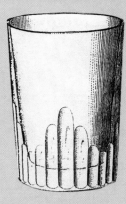

No. 752 — 7½ oz.
Old No. R., 1237

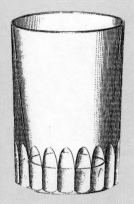

No. 753 — 8 oz.
Old Nos. R., 1230 St.;
K., 1230 St.

No. 754 — 8 oz.
Old No. R., 1230 Hotel;
K., 1230 Hotel

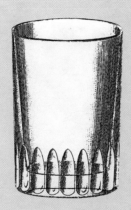

No. 755 — 9 oz.
Old No. D., 342

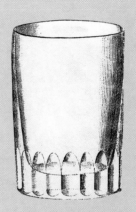

No. 756 — 10 oz.
Old No. R., 1229 Hotel

No. 757 — 10¾ oz.
Old No. R., 1229 St.

No. 758 — 9 oz.
Old No. K., 409

No. 759 — 8 oz.
Old No. K., 886

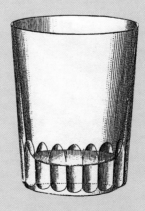

No. 760 — 10 oz.
Old No. R., 122

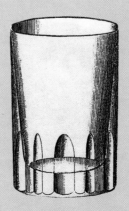

No. 761 — 9 oz.
Old No. R., 1236

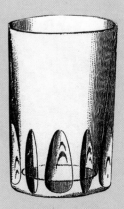

No. 762 — 8 oz.
Old No. K., 403

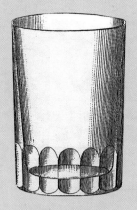
No. 763 — 10 oz.
Old No. K.,415

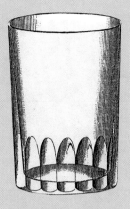
No. 764 — 8 oz.
Old No. O.,853

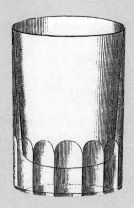
No. 785 — 10 oz.
Old No. R.,1228

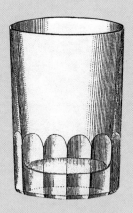
No. 786 — 9 oz.
Old No. R.,1233

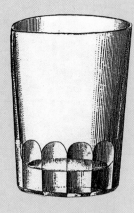
No. 787 — 9½ oz.
Old No. R.,121

No. 788 — 9 oz.
Old No. F.,4

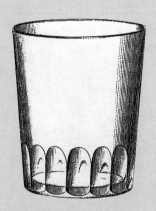
No. 789 — 9 oz.
Old Nos. R., 109; L., 125;
E., 21; O., 489

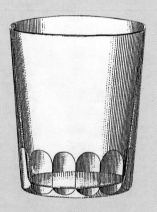
No. 790 — 8 oz.
Old No. O.,159

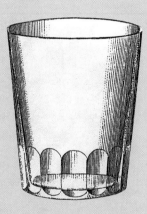
No. 791 — 8½ oz.
Old No. R., 583; H., 224;
G., 67

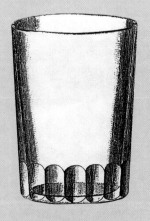
No. 792 — 8 oz.
Old No. R., 588; E., 23

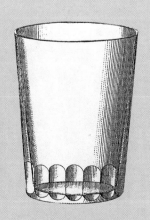
No. 793 — 10 oz.
Old No. R., 592

No. 794 — 11 oz.
Old No. R., 107; O., 69

No. 795 — 11 oz.
Old No. R., 103

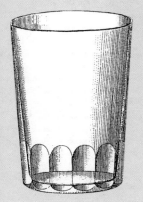

No. 796 — 8 oz.
Old Nos. O., 543;
H., 275; G., 53

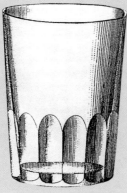

No. 797 — 9 oz.
Old No. D., 54

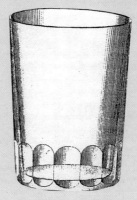

No. 798 — 8½ oz.
Old No. N., 24

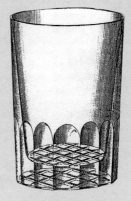

No. 799 — 8½ oz.
Old No. R., 1235

No. 800 — 9¼ oz.
Old No. R., 593

No. 801 — 10 oz.
Old No. D., ½ Pint Chicago

No. 803 — 9 oz.
Old No. R., 110

No. 804 — 8½ oz.
Old No. R., 101

No. 961 — 11 oz.
Old No. R., 102; G., 28;
H., 257

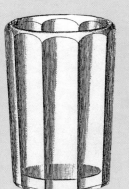

No. 962 — 9½ oz.
Old No. R., 117

No. 963 — 10 oz.
Old No. R., 111

No. 964 — 9 oz.
Old No. R., 114; K., 827

No. 965 — 10 oz.
Old No. R., 118;
D., ½ Pint Huber

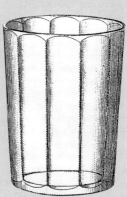

No. 967 — 8½ oz.
Old No. R., 574;
D., 51 Optic; K., 215 Optic

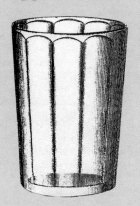

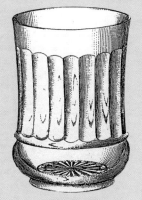

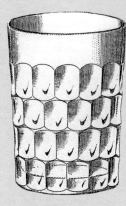

No. 968 — 10 oz.
Old No. R., 575 & 565

No. 969 — 11 oz.
Old No. P., ½ Pint, Plain
H'y. Optic

No. 970 — 8 oz.
Old No. P., 300, Fluted

No. 977 — 9 oz.
Old No. F., Duchess

No. 981 — 8 oz.
Old No. J., Tycoon

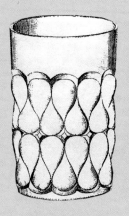

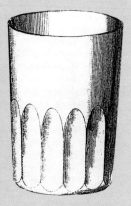

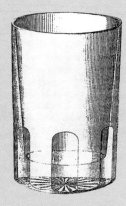

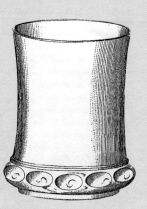

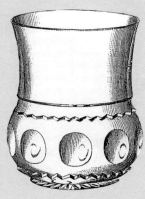

No. 982 — 7 oz.
Old No. G., 97

No. 1028 — 9 oz.
Old No. D., 314

No. 1030 — 9 oz.
Old No. R., 1238

No. 820 — 8 oz.
Old No. F., Dakota

No. 824 — 8¾ oz.
Old No. A., X. L. C. R.

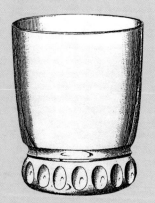

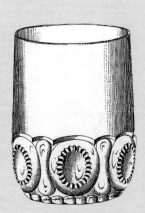

No. 826 — 10 oz.
Old No. G., 15013

No. 836 — 8¾ oz.
Old No. B., 182

No. 848 — 6½ oz.
Old No. B., Atlas

No. 850 — 9¾ oz.
Old No. N., 82

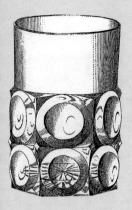

No. 853 — 9 oz.
Old No. M., 151

No. 883 — 9¾ oz.
Old No. E., 103

No. 886 — 7½ oz.
Old No. P., 2

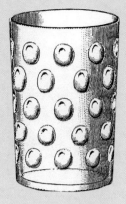

No. 979 — 9 oz.
Old No. O., 976;
K., 215 Dot; R., 569

No. 980 — 9 oz.
Old No. P., 800

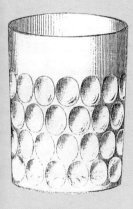

No. 999 — 7½ oz.
Old No. C., 312

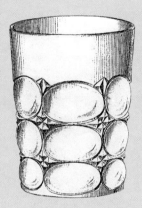

No. 1002 — 8 oz.
Old No. G., 421

No. 1021 — 11 oz.
Old No. R., 210

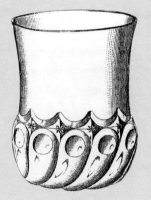

No. 827 — 9½ oz.
Old No. K., 500

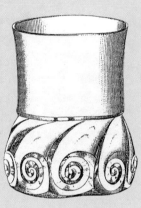

No. 829 — 8¾ oz.
Old No. D., 360

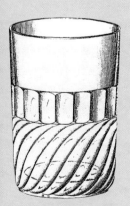

No. 841 — 8 oz.
Old No. O., 844

No. 842 — 10 oz.
Old No. O., 772

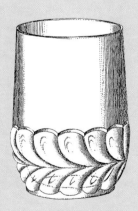

No. 845 — 10 oz.
Old No. A., Plume

No. 852 — 9½ oz.
Old No. E., 55

No. 855 — 9 oz.
Old No. R., 1201

No. 942 — 7½ oz.
Old No. N., 15007

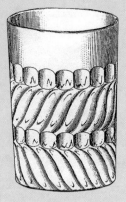

No. 960 — 8 oz.
Old No. R., 1212

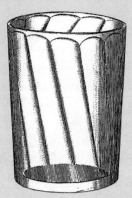

No. 966 — 8½ oz.
Old No. R., 564

No. 971 — 9 oz.
Old No. N., 26

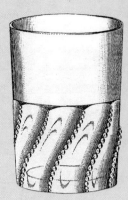

No. 823 — 8 oz.
Old No. D., 335

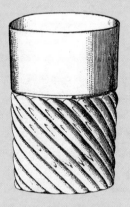

No. 973 — 9 oz.
Old No. D., 313

No. 978 — 9 oz.
Old No. K., 458

No. 974 — 8 oz.
Old No. O., 772 Small

No. 1004 — 9 oz.
Old No. R., Orinoco

No. 1013 — 10 oz.
Old No. K., 355

No. 1027 — 8 oz.
Old No. 15026

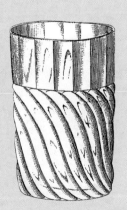

Old No. R., 1211

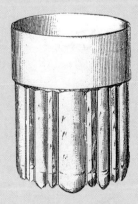

No. 766 — 9 oz.
Old No. N., 15022

No. 768 — 9 oz.
Old No. J., 15021

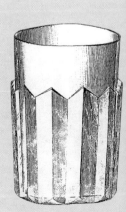

No. 769 — 9 oz.
Old No. L., 15023

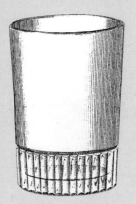

No. 861 — 8 oz.
Old No. L., 139

No. 860 — 8 oz.
Old No. J., 39; R., 1215

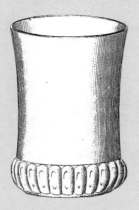

No. 802 — 9 oz.
Old No. D., 340

No. 838 — 10 oz.
Old No. H., 341

No. 840 — 8 oz.
Old No. J., 15006

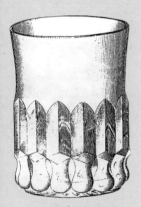

No. 843 — 9½ oz.
Old No. B., Pittsburgh

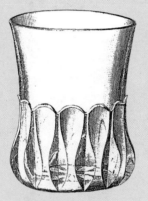

No. 844 — 8 oz.
Old No. A., Crystal Wedding

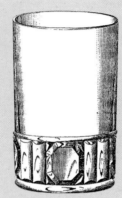

No. 854 — 9½ oz.
Old No. N., 78

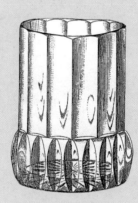

No. 849 — 9 oz.
Old No. L., Cordova

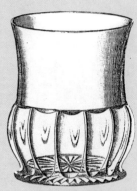

No. 851 — 8¾ oz.
Old No. J., Columbia

No. 857 — 8½ oz.
Old No. L., Crown Jewel

No. 858 — 8½ oz.
Old No. O., 15005½

No. 943 — 10 oz.
Old No. H., 337

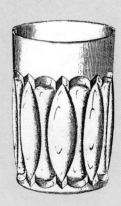

No. 983 — 7 oz.
Old No. G., 98

No. 958 — 10 oz.
Old No. D., 321

No. 976 — 9 oz.
Old No. J., 73

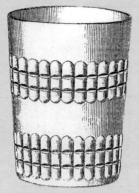

No. 1014 — 8½ oz.
Old No. J., Climax

No. 1016 — 9 oz.
Old No. B., 15003

No. 1019 — 9 oz.
Old No. B., Coral

No. 1020 — 9 oz.
Old No. B., Brazil

No. 984 — 7½ oz.
Old No. R., 100

No. 985 — 8 oz.
Old No. H., 323

No. 987 — 8 oz.
Old No. P., 150 Footed

No. 986 — 7 oz.
Old No. P., 150;
J., Dew Drop

No. 767 — 9 oz.
Old No. K., 15024

No. 765 — 9 oz.
Old No. K., 15020

No. 839 — 10 oz.
Old No. H., 339

No. 847 — 10½ oz.
Old No. L., 870

No. 856 — 8 oz.
Old No. E., Hanover

No. 868 — 10 oz.
Old No. R., 597; O., 766

No. 871 — 8 oz.
Old No. R., 596

No. 872 — 9 oz.
Old No. L., 650

No. 872½ — 8 oz.
Old No. D., 303

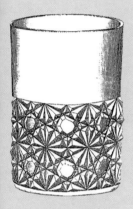

No. 873 — 11 oz.
Old No. H., 101

No. 875 — 12 oz.
Old No. G., 81 and 88;
O., 835; R., 559

No. 876 — 12 oz.
Old No. R., 558

No. 877 — 11 oz.
Old No. R., 556 and 557

No. 887 — 7½ oz.
Old No. F., 15002

No. 888 — 7¾ oz.
Old No. P., 76

No. 940 — 10 oz.
Old No. E., Oregon

No. 941 — 8 oz.
Old No. D., 15004

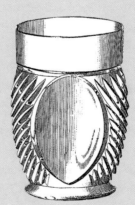

No. 944 — 8 oz.
Old No. G., 15008

No. 945 — 8 oz.
Old No. J., 15014

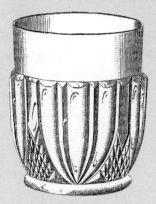

No. 959 — 10 oz.
Old No. E., Richmond

No. 988 — 8½ oz.
Old No. L., 137

No. 989 — 9 oz.
Old No. H., 101 & 102;
R., 562 & 563

No. 998 — 9½ oz.
Old No. R., 1220

No. 1003 — 9½ oz.
Old No. R., 1221

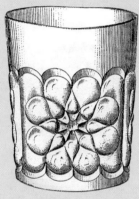

No. 1005 — 10 oz.
Old No. M., 101

No. 1007 — 10 oz.
Old No. R., 1219

No. 1009 — 9 oz.
Old No. R., 1218

No. 1011 — 9 oz.
Old No. J., 23

No. 1012 — 9 oz.
Old No. J., Eldorado

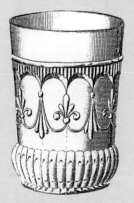

No. 1015 — 9 oz.
Old No. A., 15009

No. 1017 — 9 oz.
Old No. B., 15010

No. 1018 — 9 oz.
Old No. B., Magic

No. 1029 — 8½ oz.
Old No. A., Cottage

No. 822 — 9¾ oz.
Old No. F., Mascotte

No. 821 — 9 oz.
Old No. F., Pavonia

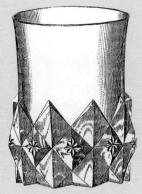

No. 828 — 9 oz.
Old No. L., 15001

No. 825 — 8¾ oz.
Old No. B., Amazon

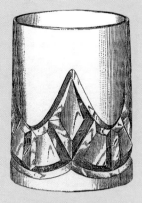

No. 830 — 9¾ oz.
Old No. D., 326

No. 831 — 9½ oz.
Old No. E., 190

No. 834 — 9 oz.
Old No. B., 177; C., 311

No. 846 — 8¾ oz.
Old No. B., 181

No. 862 — 8 oz.
Old No. D., 316

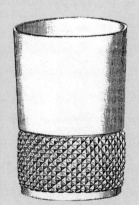

No. 863 — 8 oz.
Old No. R., 589; O., 439

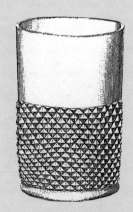

No. 864 — 8 oz.
Old No. O., 439, New Mold

No. 865 — 11 oz.
Old No. R., 590

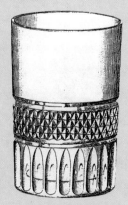

No. 866 — 9 oz.
Old No. D., 343

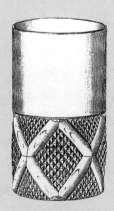

No. 878 — 9 oz.
Old No. R., 1205

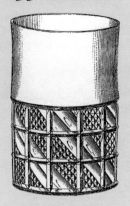

No. 880 — 9½ oz.
Old No. R., 1204

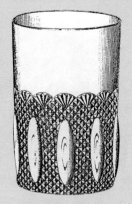

No. 882 — 9½ oz.
Old No. R., 1203 G., 404

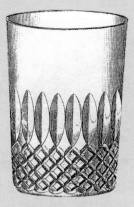

No. 884 — 8 oz.
Old No. N., 27

No. 885 — 8 oz.
Old No. P., 1

No. 925 — 8½ oz.
Old No. D., 15011

No. 926 — 8½ oz.
Old No. O., 893; D., 317

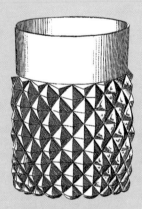

No. 931 — 9 oz.
Old No. F., Roanoke

No. 932 — 9½ oz.
Old No. L., 136

No. 946 — 8 oz.
Old No. G., 420

No. 956 — 9 oz.
Old No. L., 750

No. 957 — 9 oz.
Old No. A., Art

No. 991 — 7½ oz.
Old No. J., 27

No. 997 — 9 oz.
Old No. O., 967

No. 1006 — 10 oz.
Old No. R., 1202

No. 1008 — 8 oz.
Old No. R., 554

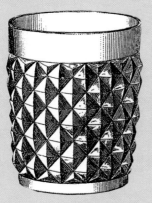

No. 1010 — 8 oz.
Old No. R., 551

No. 1023 — 8½ oz.
Old No. G., 56

No. 1024 — 9 oz.
Old No. G., 91

No. 1025 — 9 oz.
Old No. D., 827

Old No. B. — 1108

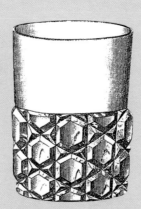

No. 832 — 8½ oz.
Old No. D., 328; P., 250

No. 833 — 9 oz.
Old No. B., 175

No. 881 — 11 oz.
Old No. R., 1209

No. 867 — 10 oz.
Old No. D., 302

No. 869 — 10 oz.
Old No. R., 595

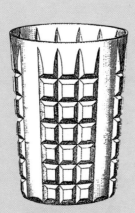

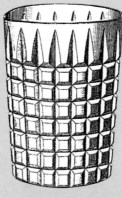
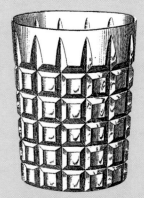

No. 870 — 8 oz.
Old No. R., 594; O., 740

No. 927 — 8½ oz.
Old No. L., 188

No. 928 — 9½ oz.
Old No. D., 318; R., 552

No. 929 — 8 oz.
Old No. R., 1214

No. 930 — 8 oz.
Old No. D., 308 & 312;
C., 10 Table; E., 8; O., 843

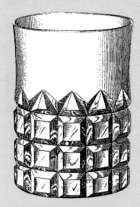

No. 933 — 8½ oz.
Old No. B., 176

No. 934 — 10 oz.
Old No. R., 1216

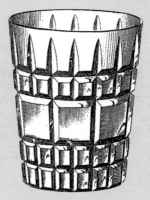

No. 936 — 8 oz.
Old No. E., 544

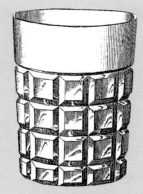

No. 935 — 9 oz.
Old No. P., 200

No. 835 — 9 oz.
Old No. H., 335

No. 837 — 8¾ oz.
Old No. D., 315

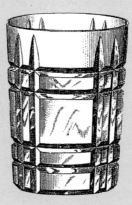

No. 937 — 9 oz.
Old No. R., 553

No. 938 — 8 oz.
Old No. G., 92

No. 939 — 8½ oz.
Old No. R., 1207

No. 947 — 9 oz.
Old No. D., 825

No. 948 — 10 oz.
Old No. R., 1217

No. 949 — 10 oz.
Old No. R., 1210

No. 950 — 10 oz.
Old No. D., 820

No. 951 — 9 oz.
Old No. J., Henrietta

No. 952 — 9 oz.
Old No. C., 309

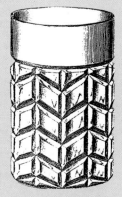

No. 953 — 9 oz.
Old No. P., 80

No. 955 — 9 oz.
Old No. N., 76

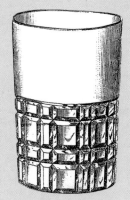

No. 879 — 8½ oz.
Old No. R., 1208

No. 954 — 9 oz.
Old No. H., 330

No. 990 — 9 oz.
Old No. D., 310

No. 992 — 8 oz.
Old No. R., 560 and 561

No. 994 — 9 oz.
Old No. N., 80

No. 995 — 9 oz.
Old No. J., 100

No. 993 — 7½ oz.
Old No. P., Shell

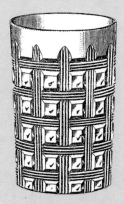

No. 996 — 8½ oz.
Old No. O., 861

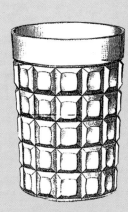

No. 1000 — 8 oz.
Old No. J., Banquet

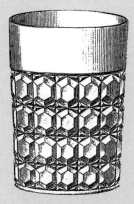

No. 1001 — 9 oz.
Old No. J., 90

No. 1026 — 8 oz.
Old No. D., 331

Westmoreland Glass Co. — Organized in 1888, as Westmoreland Specialty Co., in Grapeville, Pennsylvania. Primarily produced pressed tablewares, decorative accessories, and novelties. Factory closed in 1985.

| Floral Colonial | 1776 | 575 | 550 | 500 |

920

L. G. Wright Glass Co. — Began as a one-man operation in 1937. Wright contracted to have glass made and then sold it wholesale to dealers. Both pressed and blown wares were made. Much of the production centered around reproductions of Victorian colored glassware. Wright's blown tumblers can be identified from the earlier tumblers by the rounded corners and the noticeably concave bottoms. (Compare the two illustrations below.) The business closed in 1999.

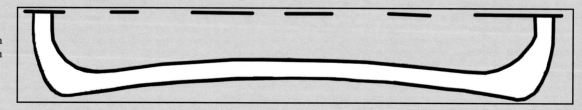

Bottom form common to many blown Victorian tumblers.

Bottom form common to L.G. Wright blown tumblers.

Appendix B

Glass Combines and Their Members

United States Glass Co. Organized in 1891 —————

Factory A	Adams & Co., Pittsburgh, PA
Factory B	Bryce Brothers, Pittsburgh, PA
Factory C	Challinor, Taylor; Tarentum, PA
Factory D	Geo. Duncan & Sons, Pittsburgh, PA
Factory E	Richards and Hartley, Tarentum, PA
Factory F	Ripley & Co., Pittsburgh, PA
Factory G	Gillinder & Sons, Greensburg, PA
Factory H	Hobbs Glass Co., Wheeling, WV
Factory J	Columbia Glass Co., Findlay, OH
Factory K	King, Son & Co., Pittsburgh, PA
Factory L	O'Hara (Lyons), Pittsburgh, PA
Factory M	Bellaire Goblet Co., Findlay, OH
Factory N	Nickel Plate Glass Co., Fostoria, OH
Factory O	Central Glass Co., Wheeling, WV
Factory P	Doyle Co., Pittsburgh, PA
Factory R	A. J. Beatty, Tiffin, OH
Factory S	A. J. Beatty, Steubenville, OH
Factory T	Novelty Glass Co., Fostoria, OH
Factory U	Built by U. S. Glass in 1894, at Gas City, IN
Factory Glassport	Built by U. S. Glass in 1894, at Glassport, PA

National Glass Co. Organized in 1899 —————

Factory No. 1	Beatty, Brady Glass Co., Dunkirk, IN
Factory No. 2	Canton Glass Co., Marion, IN
Factory No. 3	Central Glass Co., Summitville, IN
Factory No. 4	Crystal Glass Co., Bridgeport, OH
Factory No. 5	Cumberland Glass Co., Cumberland, MD
Factory No. 6	Dalzell, Gilmore and Leighton Glass Co., Findlay, OH
Factory No. 7	Fairmont Glass Co., Fairmont, WV
Factory No. 8	Greensburg Glass Co., Greensburg, PA
Factory No. 9	Indiana Tumbler & Goblet Co., Greentown, IN
Factory No. 10	Keystone Tumbler Co., Rochester, PA
Factory No. 11	Model Flint Glass Co., Albany, IN
Factory No. 12	McKee & Bros. Glass Co., Jeannette, PA
Factory No. 13	Northwood Glass Co., Indiana, PA
Factory No. 14	Ohio Flint Glass Co., Lancaster, OH
Factory No. 15	Riverside Glass Co., Wellsburg, WV
Factory No. 16	Robinson Glass Co., Zanesville, OH
Factory No. 17	Rochester Glass Co., Rochester, PA
Factory No. 18	Royal Glass Co., Marietta, OH
Factory No. 19	West Virginia Glass Co., Martin's Ferry, OH

In 1902, National built a major glass factory in Cambridge, Ohio. It was purchased from National by its own management in 1907.

By 1904, National had become a holding company, leasing operations of its plants to the management. The company was dissolved in 1908.

Glossary

Terms you ought to know that relate to tumblers....

Blown Glass: glass that has been formed on a blowpipe and expanded by air pressure.

Cased Glass: a blown tumbler that has two or more layers of glass in the gather.

Cracked Off: After a tumbler was blown and had been through the lehr, it was put on a small turntable and scribed with a diamond at the finished height. This need only have been one inch around the tumbler. The glass was then transferred to a turntable that had a ring of gas jets above it. When the heat hit the glass, the tumbler cracked along the mark, and the top portion became loose and could be lifted off. The tumbler was then either ground and polished or sent to the glazer.

Fire Polished: indicates a complete transition from interior to exterior surface without interruption. The cap ring, which made tumblers possible, left concentric rings around the inside and outside of the tumbler; fire polishing smoothed these rings and left an unblemished surface. Fire polishing was also used on blown tumblers which had been cracked off, leaving a nearly perfect surface. A glazer fire polished the top surface, which left the glass nearly unblemished and was much less expensive than grinding and polishing.

Frit: broken, chipped, or powdered glass, usually picked up on the outside of a hot gather. It may be marvered smooth or left on the surface for texture.

Gather: this refers both to the picking up of raw glass onto a rod or pipe, and to the gob of glass itself. In the case of blown glass, the gob was about the size of an egg.

Glazer: a machine that carried a revolving tumbler through a series of gas jets, fire polishing the top surface.

Glory Hole: a small intense furnace, just large enough to admit the glass being worked upon, for warming-in.

Incomplete Fire Polish: indicates that the top surface still shows signs of the concentric cap ring joints around the diameter, either inside or out; if on a blown tumbler, signs of the original crack-off surface.

Irregular Star: means that there are varying lengths of the points. The number given, 5, 6, etc., indicates the multiples of the pattern.

Marver: now a piece of iron, originally marble, on which a hot gather is rolled to smooth the surface.

Mica: a silvery mineral that can be encased in hot glass. It imparts a sparkle to the glass that is called "spangle."

Mold: a device for forming the outside of a tumbler, either pressed or blown.

Paste Mold: a blow mold that is lined with a compound, perhaps asphalt and powdered cork, that holds water. When the hot glass is blown into the cavity, the steam formed between the glass and the water prevents the glass from touching the surface and leaving mold marks.

Pontil: a scar on the bottom of a tumbler left by the breaking off of the punty rod, or a polished area where the scar has been.

Pressed Glass: glass that has been formed by having been pressed into a mold and then expanded to fill it with a plunger.

Pressed Mold: a mold that receives a gob of glass and into which is pressed a plunger. The glass spreads evenly throughout the mold, taking the shape of the outer surface.

Punty Rod: a rod four to five feet long, with a tiny bit of hot glass on the end, intended to be stuck to the bottom of a tumbler so the piece can be warmed-in and manipulated.

Spatter: a gather is rolled in colored frit and marvered to make it smooth. It then has another gather of crystal glass taken over it and is expanded in the final mold. This process gives the tumbler a spotted color; often, several colors mix.

Spot, Optic, or Dip Mold: a small cavity into which the gather is poked. These little molds have rudimentary patterns on their sides. They leave bumps, grooves, or ribs on the outside of the gather. When the tumbler is blown into the final mold, the thinner glass between the ribs, etc., expands, leaving evidence of the former ribs, spots, etc., on the inside.

Stuck-up: This process involved placing the tumbler on a punty rod, so that the glass could be fire polished in the glory hole. When the tumbler was removed from the punty rod, it left a scar where the glass broke. Quality work required that the scar be polished, leaving a polished punty that generally took the form of a concave circle.

Tooling: changing the shape of a tumbler with a tool, either with a cone, to expand the top, or with a paddle, to shape it in other ways.

Warming-in: putting a tumbler back into the fire to soften the glass, either to fire polish the top rim or to enable the glass to be worked another way.

Bibliography

Bickenheuser, Fred, and William Heacock. *Victorian Colored Pattern Glass, U. S. Glass from A to Z.* Marietta, OH: Antiques Publications, 1978.

Bond, Marcelle. *The Beauty of Albany Glass.* Self-published, 1972.

Bredehoft, Neila, George A. Fogg, and Francis C. Maloney. *Early Duncan Glassware.* Self-published, 1987.

Bredehoft, Neila and Tom, and Jo and Bob Sanford *Findlay Flint Glass Co.* Cherry Hill Publications 1994.

———. *Glass Toothpick Holders,* Paducah, KY: Collector Books, 1999.

Bredehoft, Neila and Tom. *Heisey Glass.* Paducah, KY: Collector Books, 2001.

———. *Hobbs, Brockunier & Co. Glass.* Paducah, KY: Collector Books, 1997.

Elmore, JoAnn and William Heacock. *Opalescent Glass from A to Z.* Marietta, OH: The Glass Press, 2000.

Gorham, C. W. *Riverside Glass Works.* Heartlights, 1995.

Heacock, William. *Victorian Colored Pattern Glass, Ruby Stained Glass from A to Z.* Marietta, OH: Antique Publications, 1986.

———. *Harry Northwood, The Early Years.* Marietta, OH: Antique Publications, 1990.

———. *Harry Northwood, The Wheeling Years.* Marietta, OH: Antique Publications, 1991.

Heacock, William, James Measell, and Berry Wiggins. *Dugan/Diamond.* Marietta, OH: Antique Publications, 1993.

Jarves, Deming. *Introduction to Glass Making.* Reprinted by Grace C. Weinstock, 1968.

Knittle, Rhea Mansfield. *Early American Glass.* The Century Press, 1927.

Lee, Ruth Webb. *Early American Pressed Glass.* Self-published, 1946.

———. *Sandwich Glass.* Lee Publications, 1966.

———. *Victorian Glass, Seventh Edition.* Self-published, 1944.

McCain, Mollie Helen. *Field Guide to Pattern Glass.* Paducah, KY: Collector Books, 2000.

Measell, James. *Greentown Glass.* Grand Rapids, MI: The Grand Rapids Public Library, 1979.

———. *Imperial Glass Encyclopedia, Vols. 1, 2, 3.* Marietta, OH: Antique Publications, 1995.

———. *New Martinsville Glass, 1900 – 1944.* Marietta, OH: Antique Publications, 1994.

Metz, Alice Hulett. *Early American Pattern Glass, Vol. 1, 2.* Paducah, KY: Collector Books, 1978.

M'Kee Victorian Glass. Mineola, NY: Dover Publications, 1981.

Murray, James, ed. *The Oxford English Dictionary,* Vol. 2. Oxford, England: Oxford University Press, 1933, 1961.

Murray, Melvin L. *Fostoria, Ohio Glass II.* Self-published, 1992.

Pennsylvania Glassware, 1870 – 1904, catalog reprint. Princeton, NJ: The Pyne Press, 1972.

Revi, A. C. *American Pressed Glass and Figural Bottles.* Thomas Nelson & Sons, 1964.

———. *Nineteenth Century Glass.* Galahad Books, 1967.

Shuman, John A., III. *American Art Glass.* Paducah, KY: Collector Books, 1988.

Simon, Leroy C. and Mertie B. *Tumblers with a Past.* Self-published, 1967.

Smith, Don E. *Findlay Pattern Glass.* Hancock Historical Museum Association; 1970, 1989.

Stevens, Gerald. *Canadian Glass.* The Ryerson Press, 1967.

Stout, Sandra McPhee. *The Complete Book of McKee Glass.* Trojan Press, 1972.

Teal, Ron, Sr. *Albany Glass.* Marietta, OH: The Glass Press, 1997.

Welker, John and Elizabeth. *Pressed Glass in America.* Antique Acres Press, 1985.

Index

288